international
review of
social history

Special Issue 22

Labour in Transport: Histories from the Global South, c.1750–1950

Edited by Stefano Bellucci, Larissa Rosa Corrêa, Jan-Georg Deutsch, and Chitra Joshi

T0370778

CAMBRIDGE
UNIVERSITY PRESS

University Printing House, Cambridge CB2 8BS, United Kingdom

One Liberty Plaza, 20th Floor, New York, NY 10006, USA

477 Williamstown Road, Port Melbourne, VIC 3207, Australia

314-321, 3rd Floor, Plot 3, Splendor Forum, Jasola District Centre, New Delhi - 110025, India

79 Anson Road, #06-04/06, Singapore 079906

Cambridge University Press is part of the University of Cambridge.

It furthers the University's mission by disseminating knowledge in the pursuit of education, learning and research at the highest international levels of excellence.

www.cambridge.org
Information on this title: www.cambridge.org/9781107521179

A catalogue record for this publication is available from the British Library

ISBN 978-1-107-52117-9 Paperback

CONTENTS

Labour in Transport: Histories from the Global South,
c.1750–1950

Edited by
Stefano Bellucci, Larissa Rosa Corrêa, Jan-Georg Deutsch,
and Chitra Joshi

IRSH 59 (2014), Special Issue, pp. 1–10 doi:10.1017/S0020859014000364

Introduction: Labour in Transport: Histories from the Global South (Africa, Asia, and Latin America), c.1750 to 1950

STEFANO BELLUCCI

International Institute of Social History
PO Box 2169, 1000 CD Amsterdam, The Netherlands

E-mail: sbe@iisg.nl

LARISSA ROSA CORRÊA

Instituto Multidisciplinar, Federal Rural University of Rio de Janeiro (UFRRJ)
Av. Governador Roberto Silveira S/N – CEP: 26020-740
Centro – Nova Iguaçu-RJ, Brazil

E-mail: larissarosacorrea@hotmail.com

JAN-GEORG DEUTSCH

St Cross College, University of Oxford
Oxford, OX1 3LZ, UK

E-mail: jan-georg.deutsch@stx.ox.ac.uk

CHITRA JOSHI

Indraprastha College, Delhi University
31, Sham Nath Marg, Delhi-110054, India

E-mail: chitrajos@gmail.com

ABSTRACT: This introduction highlights the main subjects and research questions addressed in the articles making up this special issue on the labour histories of transport in the Global South. Although historiographical interest in the history of transport labour is growing, scientific knowledge on the subject is still very limited. This is especially true for histories from outside Europe and North America. Important topics and research problems covered here are: (1) transport labour as facilitating the exchange and mobility of goods but also of peoples and ideas – as such transport constitutes a noteworthy element of social history; (2) transport labour as a factor of production which is relevant for industrial and agrarian societies, as well as for market-driven and socialist economies; (3) the extent to which the processes of globalization, imperial expansion, and the emergence of global capitalism owe a debt to transport labour of the Global South and its micro-histories.

This special issue 22 of the *International Review of Social History*
(*IRSH*) seeks to explore new frontiers in the labour history of different
transport sectors from the mid-eighteenth to the mid-twentieth century.
The contributions to this volume focus on what one might loosely call the
"Global South" – the colonial and semi-colonial societies in Africa, Asia,
and Latin America that were once part of European empires.

Connecting people and markets is a prerequisite for the functioning
of capitalist economies. For this purpose, commodities need to be transported and thus transport is a "necessary moment" (Marx) in the exchange
process. As many contributors to this special issue have shown, this is true
whether the seller is an industrial capitalist or a merchant who has bought
to resell: transport is needed for the buyer of a commodity to acquire its
use value.

The labour involved in moving people and commodities, in loading and
unloading vehicles, and in driving or sailing them should be counted as
productive labour in the same sense as artisanal or industrial labour. In
both cases, entrepreneurs invest their capital in new kinds of machines
and new kinds of labour in order to put people to work and exact profit.
Labour creates products that realize a surplus value when (profitably)
exchanged, irrespective of whether such labour occurs in "the sphere of
production" or in "the sphere of circulation", such as transport labour.
There exist several historical works on labour in transport, but they focus
mainly on the so-called West or "Global North".[1] Very little attention
has been paid so far to studying the history of transport labour in the
Global South, both as a subject on its own or in a comparative or global
perspective.[2] One of the main questions that immediately arise in the

---

1. For a recent example, see the study by Margaret Makepeace, *The East India Company's
London Workers: Management of the Warehouse Labourers, 1800–1858* (Woodbridge, 2010).
For a comprehensive bibliography on the history of labour in global perspective, including
transport labour, see Jan Lucassen (ed.), *Global Labour History: A State of the Art* (Bern, 2006),
pp. 649–746.
2. Comparative or global transport labour studies are still very few in number. See, for
instance, Sam Davies *et al.* (eds), *Dock Workers: International Explorations in Comparative
Labour History, 1790–1970* (Aldershot, 2000). See also in Lucassen, *Global Labour History*, the
contributions of Lex Heerma van Voss, "'Nothing to Lose but a Harsh and Miserable Life Here
on Earth': Dock Work as a Global Occupation, 1790–1970", pp. 591–621, and Shelton
Stromquist, "Railroad Labor and the Global Economy: Historical Patterns", pp. 623–647. A
considerable part of the transport labour literature actually illuminates US labour history. On
railroad labour see, for example, David E. Bernstein, "Racism, Railroad Unions, and Labor
Regulations", *Independent Review*, 5 (2000), pp. 237–247; James B. Burns, *Railroad Mergers
and the Language of Unification* (Westport, CT, 1998); Joseph Kelly, "Showing Agency on the
Margins: African American Railway Workers in the South and Their Unions, 1917–1930",
Labour/Le Travail, 71 (Spring 2013), pp. 123–148; and Eric Arnesen, *Brotherhoods of Color:
Black Railroad Workers and the Struggle for Equality* (Cambridge, MA, 2001). On truck drivers
see Jane Stern, *Trucker: A Portrait of the Last American Cowboy* (New York, 1975); Shirley K.

historical study of transport labour in the Global South concerns the
degree to which the coloniality of the labour situation has shaped the
structure of work and the formation of collective identities. It is also
questionable to what extent analytical categories such as "free labour" that
have their origin in the specific historical experience of European industrial societies can be applied without modification in the historical study
of non-industrial societies in other parts of the world, especially in the
nineteenth century, where a significant part of the work was undertaken
by servile labourers and slaves. This special issue tries to address these
concerns and to fill in this historiographical gap.

Transport labour exists everywhere and has been a feature in every
epoch of humanity, in both what has now become the Global North
as well as the Global South. "Global" North and South are not mere
geographical expressions. The adjective "global" highlights connectivities
within regions as well as between regions. According to Marcel van der
Linden, global connections do not necessarily occur between continents
and countries separated by thousands of kilometres; global connection
can also materialize between places that are close in geographical terms.[3]
Any kind of connection – whether social, economic, or political – will
have been facilitated by transport and transport labour. "Global" also
refers to "globalization", of course. In our view this process is related
mostly to the relentless expansion of the capitalist economy, from the
Global North to the Global South.

The general issues that emerge from the studies selected for this special
issue are threefold. Firstly, transport labour facilitates the exchange of
goods and the related movement of peoples, ideas, plants, and pathogens
and thus constitutes a fundamental part of economic and social history.
As this volume demonstrates, transport-related activities have been conducted in a great variety of forms, ranging from porters to mail runners,
from railway workers to seafarers, and from rickshaw pullers to motor
drivers.

Secondly, transport labour has always been a necessary feature of
production; it appears in industrial and agrarian societies, in capitalist and
non-capitalist modes of production, as well as in supposedly socialist
economies; transport labour was part and parcel of the processes of globalization, imperial expansion, and the emergence of global capitalism,

Drew, *Dirty Work: The Social Construction of Taint* (Waco, TX, 2007); Shane Hamilton,
Trucking Country: The Road to America's Wal-Mart Economy (Princeton, NJ, 2008). Matthew
Josephson, *The Robber Barons: The Great American Capitalists, 1861–1901* (New York, 1934),
is also still relevant for the subject.
3. See Marcel van der Linden, "The National Integration of European Working Classes
(1871–1914): Exploring the Causal Configuration", *International Review of Social History*,
33 (1988), pp. 285–311.

regardless of the specific definition of these concepts. Transport labour was often the first form of regulated wage labour that the colonized experienced on a significant scale. Transportation can be realized through complex technological or capital-intensive as well as labour-intensive means. In the past five or six decades, a significant number of studies have been published on the history of transport and transport routes,[4] but only a few on the history of labour in transport. Just a handful of such studies have actually addressed issues related to the history of transport labour in Africa, Asia, or Latin America. With a few notable exceptions,[5] it is only comparatively recently that scholarly works have started to appear that focus exclusively on the Global South.[6]

Thirdly, through a focus on transport labour, the contributions to this volume show how it is possible to expand the boundaries of labour history, and explore ideas that new critical histories have posed.[7] This they do in several different ways. First: they reaffirm the need to move away from classical Eurocentric orthodoxies towards a more inclusive and complex understanding of labour relations, identifying the relationship between local forms and the operation of global capital. Second: they reinforce an important trend in labour history over the past two decades,

4. See, for instance, the studies on shipping companies, such as Freda Harcourt's work on P&O: *Flagships of Imperialism: The P&O Company and the Politics of Empire from its Origins to 1867* (Manchester, 2006). For maritime labour, however, see Ravi Ahuja, "The Age of the 'Lascar': South Asian Seafarers in the Times of Imperial Steam Shipping", in Joya Chatterji and David Washbrook (eds), *Routledge Handbook of the South Asian Diaspora* (Manchester, 2013), pp. 110–122.
5. See, for instance, Catherine Coquery-Vidrovitch and Paul E. Lovejoy (eds), *The Workers of African Trade* (Beverly Hills, CA, 1985), and Timothy Oberst, "Transport Workers, Strikes and the 'Imperial Response': Africa and the Post World War II Conjuncture", *African Studies Review*, 31 (1988), pp. 117–133. For more recent studies, see Stephen J. Rockel, *Carriers of Culture: Labor on the Road in Nineteenth-Century East Africa* (Portsmouth, NH, 2006), and Jan-Bart Gewald, Sabine Luning, and Klaas van Walraven (eds), *The Speed of Change: Motor Vehicles and People in Africa, 1890–2000* (Leiden, 2009). On India, see Ian Kerr, *Building the Railways of the Raj, 1850–1900* (Delhi, 1995).
6. The lack of studies on Latin American transport labour that take into account transnational and comparative perspectives as well as the free and unfree labour, ethnic, gender, and class connections has been slowly corrected by some recent and valuable investigations in this field. See, for instance, Silvana A. Palermo, "*En nombre del hogar proletario*: Engendering the 1917 Great Railroad Strike in Argentina", *Hispanic American Historical Review*, 93 (2013), pp. 585–620; Vitor W. de Oliveira, *Nas águas do Prata: os trabalhadores da rota fluvial entre Buenos Aires e Corumbá (1910–1930)* (Campinas, 2009); Jaime Rodrigues, "Mariners-Slavers and Slave Ships in Atlantic, 18th and 19th Centuries: The Perspective of Captives and the Slaveholders Logic", *Africana Studia*, 18 (2012), pp. 205–222.
7. Rana P. Behal, Chitra Joshi, and Prabhu P. Mohapatra, "India", in Joan Allen, Alan Campbell, and John McIlroy (eds), *Histories of Labour: National and International Perspectives* (Pontypool, 2010), pp. 290–314; see also Leo Lucassen, "Writing Global Labour History c.1800–1940: A Historiography of Concepts, Periods, and Geographical Scope", in Lucassen, *Global Labour History*, pp. 39–90.

a trend that shifts the focus away from factory labour – which in any case always constituted a small minority of the labour force – to the study of varieties of forms of labour. Third: the essays show the limits of working with the standard binaries between coercion and freedom, oppositions that have now been widely criticized by new labour histories in different countries. Fourth: the essays in this volume also reassert the significance of non-economic factors to the understanding of labour relations: they show how articulations of class were crucially shaped by notions of caste, gender, race, age, and other cultural mediations.

As noted above, it is not possible to understand the colonization process in the Global South without considering the complex connections between free and unfree labour. For a good part of the nineteenth century, the provision of transport services in Rio de Janeiro, as Terra's piece in the collection shows, depended to a significant degree on "wage-earning slaves" – unfree workers who had to pay a fixed income to their owners. Similarly, in the north-eastern borderlands of India, "impressed" coolie labour was widely employed in porterage and construction work (Sinha and Dzüvichü). As the essays show, we can understand the logic of such labour forms only by exploring the entangled histories of freedom and force, coercion and consent.

Transport labour is a particularly promising field for the production of challenging theoretical insights into labour history.[8] Above all, the studies in this volume emphasize the dual nature of the role of transport labour, extending the reach of colonial states as much as of capitalist markets. Porters, runners, boatmen, and construction workers building roads were all crucial to the processes through which territories were spatialized, unified, and extended. Porters in the Naga Hills in India or flag-post runners in the Cameroons penetrated interiors, accessed hilly and difficult terrain, and made possible interconnections across regions. Similarly, Mongolian lama porters provided the mobile labour force underlining the transnational connections between Russia and China. Connecting places and people, rural and urban areas, transport labourers facilitated the rapid expansion of both commerce and imperial power in diverse places such as late nineteenth-century Mongolia and early twentieth-century West Africa (Dear and Hart).

The crucial role transport labour played in commerce defined its position in relation to capital. At different points in time, compared with other forms of labour, say agricultural or industrial labour, the particular position of transport workers and their mobility gave them greater manoeuvrability in negotiating their wages and conditions of work. By

---

8. For a recent survey, see Marcel van der Linden, "The Promise and Challenges of Global Labor History", *International Labor and Working-Class History*, 82 (Fall 2012), pp. 57–76.

the nature of their work, transport workers occupied a central location in the commodity chain and thus they could not easily be replaced by their employers. Similarly, the nation state (no matter the varied forms of state-building processes) has depended very much on transport workers. Therefore, governments have tried both to control and to gain the support of these workers, sometimes conceding better labour conditions and creating specific laws.

For those dependent on transport workers, the menace of disruption was always on the horizon and they had to deal with it. There was the constant threat of flight, desertion, go-slows, and strikes. This is why, in many cases, the work was done by self-employed workers who often assumed the role of small-scale entrepreneurs (Sinha and Hart), were able to extract comparatively high wages for their work (Nkwi and de Bruijn), or were leaders of strike movements (Grandi). In periods of great economic expansion and urban development, transport workers were able to struggle for better wages and working conditions. In many cases, such as, in various countries railway workers, they created a strong tradition of militancy and insubordination.[9]

In the extreme, there was always the possibility of flight (Dzüvichü). Conversely, when such mobility was severely limited or the transport workers' bargaining power particularly weak, as in the case of seamen (lascars) on ships operated by the British East India Company, transport workers were subjected to coercion and appalling violence and treated no better than slaves by their employers (Frey). At the same time, the element of mobility involved in transport always gave workers some specific leeway. Shipping on the Ganges, for example, allowed steersmen (*manjhees*) to use their control over the space of the deck to store items that they then traded "illicitly", despite the legal monopoly of the East India Company over the trade in these commodities (Sinha). Similarly, the rowers (*dandies*) would often use the terms of subcontracts to their advantage, pressing their own demands on travellers on the boat.

The specificity of the position of transport labour is also revealed in the manner in which transport workers dealt with novel transport technologies. Rather than being completely subjected to the will of their potential employers, transport workers were sometimes able to negotiate, if not resist outright, the introduction of new technologies, when the conditions

9. In this sense, the history of railway workers in many countries of Latin America is quite representative. In Brazil, for instance, until the first half of the twentieth century, railway workers were considered to be one of the most active and combative factions in the labour movement. Highly visible as a sort of "elite" within the national labour movement, railway workers secured important labour rights that were subsequently extended to groups of other industrial workers.

of work attached to these new technologies were unacceptable to them. Technology, as we know, is laden with symbolic meanings: a defence of a particular technology gets linked up with notions of dignity, independence, and identity. In colonial Manila, for example, opposition to technology came to be associated with questions of race and nationalism. The attempt to introduce rickshaws into the American-occupied Philippines in the early 1900s failed utterly, because the potential rickshaw drivers perceived the kind of work involved in pulling rickshaws as a new form of enslavement. Consequently, they boycotted the introduction of this new form of urban transport (Pante). This might be an extreme case, but other articles in this volume hint at the possibility that transport companies at times attempted to undermine local resistance to technological change by lending support to the immigration of foreign workers, often under the auspices of both the distant imperial power and national states (Grandi and Terra).

For self-employed driver-workers on the outskirts of Accra, rickshaw pullers and *cocheros* (carriage drivers) in Manila, and railway workers in São Paulo, the savoir-faire as well as the notions of autonomy and dignity are pointed to in this volume as key elements for the process of forming their collective identity and of class organization (Hart, Grandi, and Pante). In the same way, the metaphor of slavery used by some groups of transport workers to denounce the precariousness of their working conditions represented a strategic argument that enabled them to challenge the system of discipline imposed by the employers and gain the support of public opinion (Pante and Terra).

At the same time, however, locally defined notions of dignity and what constitutes "honourable" work could be mobilized to expedite rapid change. Monasteries and monks (lamas), for instance, played a crucial role in facilitating the massive expansion of the tea trade between imperial Russia and the Qing empire in the later nineteenth century. These monks, especially the poorer ones, took enthusiastically to transport labour, partly because there was no attractive alternative available to them, but also because they (and everyone else involved in the trade) apparently believed that the expansion in trade would merely replicate traditional transport working patterns that, according to contemporary observers, had supposedly existed in the steppe since time immemorial. Yet in this part of central Asia geopolitics, commercial activities, and thus transport labour practices underwent dramatic changes in the second half of the nineteenth century (Dear). Thus, what can be learnt from this example in more abstract terms is that rather than being an obstacle to "progress and development", perceived "traditions" (invented or otherwise) can serve as a handmaiden of rapid change.

Transport workers are, of course, also directly connected with urban mobility, one of the main controversial political issues in global cities currently, particularly in the Global South. In countries such as Brazil, better and cheaper transportation in megalopolises such as São Paulo and Rio de Janeiro has been at the heart of the demands of massive demonstrations recently. Terra's article in this special issue demonstrates how this topic has had a long and contentious history since the colonial period in Brazil. In contrast to factory labour, transport workers in urban areas are in constant contact with the population. They can play an important role in the mobilization of working-class people and act as their spokespersons (as Grandi shows in his article). But they have also been well-known until today for being involved in daily conflicts in the urban spaces, provoking accidents and quarrelling with their passengers (see Terra's article). For people who commute every day in the Global South, drivers are sometimes seen as heroes, at other times they are considered to be the worst kind of daily nuisance.

At the same time, the relative autonomy and mobility of transport workers has often been accounted for by their invisibility, making it difficult for historians to recover their histories. As mobile transport workers were frequently hidden from central authority, they were also hidden from official records. This is particularly noticeable with regard to their social life. Colonial archives are excellent in revealing estimates about, for instance, the number of flag-post mail runners employed in British Southern Cameroons between 1916 and 1955 (Nkwi and de Bruijn). However, they tell us little about what people thought about their work, how they lived, whether they took pride in their work or despised it, whether they felt an affinity to those engaged in similar work or merely saw them as faceless competitors in the market place.

Still, as demonstrated in this volume, a set of "traditional" sources may illuminate many aspects of the transport workers' world. The analysis of reports written by colonial and government officials, as well as local newspapers, police records, travel diaries, among others, are key to revealing the living and working conditions of the transport workers. These records also provide us a glimpse of different conflicts, strategies, and resistance actions conducted by these workers in order to challenge the colonial power (see the examples in Frey, Pante, Sinha, and Hart). Official sources, as Sinha shows, can even tell us about the minutiae of the eating habits of river transport workers in late eighteenth-century India.

Altogether, the transport labour studies in this volume show that the entangled processes of globalization, imperial expansion, and the emergence of global capitalism were negotiated through the prism of the "local" (see, in particular, Dear, Hart, and Dzüvichü). Reconstructing the "remote" worlds of Mongolian monks and monasteries in the late nineteenth century or self-employed motor drivers in West Africa in the mid-twentieth century (let alone fierce railway union struggles in metropolitan São Paulo in the early twentieth century) has a value of its own. This is arguably one reason why transport labour histories in the Global South are such admirable and rewarding objects of comparative study. However, it also poses the challenge of not losing sight of the wider implications of such studies, especially of the fact of how deeply entangled the global processes mentioned above actually were, particularly in those parts of the world that appeared to be "remote" when seen from an imperial perspective.

Finally, an important scholarly debate on labour history centres on the appraisal that transport workers have been historically essential for the dissemination of ideas and the expansion of labour movements, especially in the colonized world. Several papers in this special issue challenge this view. Transport workers have been interesting for historians because of their high level of unionization. Owing to their crucial role in economies where the movement of goods and people is fundamental, transport workers often possessed significant bargaining power vis-à-vis capital and the state. For these reasons, and the fact that transport workers in the Global South in the eighteenth and nineteenth centuries were highly specialized, the demands of transport workers were often conceded. This led to the idea, held by many historians, that transport workers represented a force of internationalist practice.

Some articles in this volume show how these assumptions or clichés do not apply to all cases and categories of transport workers. For example, in the case of the transport workers in Brazil analysed by Terra, between 1870 and 1906 transport workers were the group holding most of the strikes in the city. Of a total of twenty-two stoppages initiated by transport workers, five were motivated mainly by local and federal laws and police regulations. Of the three most important strikes involving the greatest numbers of strikers and having the greatest impact (in 1890, 1900, and 1906), two were directly related to regulations. The mobilization organized in 1890, for example, was against Article 298 of the Penal Code, which regulated the question of accidents.

These were not internationalist claims, geared towards a radical change of society. They were demands aimed at improving specific labour conditions. It is not even clear if they served as examples to workers in other sectors. This example is quite interesting as it might explain why in early colonial Kenya – as revealed by Frederick Cooper[10] – the wages of transport workers were significantly higher than those of other wage workers, let alone of workers who were not earning stable wages in the so-called informal sector. Jennifer Hart's article argues that the appropriation by drivers of the language of trade unionism in colonial Ghana drew to a considerable degree on the trade unionism of interwar British

10. Frederick Cooper, *On the African Waterfront: Urban Disorder and the Transformation of Work in Colonial Mombasa* (New Haven, CT, 1987), p. 243.

colonial governance, and not only on African traditions of radicalism and reform. These multiple influences resulted in a unique understanding and practice of unionism among drivers, which positioned them well both in their own profession and in relation to the state in both urban and rural areas. Ghanaian drivers never became explicitly involved in politics. These two case studies help to de-romanticize the role of wage workers as a progressive force in underdeveloped economies, and indeed reinforce the idea of transport workers as potentially and specifically prone to be what was once called the "labour aristocracy".

This volume makes no claim to be a comprehensive study of labour history in different transport sectors in the Global South. Such a claim would greatly exceed the scope of any single special issue. However, as we have seen, the essays help us to understand some of the specificities of transport labour, and to see how the fluidity and mobility of labour – rather than the fixity of their location – shapes the working of capital as well as the nature of labour resistance. Some of the insights may be specific to the history of transport labour in the Global South, but many others are also applicable to global labour history in general.

The contributions in this collection have concentrated on male workers in transport. We know from other studies, however, that the work of men in transport was predicated crucially on the services provided by women in maintaining their rural linkages to where they had come from, in managing domestic arrangements, or in the actual task of carrying, as with caravan women in East Africa.[11] In writing the history of transport labour these linkages need to be explored in greater detail. That ought to be one of the aims of future work on the history of transport labour.

11. Rockel, *Carriers of Culture*, pp. 117–130.

IRSH 59 (2014), Special Issue, pp. 11–43 doi:10.1017/S002085901400039X
© 2014 Internationaal Instituut voor Sociale Geschiedenis

Contract, Work, and Resistance: Boatmen in Early Colonial Eastern India, 1760s–1850s*

N i t i n   S i n h a

*Vanbrugh College V/A/221, Department of History,
University of York
York YO10 5DD, United Kingdom*

E-mail: nitin.sinha@york.ac.uk

ABSTRACT: In the period between the 1760s and the 1850s boatmen were the most important transport workers in early colonial eastern India, at least numerically. Unfortunately, they have received little scholarly attention so far. By looking at the regime of work, which surprisingly had strong bases in the notion of contract from as early as the 1770s, this article explores the nature of work, work organization, and resistance by boatmen. It argues that although work was structured according to the wage or hire-based (*thika*) contract regime, the social, political, and ecological conditions in which contract operated were equally crucial. The centrality of contract was premised upon how effectively it was enforceable and, in fact, historically enforced. Boatmen being one of the most important "native" groups with which the British were left on their often long journeys, this article suggests that contract helps to understand the formal "structure of work", and the minute details of the journey help to understand the "world of work", of which clandestine trade, weather, wind, rain, torrents, tracking, mooring, internal squabbling, and, not least, preparing food were some of the main components.

The ecology and political economy of eastern India perhaps made boatmen the most important transport workers in early colonial India. This region is criss-crossed by a variety of bodies of water that historically made rivers the standard means of communication throughout the year. To a great extent, the ascendancy of the English East India Company (EIC) depended on the long-distance trade in imperial commodities such

* This paper is part of the larger project "The Ganga: Landscape, Community, Religion, 1760s–1960s", which was funded by the Federal Ministry for Education and Research, Germany. The archival research was carried out when based at ZMO, Berlin. The paper was written under the fellowship programme of IGK Work and Human Life Cycle in Global History, Berlin. I am thankful to all three of them for institutional support. The paper has organically grown through numerous discussions with Nitin Varma and help provided by Maria Framke.

as opium, indigo, textiles, salt, and saltpetre. This required a stable system of transportation to and from Calcutta. In 1780, James Rennell had estimated that about 30,000 boatmen were involved in the task of inland navigation in Bengal.[1] Subsequently, a text published in 1836 gave a figure of 350,000 for the whole of the river Ganga.[2] Even if these figures seem inflated, the fact that boatmen remained an important group of transport workers is beyond dispute. This is also corroborated by looking at a range of visual and textual accounts (both administrative and private) in which they start appearing early on.

The Ganga, connecting eastern and northern India, was the imperial highway both in Mughal and early colonial times. A number of European trading companies, native chiefs, and *zamindari* (landed) elites required the services of boatmen; this article discusses their relationship with the EIC. The Company required their services for a number of reasons: for conveying newly arrived cadets and officials to their joining stations; for transporting goods such as saltpetre, opium, indigo, textiles, cotton, and other bulk commodities such as grains; and for carrying troops. The sheer variety of boats, depending on the nature of merchandise, weight, and oars, proves that boating was an extremely diversified and specialized profession.[3] Further, as the navigability of some of the channels, streams, and rivers changed constantly, the boatmen's skill was complemented by their close and precise knowledge of the waterways.[4]

In south Asian transport and labour historiographies, transport workers have received little scholarly attention.[5] Only in very recent times have some of the groups become the subject of study.[6] By looking at boatmen's

1. Sabyasachi Bhattacharya, "Eastern India I", in Dharma Kumar (ed.) (with the editorial assistance of Meghnad Desai), *The Cambridge Economic History of India*, II, *c.1757–c.1970* (Cambridge, 1983), p. 271.
2. *Memoir on the Agricultural and Commercial Capabilities of Bengal in Observations with Reference to the Establishment of the East India Sugar and Agricultural Company, Extracted from Various Sources, with Original Calculations, and Remarks* (London, 1836), p. 5.
3. Robert L. Hardgrave, Jr, *Boats of Bengal: Eighteenth Century Portraits by Balthazar Solvyns* (Delhi, 2001).
4. On the changing courses, see Walter S. Sherwill, "Report on the Rivers of Bengal", in *Selections from the Records of the Bengal Government* (Calcutta, 1858), pp. 1–19.
5. Railway workers have attracted the most attention by far, but for them also the scope of future research is immense. Two important works on India's railways are Ian J. Kerr, *Building the Railways of the Raj, 1850–1900* (Delhi, 1995); and Laura Bear, *Lines of the Nation: Indian Railway Workers, Bureaucracy, and the Intimate Historical Self* (New York, 2007).
6. Recently, Chitra Joshi looked at convicts, dak runners, and palanquin bearers, all associated with road transport: Chitra Joshi, "Dak Roads, Dak Runners, and the Reordering of Communication Networks", *International Review of Social History*, 57 (2012), pp. 169–189; *idem*, "Fettered Bodies: Labouring on Public Works in Nineteenth-Century India", in Marcel van der Linden and Prabhu P. Mohapatra (eds), *Labour Matters: Towards Global Histories, Studies in Honour of Sabyasachi Bhattacharya* (New Delhi, 2009), pp. 3–21. Another group characterized

regime of work, which from as early as the 1770s had a strong basis in the notion of contract, I will examine the nature of work, work organization, and resistance by boatmen. In doing so, this article also contributes to the few existing studies on labour in the early colonial period.

CONTRACTS FOR TRANSPORTING TROOPS AND IMPERIAL COMMODITIES

In the 1770s, within the government establishment, the army's requirement for boats was greatest. In 1771 and 1772 the boat establishment cost Rs 307,922 and Rs 352,264 respectively.[7] This was the cost of the fixed boat establishment. In 1772, in addition to this, boats hired for military services cost Rs 214,926, thus bringing total expenditure to Rs 567,190. In the same year, a brigade which was on the march for four months cost Rs 18,620. The EIC therefore decided to reduce the fixed establishment and procure boats, when needed, through a system of public tenders and contracts. Arguably, the contract system had been practised at an earlier date, but due to "many difficulties and inconveniences which were found to attend it" it was discontinued.[8]

The reduced establishment of five budgerows (a contemporary anglicized word for one of the most popular boats in Bengal, the *bajrah*) of eighteen oars, fifteen boats for magazine and military stores, twelve boats for the hospital (carrying the sick and supplies), twelve common transport boats, and five small boats for each brigade (there were three brigades altogether) was proposed. To reduce the cost further, private trade using these boats was strictly prohibited; the brigades were asked occasionally to assist each other, when required; and the civil officials were promised cash in lieu of their boat expenses.[9] Mobility itself was restricted due to the seasonal navigability of rivers. In the winter months, the Hooghly

as transport workers are the *banjaras*. Both their mobility and criminality has been explored: Robert G. Varady, "North Indian Banjaras: Their Evolution as Transporters", *South Asia*, 2:1–2 (1979), pp. 1–18; Ian J. Kerr, "On the Move: Circulating Labor in Pre-Colonial, Colonial, and Post-Colonial India", in Rana P. Behal and Marcel van der Linden (eds), *Coolies, Capital, and Colonialism: Studies in Indian Labour History* (Cambridge, 2007), pp. 85–109; Meena Radhakrishna, *Dishonoured by History: "Criminal Tribes" and British Colonial Policy* (Delhi, 2001); Nitin Sinha, "Mobility, Control and Criminality in Early Colonial India, 1760s–1850s", *Indian Economic and Social History Review*, 45 (2008), pp. 1–33.
7. Home Public [hereafter, HP], B, 21 June 1773, no. 15. Subsequent information is based on this source. The HP files used in this article are from the National Archives of India, New Delhi.
8. *Ibid.*
9. For military officials, too, the rules were tightened. The commanding officers of brigades and detachments were not allowed to permit officers under their command to go to Calcutta on leave or absence without the governor's prior permission. If permitted, such passages were not allowed at the Company's expense; HP, Consultation 7, June 1773, nos 29–30.

passage was difficult to navigate; the boats usually took the circuitous route round the Sundarbans. It was therefore decided not to send any stores from the Bengal Presidency up the country between 20 November and 30 June of the following year. It was also pointed out that usually in these months troops marched over land, which rendered transporting them by water unnecessary.[10]

The exact effect of these reductions and restrictions on the employ-ability of boatmen is difficult to calculate, but it is clear that the reduction in the number of boats must have led to a significant reduction in the overall strength of the crews. Before the proposed reduction, the total estimate of boats in service was: 63 budgerows, 120 large boats, 100 small boats, and 6 Dacca *pulwars*. The cost of hiring all of these was Rs 20,060 per month. In contrast, the reduced number of boats was supposed to cost Rs 9,870 per month. For large boats, the rate of hire was also reduced, from Rs 65 to Rs 60 per boat.[11] For the 18-oared budgerows alone, this reduction meant that the total number of men employed decreased from 1,134 to 270, i.e. to less than one-quarter.

In addition, there is strong evidence to suggest that a majority of those who were employed under the new contract system ceased to enjoy better wages. For this, the contracts have to be considered. In 1774, a contract was finalized between the EIC and Mr J. Fraser, who had been living in India for seven to eight years and was described as a "peaceable and inoffensive subject".[12] He was contracted to provide for 116 boats of 4 different varieties, and therefore, was required to maintain "upwards of 5000 people, orphans and coolies".[13] However, a comparison of his tendered price with that of the government's estimation is revealing: for one budgerow "fitted with 18 oars and manned with one manjee, two golleahs and eighteen dandies completely found and equipped for service" he had offered the monthly hire rate of Rs 100. This was way below the rate of Rs 160 as fixed or estimated by the government. It is unclear how Fraser offered to supply the boats and maintain the crew at his proposed rate.

10. HP, B, 21 June 1773, no. 16. The employment of boatmen obviously varied according to the season and the amount of rain. See HP, October 1822, no. 7, and HP, 1 August 1822, no. 10, on the extra hire of boatmen during the rainy season.

11. HP, B, 21 June 1773, no. 15. It must have taken some time for the reduction to come through. In December 1773 the total number of boats employed in the military department was eight budgerows (ranging from twenty-four to fourteen oars) and fifty-six boats (from fourteen to six oars); HP, C, 16 December 1773, no. 1 (B).

12. HP, Consultation, 6 January 1774, no. 11.

13. *Ibid.* Reference to the use of orphans is quite striking and singular in the sources used in this article. Also, there is no further discussion of this in the letter written by Fraser and the contract approved by the Chief of Patna. In all probability, it could mean a pool of orphans available in the local labour bazaar of Patna or other riverine districts who could have been hired on low wages.

According to a government calculation, for one budgerow with eighteen oars the monthly maintenance and labour charges would amount to Rs 113, calculated in the following manner: monthly repair charge at Rs 2 an oar (18 × 2 = 36) and monthly pay of Rs 5 and 4 to a *manjhee*[14] and a *dandy*[15] respectively (1 × 5 + 18 × 4 = 77).[16] Without adding the cost of two *golleahs*,[17] the labour and maintenance costs alone exceeded the Rs 100 being proposed.

The sources immediately related to this contract do not explain this conundrum. There can be two possibilities: either Fraser's offer of Rs 100 did not include repair and labour costs (just the boat hire); or the maintenance of boats was not taken very seriously and the monthly wages of the boatmen were significantly reduced to increase profit margins. The wording in the contract that Fraser, *"notwithstanding the difficulty"*, would maintain upwards of 5,000 people is revelatory and implies that the second reading could be correct, even more so since a monthly hire rate of Rs 100 just for boats seems untenable in the light of other evidence from the early nineteenth century. Additionally, these sources also indicate that dandies were likely to receive almost half the wage the government had fixed or estimated. To quote from the author of a two-volume guide for newcomers to India, the wages varied "from two and a half to three and a half, or even four [Rs]; all according to the kind of the boat, and the dignity of the employer".[18]

---

14. The *manjhee* was the master or steersman of a boat; Henry Yule and A.C. Burnell, *Hobson-Jobson: A glossary of colloquial Anglo-Indian words and phrases, and of kindred terms, etymological, historical, geographical and discursive*, new edn by William Crooke (London, 1903), p. 558.

15. The word dandy, meaning boatman, was peculiar to the river Ganga in the Hindi and Bengali languages; the word derived from *dandi* or *dand*, meaning a staff or an oar; Yule and Burnell, *Hobson-Jobson*, p. 296.

16. Cost calculated from HP, B, 21 June 1773, no. 15.

17. Surprisingly, *Hobson-Jobson* has no entry for *golleah*. Nonetheless, other contemporary sources do refer to this workforce: Thomas Williamson described the *manjhee* as the steersman and the *golleah* as the bowman; A. Deane, who provided a list of necessary words and commands for river travel, described the *golleah* as the steersman, and the *manjhee* as the captain of the boat crew. See Thomas Williamson, *The East India Vade-Mecum; or, Complete Guide to Gentlemen Intended for the Civil, Military, or, Naval Service of the Hon. East India Company*, 2 vols (London, 1810), I, p. 283; A. Deane, *A Tour through the Upper Provinces of Hindostan; Comprising a Period between the Years 1804 and 1814: with Remarks and Authentic Anecdotes to which is Annexed, a Guide up the River Ganges with a Map from the Source to the Mouth* (London, 1823), pp. 290–291.

18. Williamson, *The East India Vade-Mecum*, I, p. 284. A Christian missionary who travelled up the river in 1834 mentioned that the general monthly wages of a dandy and a *manjhee* were Rs 3 and Rs 4 respectively; John C. Lowrie, *Travels in North India [...]* (Philadelphia, PA, 1842), p. 91. Balthazar Solvyns also gave the figure of Rs 3 a month for the dandy. For the ill-fed and ill-paid conditions of "boys" employed on towboats helping incoming ships to enter into the Ganga and Hooghly, see Hardgrave, *Boats of Bengal*, p. 116; for reference to dandies' wages, see p. 30.

One thing that clearly emerges from this discussion is that boatmen, especially dandies, received lower wages under a private contract system than under the direct hiring done by the government. Also, some form of personal perquisites that these men would have obtained through the provision of repair charges might have ceased to exist under the private contract system.

The choice of speculative phrases such as "might have", "must have", and "would have" is deliberate. It reflects the scarce and sketchy nature of the materials one is dealing with in constructing the history of work and work relationships between boatmen and their employers (the EIC). It was probably this, and the seductive strength of the "continuity" framework to understand the early colonial period, that led Michael Anderson to claim that the question of labour in this period did not become an independent topic of concern for early colonial administrators. According to him, they followed the available pre-colonial frameworks of kin, caste, family, and village communities to "manufacture the consent for highly coercive labour processes".[19] Ravi Ahuja's work on early colonial Madras convincingly refutes this argument and brings back the focus on the colonial state in not only advancing a labour policy but also, through its interventionist practices, shaping labour relationships.[20]

One such instrument was the contract between the worker and the employer. Once again, turning to another of Ahuja's essays, it becomes clear that the notion of contract as premised upon free wage labour and an agreement supposedly formed between formally equal parties was not the only form of labour relationship. Heterogeneity, ranging from slavery and forced labour to that of contracted work, was the hallmark of early colonial labour relations.[21] This kind of observation is possible when one covers a range of occupations, as Ahuja did. Working on a specific group of workers has its advantages and limitations. One advantage is the clear identification of the centrality of the contract system, at least for those boatmen who worked directly for the EIC. In fact, it was also crucial in the sphere of private travelling (as elaborated in the next section). One of the limitations, however, is the impossibility of determining the "coloniality" of this practice. Given the lack of studies on pre-colonial times, it would be highly dubious to claim that the contract system for boat hiring was a colonial novelty.

---

19. Michael R. Anderson, "Work Construed: Ideological Origins of Labour Law in British India to 1918", in Peter Robb (ed.), *Dalit Movements and the Meanings of Labour in India* (New Delhi, 1993), p. 90.
20. Ravi Ahuja, "The Origins of Colonial Labour Policy in Late Eighteenth-Century Madras", *International Review of Social History*, 44 (1999), pp. 159–195.
21. Idem, "Labour Relations in an Early Colonial Context: Madras, c.1750–1800", *Modern Asian Studies*, 36 (2002), pp. 793–826.

Prabhu Mohapatra has recently looked at the working of contracts in the production of textiles and indigo.[22] He argues that although contracts were theoretically based on the idea of free choice, they contradictorily induced the production or reproduction of unfree labour conditions. Before teasing out the implications of the contract, in the context of this article it is important to ask why the government resorted to contracts for procuring boats.[23] Evidently, it wanted to cut its expenses. In other words, it intentionally used contracts as a cost-saving mechanism, with repercussions for the wages of boatmen.

At the same time, it is equally necessary to ask how far this system helped the state beyond mere cost-saving. To what extent were contracts successfully enforceable and actually enforced? It is important to realize that the system was subject to the political and administrative limitations of the early colonial state; because of the nature of this occupation seasonal and ecological constraints were also significant. The fundamental question to begin with is: did the parcelling of the authority and responsibility which contracts engendered (for instance, from the military board of the EIC to Mr Fraser) help the Company to secure boats easily? Complaints, in any case, about the insufficient availability of boats were frequent. In 1781, the revenue chief at Patna complained about the unavailability of boats for transmitting the treasury (district revenue) to Calcutta. This might have been because of the season; it was already April and the hot season had set in.[24] In another incident in 1799, fifty-two boats laden with grain for the Allahabad fort were detained at Patna. The boats were sailing under the charge of the Company and under the command of one *naik* (police supervisor) and six sepoys, but a dispute among *manjhees* caused a hold-up.[25]

For transporting high-end commodities such as saltpetre and opium, either contractors or manufacturers were made responsible. The transportation depended on how the production was organized. Opium serves as a good example to show the indeterminate position of the colonial state.[26] The EIC in Bengal had enjoyed a monopoly of the trade in opium

22. Prabhu P. Mohapatra, "From Contract to Status? Or How Law Shaped Labour Relations in Colonial India, 1780–1880", in Jan Breman *et al.* (eds), *India's Unfree Workforce: Of Bondage Old and New* (New Delhi, 2009), pp. 96–125.

23. This discussion of the notion of contract is unrelated to Mohapatra's point concerning the contradictory nature of contractarian philosophy in producing unfree labour. My intention is to situate contract within the prevailing economic, administrative and ecological settings of the late eighteenth and early nineteenth centuries, which, by any estimate, were "dynamic".

24. John Francis William James, *Selections from the Correspondence of the Revenue Chief of Bihar, 1781–1786* (Patna, 1919), p. 65.

25. Kalikinkar K. Datta (ed.), *Selections from Unpublished Correspondence of the Judge-Magistrate and the Judge of Patna, 1790–1857* (Patna, 1954), p. 192.

26. The following account is based on *ibid.*, pp. 25–28.

since 1761. In 1765, this trade and its profits were put in the hands of the
Company's Patna factory. However, in 1773 the Governor-General
Warren Hastings granted the contract to two natives, Meer Muneer and
Ramsharan Pundit. Due to their irregularities and the oppression of the
raiyats (peasants), on 11 July 1785 the EIC resorted to the public sale of
the contract to the highest bidder for a term of four years. The revenue
from the opium trade declined. Its quality also reportedly suffered. As a
result, in 1797 the contract system was abolished. In 1799 an agency of a
covenanted servant of the Company was established. The Company
began to deal directly with opium manufacturers through its servants.
Under the contract system, the seventh clause made it clear that
"the charges of package and manufacture and the charges and risk of
transportation and delivery are to be on account of the contractor".[27] The
manufacturers privately arranged to transport opium to Calcutta. Boats
were procured on the basis of contracts with *manjhees.*

   Although any delays may thus appear to have been a private affair,
saltpetre and opium manufacturers frequently petitioned the EIC. These
petitions reveal that that the contract did not ensure efficacy. In 1826 one
Ramdayal, a saltpetre manufacturer based in the United Provinces, petitioned the EIC resident at Lucknow, who then forwarded his complaint
to the magistrate at Patna. In the petition, Ramdayal accused *manjhees* of
holding up his boats at Patna even after they had been paid for in full and
contracted to unload the saltpetre in Calcutta.[28] In another case, from
Bihar, the boats contracted by the EIC for transporting saltpetre to
Calcutta were pressed into service by private merchants based at Patna.[29]

   The first example is of the private contract; the second involves the
state. Both relate to disputes over and deviations from the terms of the
contract. Both show the complexity of the socio-economic and political
set-up in which the contract worked. Its successful realization depended
upon different stakeholders involved in the production and transportation
of commodities. A Company monopoly in the trade of certain commodities existed alongside the private trade clandestinely carried in those
very commodities and in others for which private traders also needed
boats. However, these cases also highlight the way the state authorities
were drawn into resolving disputes. Contracts of a private nature did not
mean the marginality of the state.[30] The reasons why the state got deeply
involved were twofold. First, even if the matter related to a private
contract, the nature of commodities (usually the EIC monopoly ones)

---

27. *Idem* (ed.), *Selections from the Judicial Records of the Bhagalpur District Office (1792–1805)*
(Patna, 1968), p. 37.
28. *Idem, Selections from Unpublished Correspondence.*
29. *Ibid.*, p. 168.
30. As has also been convincingly shown by Mohapatra, "From Contract to Status?".

demanded direct state action. Walter S. Sherwill's account of the production and transportation of opium from the Patna factory is illustrative. The Opium Fleet, as he called it, was "preceded by small canoes, the crews of which sound the depth of water, warn all boats out of the channel by beat of drum, and proclaim that the Opium of the 'Companee Bahadoor' claims a passage down the river".[31] The state directed the local authorities to prevent private merchants from seizing the Company's contracted boats. Second was the notion of the contract itself, which was based upon the twin principles of parcelling authority and responsibility on the one hand but drawing upon the state's enforcing authority on the other.

The impulse to ensure the enforcement of the contract demanded that the state play an active role. Mobility of troops was of crucial political importance, and, even when contracted, this remained an active field of state engagement. It is worth following the debates closely to see what effect the state's measures had on the workforce. The civil authorities of the Gangetic districts complained about the frequent irregularities and improprieties committed by military officials when troops passed through.[32] The army needed coolies, boatmen, boats, and supplies, which they forced the neighbouring villages to provide, often without making adequate payments. This led to peasants deserting the villages. The military complained about the shortage of workers, but civil officials drew an interesting parallel by pointing out that private individuals did not complain about the shortage of coolies or dandies. Clearly, responsibility for this highhandedness was placed at the door of the military.

The government took notice of such complaints and framed a regulation in 1806 to assist both troops and private travellers.[33] It directed collectors (a civil authority in the district) and magistrates (a police authority) to help in providing troops with supplies but also in ensuring that any damage done by them should be enquired into and adequately compensated for. A native official was deputed to supply bearers, coolies, boatmen, carts, and bullocks from landholders, farmers, and other relevant persons. The cost of labour and commodities provided for was

31. Walter S. Sherwill, *Illustrations of the Mode of Preparing the Indian Opium Intended for the Chinese Market, from Drawings by Captain Walter S. Sherwill* (London, 1851), text opposite "The Opium Fleet".
32. Datta, *Selections from the Judicial Records*, pp. 363–364.
33. "Bengal Regulation XI of 1806", in F.G. Wigley (ed.), *The Eastern Bengal and Assam Code*, 3 vols (Calcutta, 1907), I, pp. 87–93. I am grateful to Prabhu Mohapatra for extensively discussing this piece of regulation with me, and for pointing out that this regulation needs to be seen as part of the colonial state-formation as reflected in the contesting authority between the civil and military branches. I agree with him; in fact, I would tentatively extend his argument by claiming that this regulation also shows how control over the workforce was a crucial site of that contestation and processes of state-formation.

calculated on the basis of the prevailing bazaar prices. The police authorities were strictly forbidden (leading to dismissal, if found guilty) "to compel any persons not accustomed to act as bearers, *coolies*, or boatmen", or to furnish any bullocks or carts kept for private use or exclusively for agricultural purposes. Attempts to protect the workforce (coolies and boatmen) and *raiyats* (by protecting them against military highhandedness) and ensuring the smooth passage of the troops and individuals were the twin objectives of this regulation. The market played a crucial role. The cost of hire was to be market-based. Should the coolies and boatmen desire, they could enter into a "voluntary exchange" for distances exceeding the jurisdiction of the mediating district official. However, this was to be regulated and enforced by the state. Crucially, in the case of private individuals (both European and native), the police could demand that they give boatmen full or partial advance payment. Refusal to do so meant denial of government assistance.

Shades of freedom, protection, and violation were enshrined in this regulation and more broadly in conceptual categories such as the market and contract as they historically unfolded through the state's regulative measures. Adherence to the practice of market rate and wilful exchange was tempered with the administrative and political demands of a state that was still in the process of stabilizing itself. As a result, the apparent benevolence of the state in protecting the workforce intensified the "highly injurious practice" of *begari* (forced labour) because state officials were invested with the authority and responsibility to provide men and material for convenient passages of troops and individuals.[34] It can be seen as an abuse of authority, or the limitation of a state that failed to realize its ideological objectives.

Another way of looking at it is by recognizing the centrality of labour mobilization in the state-formation process, in which the regulative mechanisms of the state not only shifted and changed but also produced unintended results. There remained an indistinct zone between regulations and practices, which explains why, in spite of the regulative commitment to observe adequate payment and compensation, and also not to indulge in unnecessary force, the practice of *begari* became widespread. The clause that purported to punish subordinate state officials for the forceful extortion of labour seems to have had little effect. However, the structure of command and organization for facilitating help as enshrined in this regulation itself provides clues as to why the fuzziness would arise in the first place. On receiving requests from military commanders, the

---

34. "Bengal Regulation III of 1820", in *Papers Relating to East India Affairs: viz. Regulations passed by the Governments of Bengal, Fort St George, and Bombay, in the Year 1820* (London, 1822), pp. 6–7.

collectors would issue "necessary orders" (with the provision of fines for disobedience) to "landholders, farmers, tahsildars and other persons in charge of the lands through which the troops are to pass" to arrange for supplies.[35] A "creditable native officer" would accompany the troops to make sure that men and material were duly provided; in the case of difficulties, he would seek the assistance of the nearest police officer. Two things are noteworthy here: first, nowhere in the regulations was the phrase "necessary orders" explained, meaning that the group of providers (landlords and others) had no opportunity of saying "no". Second, although the whole organization was done under civil authority, the on-the-spot resolution of difficulties through the involvement of police authority might have opened the space for the temporary criminalization and coercion of a reluctant workforce.[36]

In 1820, therefore, the authority vested in local officials to provide men (coolies and boatmen) was rescinded. That marked the official termination of the practice of *begari* but it does not mean that historical reality would have changed overnight. Rather, it appears that the state compensated for this abolition with a regulation strengthening control over the providers. In 1825, it passed another regulation that made any "wilful neglect or disobedience" (which had to be proved to the "satisfaction" of the collector) on the part of "landholder, farmer, tahsildar and other person" in providing supplies (including boats) punishable, not criminally but through the imposition of fines not exceeding Rs 1,000.[37]

PRIVATE TRAVELLING AND CONTRACTS

While individuals like Fraser became contractors for supplying boats to the government, business agencies sprung up in Calcutta to organize up-country travel for both officials and non-officials. On a typical up-country trip from Calcutta on a budgerow (of sixteen oars) usually accompanied by a luggage boat, a cook boat, and also often separate boats for horses and servants, the crew altogether consisted of thirty to forty men.[38]

The widespread practice of river travel must have created lucrative business opportunities and rivalry. As early as 1774, the government had to put out a public disclaimer declaring that it had not offered any contract

---

35. "Bengal Regulation XI of 1806", in Wigley, *The Eastern Bengal and Assam Code*, I, p. 88.
36. This is one way of understanding the "privatisation of regulation" as pointed by Chitra Joshi in "Histories of Indian Labour: Predicaments and Possibilities", *History Compass*, 6 (2008), pp. 439–454, 447–448.
37. "Bengal Regulation VI of 1825", in Wigley, *The Eastern Bengal and Assam Code*, I, pp. 221–223.
38. By one estimate, it could reach 100, excluding an equal number of servants; Hardgrave, *Boats of Bengal*, p. 19. This seems inflated, though.

or exclusive privilege to one Messrs Share and Dellial. It was forced to do so to steer clear of the complaints made regarding the supply of boats.[39] Organizing travel through an agency was in fact recommended; it supposedly provided security against dandies' desertion, "a circumstance by no means unusual on this voyage".[40] The traveller paid the agency in advance; the boatmen also received one-half of their payment in advance. Advance payment was also an established practice for sending troops and commodities.[41] The difference in the case of private travelling, therefore, was the absence of the state as a contracting party. However, as seen above, it was not entirely absent; it actively tried to secure the comfort of the travellers. Also that native officials were given the power to direct travellers to pay boatmen in advance might be recalled.

For private travellers, the contract system worked in two ways. First, according to the *thika* (literally, a contract, similar to the system of piece wages) given for a said amount according to the distance, with provisions for demurrage; and second, a monthly hire of the vessel, usually at the rate of Rs 10 an oar. In both cases, "the person hiring has nothing to do with the pay, or provision, of the several men employed in navigating the vessel".[42] Deane, in her guide up the river Ganga, mentioned that although a budgerow could be hired at a monthly rate varying from Rs 97 to Rs 176, the one fitted with sixteen oars cost Rs 157 a month, thus almost corroborating the practice of Rs 10 an oar.[43] I will return to the relationship between these contracts and work, but before that an introduction to the variety of labour forms that existed within the boat is necessary.

There were three types of worker that shared the space of the boat. The *manjhee*, or the steersman, was the highest ranked. His pay was between Rs 5 and 7.[44] Being the steersman, he was the leader of the crew. Williamson writes about him: "[K]nowing that his services cannot be dispensed with, [he] will, in most cases, adhere to his way of thinking, until peremptorily compelled by the master's interference, to submit to orders; or overcome by absolute force."[45] He also established the superiority of his position by claiming the forepart of the budgerow, which he generally considered to be his privilege.[46] He was also responsible for the conduct of the dandies. However, Williamson points out that each of the crew had his

39. HP, C, 27 June 1774, no. 6.
40. Deane, *A Tour through the Upper Provinces of Hindostan*, p. 269. Deane had recommended Messrs Barber & Co. at the Old Fort Ghaut in Calcutta to the newly arrived Company employees.
41. HP, Consultation, 13 January 1772, no. 2 (B).
42. Williamson, *The East India Vade-Mecum*, II, pp. 368–369.
43. Deane, *A Tour through the Upper Provinces of Hindostan*, p. 269.
44. Discrepancies existed; see n. 17.
45. Williamson, *The East India Vade-Mecum*, I, p. 284.
46. *Ibid.*, II, p. 377.

own opinion and it was not always easy for the *manjhee* to enforce his wishes. Travellers frequently wrote of the abuse the *manjhee* and the crew showered at each other during the commotion of setting sail or tracking.[47]

Next in the hierarchy came the *golleah*, or bowman, whose pay was between Rs 4 and 5. Working with a bamboo pole, *golleahs* kept "the boat from running against the bank, or upon shoals".[48] An interesting passage brings out the nature of their work:

> Those who have not witnessed the dexterity of this class of people, and the rapidity with which they recover their poles, so as to make repeated resistances in dangerous situations, can form no idea of the strength, activity, and judgement, necessary to qualify a man for this arduous situation. Often the fate of a boat depends on the certainty of the *goleeah's* throw [...].[49]

Dandies, the actual rowers, were in significant numbers on the boat. They were hired on contract; *thika*-dandies, as Williamson called them, were procurable at river ghats. In all probability, each *manjhee* had his set of preferred dandies and recruited them on getting a contract. The fact that the person hiring the boat was not responsible for pay and provision suggests that for dandies the system of contract worked through the intermediary position of the *manjhees*.[50]

A rather rare and occasional presence was that of a fourth group, called *khalasies*. The *khalasie* was a generic labouring term (very much like coolie) to describe those primarily engaged in the transportation of army equipage in the department of the quartermaster-general. When employed on the budgerow they were "confined entirely to the aquatic equipages of great men".[51] Interestingly, they found it beneath their dignity to row a boat unless it happened to be a "jolly-boat furnished with oars on the European plan".[52]

In addition to these four types, another internal differentiation existed on the basis of employment. The government had a retinue of boats for the movement of the Governor-General and his entourage. The main fleet

47. Edward Ward Walter Raleigh, Mss. Eur. D 786, p. 4, British Library. All the Mss. Eur. sources used in this article are from the British Library.
48. Williamson, *The East India Vade-Mecum*, I, p. 285.
49. *Ibid.*
50. For certain commodities and services such as jute, textiles, tea, and lascars, the role of intermediaries (variously called *sardars*, *muqaddams*, jobbers, and *serangs*) is well explored in the historiography. Sources relating to boatmen are too sparse to construct a detailed history of the *manjhees'* role as intermediaries. This, therefore, lies outside the scope of the present article.
51. Williamson, *The East India Vade-Mecum*, I, p. 283.
52. *Ibid.* Wealthy Europeans and natives kept their own richly ornamented boats with handsomely dressed crew. Some of them, such as the *Morphunky* (a peacock-headed boat), were typical pleasure boats; "jolly boats" could be a reference to those, and *khalasies*, who are said to have worn clothes and jackets of English manufacture, might have drawn pride from this association; Hardgrave, *Boats of Bengal*, pp. 7, 25; Williamson, *The East India Vade-Mecum*, I, pp. 281–283.

consisted of the Governor-General's budgerow (the state yacht), called
the *Sonamukhee*; an attendant state barge, the *Philcharee*; the state band
boat, the *Bon Vivant*; a large mess boat, the *Elvira*; and many other
rowing boats (*bauleahs*).[53] When the decision to sell off the *Philcharee*
and some of the rowing boats was taken in 1828–1829, a number of the
boatmen were transferred to other boats and some discharged and given a
pension.[54] A list of pensioners gives some interesting details. First, all
boatmen were aged fifty to sixty; barring a few, all of them had been
employed in the 1790s, thus signifying an average service career of more
than thirty years. And secondly, family played an important role. Some of
them worked together with their brothers; others were substituted by
their brothers when on short leave.[55] The difference in salary from other
boatmen is noticeable: a *manjhee* who would otherwise receive anything
between Rs 4 and 7 got Rs 10 per month, and a dandy, who would
normally receive anything between Rs 2 and 4, was paid Rs 4 and 8 annas.
Better pay obviously implied a better pension too.

In a significant revisionist intervention, Mohapatra has challenged the
earlier argument put forward by Bernard Cohn that colonialism engendered
a movement from social status to contract.[56] The employment-based division
among boatmen corroborates his point. The differential status arose
because of the nature of employment shaped through active state policies,
such as pension, and not through any caste or kinship ties. The two
images below illustrate the contrast between dandies working under the
two different systems.

To summarize, different types of contractual arrangement (if not the
contract per se) structured the work regime of boatmen. One existed
directly between the Company and the boatmen, another between the
Company and wealthy and enterprising individuals. The third existed
between agencies and private individuals, the fourth between agencies and
the *manjhees*. For dandies, another level existed between them and the
manjhees. Having said this, it is equally important to bear in mind that the
ways in which merchants, traders, travellers, and the state tried to enforce
the contract was highly complex and an arena of intense negotiation
between them and the boatmen. The normative centrality of contract

---

53. The *Sonamukhee* [golden-faced] was built during the period of Warren Hastings
(1773–1785); the *Philcharee* [elephant-headed] in 1813. On the latter, see HP, 17 July 1828, nos
14–15, and HP, 18 September 1828, nos 19–23. See also *The European in India; From A
Collection of Drawings, by Charles D'Oyley [...] with a Preface and Copious Descriptions, by
Captain Thomas Williamson [...]* (London, 1813), Plate XII and its accompanying text. Edward
Walter Raleigh, who was part of this fleet, provides an interesting account in his diary; Mss. Eur.
D 786.
54. HP, Consultation, 14 July 1829, no. 11.
55. HP, Consultation, 26 February 1829, no. 2/4.
56. Mohapatra, "From Contract to Status?".

Figure 1. A state boat establishment dandy.
The European in India, Plate XII.

needs to be seen in the light of how the work was done and the challenges that were faced by both employers and employees.

WORLD OF WORK: HARD-WORKING DANDIES

Work involved twin aspects of skill and physical exertion. For *manjhees*, being the master and thus in a privileged position, the latter was not of such importance. The *golleahs*, as observed in the above passage, combined both skill and physical faculties. For dandies, it was their physical

a Dandy of the River Ganges or Exquisite of
the first Water —

Figure 2. A dandy working on the river Ganges.
Francis James Hawkins, Diaries and Letters, *Mss. Eur. B 365/4 ff. 2.* © *The British Library Board, EUR B 365 f2–4. Used with permission.*

labour that was most frequently referred to. For the journey between Calcutta and Allahabad, which normally took three months, these dandies, owing to unfavourable stream currents, had often to track boats from the shore. Neck deep in water, pulling the shore ropes and frequently forced to swim with ropes tied to their waist, their work left an imprint on their bodies. Bishop Heber had observed:

> Our own men, though all in the prime of youth, well fed, and with figures such as statuary might delight to model after, themselves show too many symptoms of the ill-effects occasioned by their constant vicissitudes of water, sun, and toil. The backs and skin of many of them were scaly, as if with leprosy, and they spoke of this complaint as a frequent consequence of their way of life [...].[57]

57. Reginald Heber, *Narrative of a Journey through the Upper Provinces of India from Calcutta to Bombay, 1824–25* (London, 1828; repr. New Delhi, 1993), I, p. 120. For the hard toil and skill of dandies as well as their knowledge of waterways, see also Henry T. Bernstein, *Steamboats on the Ganges: An Exploration in the History of India's Modernization through*

Or consider the account given by Charles Ramus Forrest:

> These are a hardy race of beings, wear but little clothing, and though exposed in towing the boat for the whole day to a burning sun, and frequently up to the middle in water, their heads are not only without any turban or covering, but literally shaven quite bare. Their skull, probably from constant exposure, becomes hard and thick enough to resist the rays of the sun thus pouring on their naked scones.[58]

The labour and skill involved in rowing depended on the nature of the merchandise, boats, and oars. For instance, rowing a flat-bottomed merchandise boat (*patella*) required ten to twelve men working in a standing position with bamboo oars almost eighteen feet in length with a broad round blade at the end.[59] In contrast, many a variety of pleasure boats required dandies to be seated and to use paddles. Apart from rowing and tracking, mooring the boat safely on a soft sandbank was also physically demanding. An anonymous traveller thus described how:

> The operation of securing the boats to the shore which is a work of some time and labour and is performed by driving heavy piles into the earth both before and after the vessel so as to moor Her securely to them against the force of the water, took up about half an hour.[60]

This physical hard work was aggravated by the changing and difficult weather conditions. Unlike dak (mail-delivery) travelling, which was frequently done during the night, river travel was restricted to daytime because "the shifting nature of the land banks and violent currents renders it impossible to go on in the dark".[61] On the basis of hard work and "consummate drudgery", Williamson compared the dandies' hard life to that of a scavenger's carthorse, symbolizing the equation of human to animal power. Taking into account this laborious employment, aggravated

---

Science and Technology (Calcutta, 1960), pp. 16–17. For tracking a boat with a combined crew of three yet yielding no results, see Raleigh, Mss. Eur. D 786, pp. 7, 14.

58. Charles Ramus Forrest, *A Picturesque Tour along the River Ganges and Jumna in India [...]* (London, 1824), p. 124. The examples can be multiplied. John Luard described dandies in the following manner: they "work laboriously from sunrise to sunset, frequently in the water for hours, up to their middles, shoving with their backs the boats over sand banks"; John Luard, *A Series of Views in India [...]* (London, 1833), Part II, text accompanying "A Budgerow", p. 1037. Lowrie, a missionary, described them as "a peaceful, hard-working, and obliging race; [who] are compelled to live nearly at the lowest point of human subsistence"; Lowrie, *Travels in North India*, p. 92; on the toil of tracking and his fear of drowning, see pp. 68, 99–100.

59. Hardgrave, *Boats of Bengal*, p. 88.

60. Anon., *Journal of a Voyage of Exploration of the River Ganges Upstream to Patna, 28 July–30 August 1821*, Mss. Eur. E 271, p. 12. Strong winds weakened the moorings; in such a situation, the boatmen's alacrity, even at midnight, was indispensable to save the boat from being either carried away or sunk; Lowrie, *Travels in North India*, p. 83.

61. Raleigh, Mss. Eur. D 786, p. 3.

by uncertain and unfavourable weather, he invited his readers to empa-
thize with the bodily exertion of this class:

> Imagine the effects, even upon the most hardy constitution, of exposure to all
> weathers; at one moment under a burning sun, or numbed by a cold northerly
> blast; by turns on board, or at the track rope; moving at a slow pace against a rapid
> current; and wading, without the smallest hesitations, through a million of puddles,
> often up to the neck, or even obliged to swim: the footing perhaps rugged, or along
> a heavy sand, or a deep mud; and the path lying through briars, bordering steep
> precipices! All this the dandy undergoes for the small wages [...].[62]

There are numerous instances recorded in the administrative papers and
travel writings of the period to suggest that the loss of men and material
was not an infrequent occurrence. In spite of the high romanticization of
landscape and river journey, the risk involved was evident from frequent
textual and visual representations of squalls and thunder storms on the river
Ganga.[63] Raleigh, who accompanied Lord Amherst's royal entourage as a
surgeon, reported frequent sinking of boats and supplies, and the drowning
of native soldiers. While describing the drowning of a soldier during a
squall, he compared the Ganga to a sea and presented the difficulties of
navigation in the following manner: "although it may appear absurd to talk
of 'sea' in the river, a squall on the Ganges in flat-bottomed, unwieldy
pinnaces and budgerows is no joke, and a far more dangerous position than
in a gale at sea in a good tight ship".[64]
The rainy season had a favourable wind blowing from the south-east
but was nevertheless hazardous because of rains and squalls.[65] On the
other hand, the hot season, when the water level was low, made tracking
inevitable. For certain stretches of the river, such as that between
Berhampore and Murshidabad, the river was low at all seasons. Here,
tracking took almost seven hours for a distance of seven miles, which by
dak travelling took about one hour.[66] The sand blowing off the banks also

---

62. Williamson, *The East India Vade-Mecum*, I, p. 286.
63. Henry Salt's 1803 drawing, reproduced below, is illustrative of this; the British Library online gallery has titled it "Scene on the Ganges near Sahibgunge". In Mildred Archer, *British Drawings in the India Office Library* (London, 1969), II, Plate 67, it is titled "A Storm on the Ganges, Near Sahibgunge". On the back of the painting itself, however, Salt had written "Ganges. Where Boatmen were nearly drowned". The incident he referred to took place during Lord Valentia's travels, in which two men, while trying to row the boat, were nearly drowned by the currents; http://www.bl.uk/onlinegallery/onlineex/apac/other/019wdz000000104u00000000.html, accessed 25 November 2013. Rains and waves wetting the interior of the cabin were often reported. See Anon., *Journal of a Voyage of Exploration of the River Ganges*, pp. 67, 87–88; Hawkins, Mss. Eur. B 365/4 ff. 1–28, pp. 7–8.
64. Raleigh, Mss. Eur. D 786, p. 6.
65. A sudden spring tidal rush, locally called *ban* in Bengali, in which the water rose up to five feet on the shore, was deeply feared; Hardgrave, *Boats of Bengal*, pp. 39–41.
66. Deane, *A Tour through the Upper Provinces of Hindostan*, p. 275.

Figure 3. Henry Salt, "Ganges. Where Boatmen were nearly drowned".
http://www.bl.uk/onlinegallery/onlineex/apac/other/largeimage65774.html; © *The British Library Board, WD 104. Used with permission.*

made the work difficult.[67] *Kaal-Baisaki* (disaster of May), as it is known locally in the region, or the north-westerly winds, as they were called by Europeans, was a feature of the months between April and June. These winds were particularly disastrous because of their suddenness and strength.[68] Frederick Augustus Barnard Glover, a Bengal civil servant living in a town situated on the banks of the Ganga, explained to his wife the impossibility for those who have not been to India to imagine the difference in the streams during the hot and rainy seasons.[69]

Although a lot of accounts did present the physical exertion and hard work of dandies in a sympathetic way, there is, at times, a lurking hint at a cultural understanding of their work. One of them was the disapproving tone in which travellers described dandies' antipathy towards each other in times of distress. They were accused of being cold and indifferent towards their fellows' misery, particularly when it came to saving those drowning.[70] Their skill was also questioned; surprisingly, after giving a

67. The anonymous traveller mentioned the difficulty this presented to the travellers, but the same can also be said for the boatmen; Anon., *Journal of a Voyage of Exploration of the River Ganges*, p. 76.
68. Hardgrave, *Boats of Bengal*, p. 14.
69. Frederick A.B. Glover, *Four Letters from Frederick Augustus Barnard Glover*, Mss. Eur B 371, p. 6.
70. On the wreckage eliciting no excitement, see Anon., *Journal of a Voyage of Exploration of the River Ganges*, pp. 84–85; on the indifference of dandies to saving their fellows from drowning, see Raleigh, Mss. Eur. D 786, p. 6.

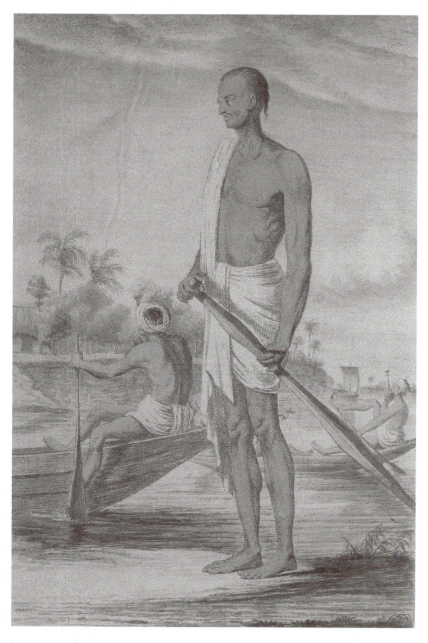

Figure 4. "Dandi, Boatman".
Etching from Balthazar Solvyns, A Collection of Two Hundred and Fifty Coloured Etchings *(Calcutta, 1799). Reproduced, with permission, from the collection of Robert L. Hardgrave, Jr. For a discussion of the Dandy, see Hardgrave*, A Portrait of the Hindus: Balthazar Solvyns and the European Image of India: 1760–1824 *(New York [etc.], 2004), pp. 218–219.*

long vivid account of torrents and rain, the wreckage of boats, and almost facing death, Lowrie caustically remarked that boatmen were unskilful and reckless.[71] Another was the practice of hookah smoking, which Solvyns pictorially depicted (Figure 4) as the chief characteristic of dandies (both dandies in the background are smoking hookah).

Ahuja has argued that the dominant strand of colonial culturalist representations depicted workers in Madras city as lazy and in need of "restraint, authority and even compulsion to be roused from apathy".[72] Without saying this in so many words, his account shows how cultural traits legitimized colonial interventions in areas of wage fixation and labour regulation. Surely, for boatmen in eastern India this was not the case. In spite of the cultural hues of secondary importance that coloured some accounts, a majority of them boldly took note of the hard work that dandies performed. It is thus pertinent to ask if plausible explanations of these cultural readings can be offered which stem from within the work process that involved rowing, tracking, and mooring. Do indirect references to skill explain direct observations on work practices, including culturally situated representations?

A range of commentators described dandies as amphibious. Lowrie noted that they were of "an almost amphibious race", not to be drowned easily.[73] Said in the context of a personal fear that he alone would drown, this characterization should be read as a description of the relationship between dandies' skill and their working conditions. Constant storms and rains that led to the frequent wreckage of boats and loss of property may have honed the skill but also plausibly eroded the sense of loss or fear. For some Europeans, the superior level of dandies' skill in dealing with difficult working conditions thus coalesced into a cultural reading of them as indifferent to their own lot.

Contract, bad weather, difficult and uncertain navigable conditions, and the physically demanding nature of work informed the working conditions of boatmen, particularly for dandies. There was, nevertheless, one more factor. Correspondence from this period is very much concerned with preventing delays. Delays, which otherwise appear to, and did in fact, occur due to factors producing uncertainties, can also be understood as depicting anxiety arising from the structured relationship between

71. Lowrie, *Travels in North India*, p. 73. Perhaps, being a missionary, he was compelled to acknowledge the saving grace of the Lord rather than the efficient rowing hands of his boatmen; see pp. 73–74, 87.
72. Ahuja, "Origins", p. 170.
73. Lowrie, *Travels in North India*, pp. 68–69. Another missionary reported a native boat crashing into his own and getting completely splintered. He noted that boatmen "swam like ducks, and none were lost"; Zebina Flavius Griffin, *India and Daily Life in Bengal* (Buffalo, NY, 1896), p. 110.

time, money, and distance. This relationship upon which the work of dandies was judged was related to the regime of contract that existed between the government and Company individuals. Officials of different ranks, ranging from a colonel to a cadet, received a fixed boat allowance.[74] This was accompanied by a table of distances from one station to another calculated in terms of months. The difficulty in procuring boats was not treated as constituting a delay.

What we have here is a strict if not fixed understanding of travel time. The fixed monetary allowances paid to Company employees must have enforced the pressure on *manjhees* and dandies to finish their work in the time stipulated. This also explains why the *thika* system was used. According to Williamson, *thika* hire ensured that *manjhees* would finish their work as speedily as possible. For this, they would hire a good crew of dandies. In contrast, he claimed that under the monthly contract system "there will be no end to excuses, delays, and evasions: the *dandies* will generally be wanting in number, and their quality be very indifferent".[75]

A critical appraisal of the category of delay reveals the interlinked economic conditions which were not directly imposed on boatmen. For, even if we accept Williamson's observation, there could only be so much delay intentionally engineered by boatmen and contested as permissible and negotiable within the broader framework set by the officials' monetary allowances and the time stipulated for arriving at the specified destination. The category of "delay" was premised upon the idea that there was a standard ideal speed that needed to be adhered to. In cases of unspecified rates, ten miles against the current and fourteen with was taken as standard.[76] The officials themselves wanted to finish their journeys in time, as delays were not compensated. One can, therefore, argue that the cultural idiom of laziness which the natives were often imputed with, or the wilful act of resistance designed to intentionally delay, had its roots in part in the nature of the fixed allowances that European officials received from the Company.

"MUTINOUS" DANDIES

Hard work as a "way of life", as Heber described it,[77] was mediated through contract, advance payment, time–money relationships, and difficult work environments. The question of delay created a suspicious relationship between the traveller and the boatmen. However, long periods of travelling

---

74. See HP, Consultation, 7 June 1773, nos. 29–30; Williamson, *The East India Vade-Mecum*, II, pp. 369–370. Unless indicated, the following account is based on these two sources.
75. Williamson, *The East India Vade-Mecum*, II, p. 374.
76. *Ibid.*, p. 370.
77. Hawkins described it as "tedious work"; Mss. Eur. B 365/4 ff. 1–28, p. 2.

made Europeans dependent on these dandies for knowing places and gathering general information about the country.

These constellations are nonetheless important in understanding the context in which dandies were called "mutinous". In other words, the extent to which dandies would have adopted a "mutinous" attitude obviously hinged upon aspects of wage and payment but it was also influenced by the realization and exploitation of the extent to which they could push their bargaining power in the zone of asymmetrical proximity. Many travellers carried guidebooks, grammar books, and other "scientific equipment", such as telescopes, but informal conversational exchange was a regular feature on the boat. Heber was informed about a variety of matters by his boatmen.[78] In times of crises, for instance during Chait Singh's rebellion in Benares in 1781, boatmen became a major source of information and intelligence.[79] Mobility allowed them to possess not only specific skills related to navigation but also information deemed important for political control. Due to this, they also became victims of political rivalry.[80]

When his dandies refused to take him further without an advance payment, William Parry Okeden labelled it a "boatmen mutiny". He was eventually forced to comply with their wishes.[81] This was not an isolated case; other travellers also mentioned mutinous moments, which were sometimes avoided by accepting dandies' demands and at other times by using force or the threat of force. The fact that delays and mutinous conditions could also be caused by bad weather did not go unnoticed; the anonymous traveller and his friends had reluctantly to accept the decision of the majority of *manjhees* to halt their journey due to bad weather.[82] However, in most colonial accounts the alleged wilful delays act as a precursor to mutiny by dandies, which would usually be based upon a demand for advance payment.

An interesting "mutinous" situation developed on the boat of the anonymous traveller's friend. He had prohibited the crew from preparing their morning meal in his presence. The reason was the noise and smoke (including smoke coming from the hookah). Usually, by nine o'clock in the morning he would join his friend and leave the crew to do their

78. Heber, *Narrative of a Journey through the Upper Provinces of India*, pp. 105, 107.
79. On matters related to revenue, the Raja of Benares had militarily challenged the authority of the EIC. His rebellion can be described as one of the most serious challenges the EIC faced in the late eighteenth century. Boatmen again became strategically important during the 1857 "Mutiny".
80. Reportedly, dandies of the governor-general's fleet were captured and either drowned or were killed; James, *Selections from the Correspondence of the Revenue Chief of Bihar*, pp. 79–80.
81. *Diary and Sporting Journal of William Parry Okeden, India, 1821–41*, Mss. Eur. A 210, p. 16.
82. Anon., *Journal of a Voyage of Exploration of the River Ganges*, p. 37.

chores. This order, however, was allegedly often disobeyed and hence the officer threatened to break all the cooking pots of the dandies. The latter then threatened to desert; the *burkandazes* (guards, usually with matchlocks) were called in to arrest the "mutineers" in case they persisted with their threat.[83] Thus, amidst the informal exchange between travelling Europeans and rowing dandies, a zone of mutual suspicion and dependence existed. On the threat of desertion, the traveller remarked that "[t]his was not to be allowed of course, either for their sakes or ours".[84]

Violence and threats were often resorted to in order to reinstate control. It is thus no surprise to see Heber commenting that "one fertile reason of boatmen's desertion was the ill conduct of Europeans, who often stimulated them [dandies] to do things which, in their weak and clumsy boats, were really dangerous, and against all law or right, beat them when they refused or hesitated".[85] Insistence by European masters on doing something that potentially threatened the boats and the dandies' means of livelihood, as well as the prohibition of certain practices such as preparing morning meals, thus constituted two sides of the volatile relationship forged between dandies and their masters on the space of the boat. Keeping such mutual dependence in mind, Williamson advised travellers to strike a balance of resolution and conciliation that would realize the desired effect without coming across as brutal and harsh.[86] Lowrie's description of his conduct based on "mild firmness" comes close to what Williamson had suggested.[87]

This firm but mild temperament was required not only to reaffirm authority but also to secure personal comfort. In a colonial situation, a public display of authority always needed to be balanced with private comfort, especially during long sojourns and journeys. Deane warned her readers: "It is always desirable to keep him [*manjhee*] in good humour, by attending a little to his advice, as on his depends in a great measure both your expedition and comfort of the voyage."[88] It must, however, be said that for many newcomers, officials, and Europeans living in India, river journeys became pleasant and bearable owing to constant visits to and from friends and acquaintances residing in places along the Ganga. The cultural "zone of contact" that existed between them and the boatmen was sprinkled all around with "zones of comfort" forged by meeting dispersed members of the British community. A slightly different feature is observable in missionary writings though; surrounded by "strange and

83. *Ibid.*, p. 38.
84. *Ibid.*
85. Heber, *Narrative of a Journey through the Upper Provinces of India*, p. 211.
86. Williamson, *The East India Vade-Mecum*, II, p. 375.
87. Lowrie, *Travels in North India*, p. 64.
88. Deane, *A Tour through the Upper Provinces of Hindostan*, p. 273.

heathen people", they saw the journey itself as an opportunity to reassert their faith in missionary activities.[89]

Partly because of this sense of dependence and anxiety, but also because of the fact that "travel by the river was literally confined to the river",[90] where the only long association with the natives was through the group of boatmen (and servants), there were moments of jocular exchange. When the wind blew off Raleigh's hat, one of the dandies made to catch it and fell overboard with the hat in his hand. Raleigh commented, "[h]owever, he was soon up again like a duck. These men are perfectly amphibious, and would as soon as be in the water as out."[91] Again, when he claimed to have called the bluff of a gunpowder seller who falsely tried to impress Raleigh, the latter gave him a thump on his head and the dandies who joined "in the joke, pitched my friend [the seller] overboard, to the great amusement of the people on the shore".[92] Sometimes, even physical contact was unavoidable. While traversing the landscape of Bengal, the missionary Griffins couple had to sit on the hands of the boatmen to be ferried across to dry land. They noted, "We do not so much object to putting our arms around the neck of each of these men, but sometimes the ladies would rather be excused. But it must be done, all the same."[93] The whole group consisting of dandies, *manjhees*, and servants were a constant source of information, amusement, and chat. Sometimes, they also asked their British masters about their lives and friends back in Britain.[94]

It is important to recognize that while work in its stricter economic sense was premised upon the notion of contracts and wages, the experience of being at work did not necessarily depend on these factors alone. Anxiety and amusement were part of the same relationship forged on the space of the boat, as were the elements of authority and desertion. A lot of Europeans talked about dandies in functional terms of work, but they also shared their routinized lives on the boat and ashore. For them, the dandy's curry was perhaps avoidable but not untouchable. In any analysis of the relationship between travelling Europeans and their rowing dandies, the shared space of the boat has to be taken into account because it allows us to understand the nature of work within the context of worksites, which were precisely the river, the banks and the boat. This relationship between work and worksite is also important in understanding the moments of solidarities and differentiations formed among the boatmen.

89. Lowrie, *Travels in North India*, p. 61. For a more direct observation on the missionary benefits of boat journeys, see pp. 105, 108–109.
90. Deane, *A Tour through the Upper Provinces of Hindostan*, p. 226.
91. Raleigh, Mss. Eur. D 786, p. 10.
92. *Ibid.*, p. 11.
93. Griffin, *India and Daily Life in Bengal*, p. 41.
94. Hawkins, Mss. Eur. B 365/4 ff. 1–28, pp. 7–8.

When Lowrie hired his budgerow and luggage/cook boat from the agency at Calcutta, little did he know that he would soon be enforcing his "mild firmness". The boatmen of the budgerow insisted on cooking on the boat, which he firmly denied but allowed them to do on the cook boat. This, nonetheless, was resisted by the boatmen of the latter. Lowrie felt compelled to explain this resistance by pointing to caste restrictions, but soon he referred to it as a "matter of convenience", which indeed seems to have been the case. Finally, three cooking places were set up on the cook boat: one each for Lowrie and his servants, the crew of the budgerow, and the boatmen of the cook boat.[95]

"THIEVISH" DANDIES: WORK AND REGULATION

While introducing the dandy serving in the governor-general's boat establishment (Figure 1), the author noted,

> The person exhibited in this Plate must not be viewed as the ordinary *Dandy*, or boatman, employed in the vessels trading throughout the country; these being generally poor naked wretches, whose avocation is, perhaps, the most laborious of any yet known, and whose depravity and thievish habits are absolutely proverbial.[96]

Williamson also warned his readers of the *manjhees'* profit-making tactics. Newcomers, in particular, were asked to remain vigilant of the boatmen. But this was said in the context of occupational privilege (or extortion) involved in by helping the newcomers; otherwise, it would be erroneous to read a culturally essentializing tone in this characterization. Williamson himself made it clear that,

> It would not be just to infer from [...] the readiness with which the boatmen avail themselves of the necessities of persons desirous to leave a ship, that they are particularly covetous, or prone to imposition: we need only look at home, where we shall find that no mercy is shewn to such unfortunate persons as become the prey of our watermen, along the whole extent of our coast.[97]

Rather than invoking any independent ideological bases of civilizational inferiority (such as Asiatic despotism), Williamson's characterization of physical appearance and morality is inseparable from the context of work. The outer physical appearance, which was full of ringworms, itch, and herpetic eruptions all over the back, chest, and arms, made a Bengal dandy the most disgusting mortal. But the hard work and modest wages that explained this physicality also explained why "the European must blame

---

95. Lowrie, *Travels in North India*, p. 64.
96. *The European in India*, text accompanying Plate XII.
97. Williamson, *The East India Vade-Mecum*, I, p. 148.

himself, should his valuables be missing in consequence of an ill-placed confidence, or of neglect in regard to securing his property, so far as may be practicable".[98] By this understanding, a thievish nature arose out of an impoverished condition. For *manjhees*, who were relatively better off, mobility became the factor that encouraged "depravity". The boats carrying colonial officials were seldom checked at river outposts. *Manjhees* allegedly used this immunity to carry out illicit trade. The space of the boat under the deck (from the veranda to the stern), which he allegedly zealously guarded as his privilege, was used for storing commodities such as salt and opium.[99]

Moral depravation of boatmen developing due to poverty or privilege conditioned by work was often reported. However, it was the constant evidence of their mutinous character exhibited either in a refusal to row or in simply "absconding" that led to stringent policing measures. It was already noted how *burkandazes* were summoned to use the threat of arrest. In such cases, it was advisable for the traveller to report the matter to the police, who would place a *burkandaz* or a *peon* (an attendant, usually without a matchlock) on the boat at the expense of the *manjhee*.[100] Meanwhile, public ferries and other boats gradually came under regulative scrutiny. Under Regulation XIX of 1816, collectors (district civil officials) had to report on the number of public ferries, tolls levied, and the number and size of boats maintained at the various ghats.[101] The private keepers of boats and boatmen were also made accountable; for instance, indigo planters had to submit statements giving the number and size of boats employed at their factories, together with the names of the *manjhees*.[102] Under the same regulation, collectors were also directed to fix the wages of the boatmen.[103] Regulation VI of 1819, however, rescinded the parts dealing with the management of public ferries.[104] The number of public ferries was reduced, but most importantly they were now put under the supervision of magistrates (district police officials).

The stated objectives were to strengthen policing, promote the safety of travellers, and facilitate the conveyance of troops. In all these, *manjhees* became the centre of regulation. In the event of misconduct, the magistrates

98. *Ibid.*, p. 287. For his related views see also pp. 148–152, 286–288.

99. Williamson, *The East India Vade-Mecum*, II, pp. 377–380. Lowrie reported an incident when a *manjhee* of another boat had come to him selling European goods which consisted of "a box of old Windsor soap and a cracked bottle of arrow root"; Lowrie, *Travels in North India*, p. 91.

100. Williamson, *The East India Vade-Mecum*, II, pp. 374–375.

101. Pranab Chandra Roy Chaudhury, *Muzaffarpur Old Records* (Patna, 1959), p. 304.

102. *Ibid.*, p. 309.

103. *Ibid.*, p. 306.

104. "Bengal Regulation VI of 1819", in *Papers Relating to East India Affairs: viz. Regulations passed by the Governments of Bengal, Fort St George, and Bombay, in the Year 1819* (London, 1821), pp. 19–22.

had the power to replace them. *Manjhees* were also obliged to ferry troops free of charge (with their baggage and stores), policemen, and other native government officers travelling on public duty. In cases of drowning and accidents, if it could be proved that the reason was the overloading or the bad condition of the boat, *manjhees* could be imprisoned for a period not exceeding six months or charged a fine of Rs 200.

The idea of promoting free commercial intercourse was aired by professing non-interference in the management of private ferries, but, once again, magistrates could interfere if matters related to the "general maintenance of the police" and the "safety of passengers and property".[105] The discussion on the conveyance of troops should be recalled here. While Regulation XI of 1806 tried to protect coolies and boatmen available at the river ghats from the excesses of travelling military men, it also made those who were part of the fleet accountable for carrying out their work. *Manjhees* "were required to deliver a list of names and places of their dandies, and sign the agreement", which read:

> I will not permit or induce any of the dandies of my boat to abscond during the voyage under the penalty of forfeiting the sum of [...] payable to me at (the destination), and that in the event of the Hon'ble Company being put to any expense for the hire of dandies in consequence of any of my people absconding my boats shall be liable to confiscation.[106]

Regulation VII of 1819 has been identified as one of the early ones absorbing the essence of master and servant law that made workmen criminally accountable for breach of contract.[107] In such cases, workmen, if found guilty, faced one month's imprisonment (with the possibility of two further months in prison), whereas masters, if guilty, had only to compensate through the payment of wages and arrears. This regulation, it should be noted, was theoretically premised upon two parties voluntarily entering into a contract. Boatmen must have come under the ambit of this regulation as the practice of private travelling and also transporting troops and merchandise was based on contracts. However, for boatmen the two aspects of regulation of work, the payment of damages due to desertion and imprisonment, predated the 1819 Regulation.[108]

The strength of these regulations definitely derived from the notion of contract and its breach, but the framing of the regulations was itself part

---

105. *Ibid.*, p. 21.
106. "Rules and Regulations for the Transport of Troops", *Board of Control*, CLXXXI, 1806–07, F/4/191, 4260, Asia, Pacific and Africa Collections, British Library.
107. Mohapatra, "From Contract to Status?"; "Bengal Regulation VII of 1819", pp. 23–24.
108. There are examples from the period before this regulation was passed that show dandies put to hard labour on road construction as part of penal punishment; "Letter from R. Graham, Acting Collector of Tirhoot to Charles Buller, Sub-Secretary to the Board of Revenue", 30 May 1800, in Chaudhury, *Muzaffarpur Old Records*, p. 176.

of the broader political context in which the early colonial state operated. This context was one of state consolidation of power through the efficient movement of troops. The ideological context was also present; this related to providing safe travelling conditions for individuals and troops, but also to protecting the workforce against any sort of highhandedness. Work enforcement and protection as mediated through the authority of the police had two interrelated aspects. First, police authority was used to enforce the contractual arrangement, leading to the possibility of the workforce being criminalized; second, the police were very much part of the process through which contractual arrangements were finalized.

According to the clauses of Regulation XI of 1806, the police officers were not only supposed to enforce carefully the just compensation for using bearers, coolies, boatmen, carts, and bullocks but also "authorized to adjust the rate of hire [...] as well as demand that the whole or a part, according to the circumstances of the case, be paid in advance".[109] The advance system was used and explained differently by the parties concerned. For travellers like Deane, advance payment emboldened boatmen to press their demands and hence made them rebellious; for the state, to make sure that boatmen were paid due advances was part of the protective shades of regulations; and for boatmen themselves, advance was a way to provide for their families when they were away at work. However, the part payment of wages as advance that formalized a contract was also, as Mohapatra has argued, an instrument "to tie down workers" by limiting their options of free exit.[110]

So far, I have looked at work and its structuring constituents to understand the regulative policies of the colonial state. The period of this study was nonetheless also marked by frequent incidences of crime, in particular those committed during travel. A lot has been written on the theme of *thugee* and highway crimes, but the Ganga (being the highway connecting eastern and northern India) was also an active and a rather difficult to control scene of crime.[111] Like other peripatetic groups, such as *banjaras* and *gosains*, boatmen came under colonial suspicion and scrutiny, at least for being collaborators if not direct perpetrators. The state envisioned the involvement of dandies in two ways: first, directly committing river dacoities, second, aiding the dacoits and criminals. In addition, criminals might disguise as dandies, making all of them, in the eyes of the authorities, suspicious.[112] An extensive system of river patrolling

109. "Bengal Regulation XI of 1806", in Wigley, *The Eastern Bengal and Assam Code*, p. 92.
110. Mohapatra, "From Contract to Status?", pp. 120–121.
111. As late as the early twentieth century, it was estimated that about 50 to 75 per cent of river crime went unreported to the police; F.C. Daly, *Manual of Criminal Classes Operating in Bengal* (Calcutta, 1916), p. 88.
112. On criminals disguising themselves as either passengers or dandies, see Datta, *Selections from the Judicial Records*, p. 296.

was organized in the all-important riverine districts of Bihar and Bengal.[113] To help combat crime, magistrates were given additional powers to search boats.

From the mid-nineteenth century on, the nexus between colonial ethnography (primarily caste-based) and the understanding of the occupational history of different professional groups reified into the notion of hereditary criminality. The river dacoities, which in Bengal became a major subject attracting recurrent administrative attention, continued throughout the nineteenth century.[114] This aspect lies outside the purview of this article, but it must be pointed out that by 1872 the Mallah caste, a prominent boatmen caste, had been added to the list of "criminal tribes".[115] It was, nevertheless, a long-drawn-out process. Even as the police understood it, the Mallah caste was, until late, seen as a professional-occupational category comprising a number of sub-castes working on rivers as traders, boatmen, or fishermen. It was only in 1914 that some of them coming from the different districts of the United Provinces were declared to be criminal tribes (under the Criminal Tribes Act of 1871, CTA).[116] Furthermore, as Smita Tewari Jassal's study shows, Mallahs were classified under Class B of the CTA, meaning that although they were "criminals" they had recently settled down to agriculture, in contrast to tribes classified under Class C, which required resettlement and transportation.[117] The upshot of this argument is that the occupational diversification, including settlement in agriculture, had taken place before the 1871 census and the passing of the CTA. I have elsewhere explored the implications of this diversification from being mobile to settled,[118] but the factor of the regulation of boatmen was something conspicuous throughout the period. A set of rules for river navigation passed in 1867 required each boatman to "provide details, such as caste, patrilineal descent, place of residence and the 'length of the river under his pilotage'".[119]

The caste composition of criminals in colonial accounts was not something novel to the second half of the nineteenth century. Nor, as

113. I have covered this theme in detail elsewhere; see Nitin Sinha, *Communication and Colonialism in Eastern India: Bihar, 1760s–1880s* (London [etc.], 2012), pp. 144–149.

114. For instance, see Home Police, A, January 1868, nos 14–16, National Archives of India, New Delhi; Arun Mukherjee, "Crime and Criminals in Nineteenth Century Bengal (1861–1904)", *Indian Economic and Social History Review*, 21 (1984), pp. 153–183, 164–166.

115. Assa Doron, *Caste, Occupation and Politics on the Ganges: Passages of Resistance* (Farnham, 2008), p. 30.

116. Daly, *Manual of Criminal Classes*, pp. 87–88, 93.

117. Smita Tewari Jassal, "Caste and the Colonial State: Mallahs in the Census", *Contributions to Indian Sociology*, 35 (2001), pp. 319–354, 340–342.

118. Sinha, *Communication and Colonialism*, 191–192.

119. Doron, *Caste, Occupation and Politics*, p. 39.

Arun Mukherjee has argued, was the involvement of the up-country Mallahs coming into Bengal from the North-Western Provinces (NWP) and Bihar a new feature.[120] However, as far as caste-based description in ascertaining the role of boatmen was concerned, a shift is discernible from the earlier period. Barring few instances, the late eighteenth- and early nineteenth-century accounts usually use the work-based categories of *manjhees*, *golleahs*, and dandies. In the sources used in this article, only one reference each to Mallahs of the NWP and Kaibarta of Bengal has been found.[121] Whether this signifies a radical move from a work-based to a caste-based understanding of Indian society remains a question for further research, but these sources provide an interesting entry point to look at work, caste, and ritual purity together.

The above point relates to accounts of the dietary practices of boatmen. In late nineteenth-century caste-based accounts, such as that of William Crooke, Mallahs were associated with a ritually inferior position in the caste hierarchy; this was shown by giving details of their "polluting" dietary habits. Apart from fish and meat, they allegedly also ate rats, tortoises, crocodiles, and practised excessive alcoholic consumption.[122] However, looking at descriptions of cooking practices as reported by several travellers of the earlier period, no trace of the dandies' "derogatory" and "polluting" practices can be found. There are two conflicting accounts of how they prepared their food. According to one, boatmen reportedly did not cook their food on board; they ate only parched rice while on board and prepared their dinner ashore in the evening after mooring their boats. This practice was so strictly observed that at times, when rain did not permit them to prepare their dinner, they did not eat at all. This was true for the "Hindu" members of the crew; the Muslims reportedly ate on board.[123] The second view suggests that they did prepare their food on board, and this was in fact, at times, the reason behind the conflict between European travellers and boatmen.[124] Whatever might

120. Mukherjee, "Crime and Criminals", p. 165. On the use of caste to understand criminality and on up-country mobile gangs in the earlier period see Sinha, "Mobility, Control and Criminality", pp. 22–25.

121. In one of the preliminary studies on fisheries, Peter Reeves has argued that there was not much of a difference between Kaibarta and Mallah castes in the two provinces; Peter Reeves, "Regional Diversity in South Asian Inland Fisheries: Colonial Bengal and Uttar Pradesh Compared", *South Asia: Journal of South Asian Studies*, 25 (2002), pp. 121–135, 127.

122. Doron, *Caste, Occupation and Politics*, pp. 32–33.

123. Caleb Wright and J.A. Brainerd, *Historic Incidents and Life in India* (Chicago, IL, 1867), p. 39; Forrest, *A Picturesque Tour along the River Ganges*, p. 124; Deane, *A Tour through the Upper Provinces of Hindostan*, p. 11. This was also a frequent theme of pictorial representation. In one of the eastern-India-style watercolours dated 1785–1790, a dandy is shown preparing his dinner on the banks of the river; Shelfmark: Add. Or. 2732, Prints & Drawings, British Library.

124. Lowrie, *Travels in North India*, p. 64.

have been the dominant practice, in both types of account the strict observance of the ritual purity of food preparation is highlighted. Rather than being lowly and polluted, the dandies were said to be the zealous practitioners of ritual purity, something which was, in fact, also applicable to Muslim boatmen.[125]

CONCLUSIONS

Boatmen's work was primarily based upon the practice of contract and wage payment. Both factors suggest that there was a labour market based on the system of open hiring. The fact that the boatmen themselves were responsible for buying provisions for the long journey (they usually bought rice at two places between Calcutta and Allahabad) attests to the fact that they were wage-dependent. The duration of contracted work is important to underscore the implications of the contract. In agro-industrial production, such as that of indigo and tea, or even in the case of weaving, contracts created generational conditions of unfreedom. This seems highly unlikely to have happened for boatmen, whose duration of one "cycle of work" was much shorter.

This article has deliberately attempted to bring together two types of material: one related to work (explored through the practices of the state, regulations, market, contract, and so on) and the other to journeys (using travel accounts). The degree of dependency that existed between travelling Europeans and rowing dandies was high. This created a zone of familiarity but also mutual suspicion. The framework of the contract helps in understanding the formal "structure of work"; the minute details of the journey allow to enter into the "world of work". Clandestine trade, weather, wind, rain, torrents, tracking, mooring, internal squabbling, jocular exchanges, and, not least, preparing food were some of the main components. These details help in understanding that, within the rubric of wage relationship, other social and economic practices also thrived. The *manjhee*'s role in illicitly carrying contraband commodities is one example. Another was the habit of dandies placing some reliance "on the produce of the fields he passes through, appropriating it, together with fire wood, and, occasionally, some stray poultry, or a kid, to the participation of his companions".[126] Wages seem to have been supplemented by extra-wage earnings or appropriations.

Baksheesh (in modern-day parlance, tipping) was an important form of customary extra-wage earning. However, we do not hear of boatmen, unlike palanquin bearers, insisting on receiving *baksheesh* from travellers.

---

125. Lowrie expressed his surprise because all his boatmen were Muslims, but still he said, "I have to be as careful not to pollute their food by touching it in any way as if they were Hindus"; *Travels in North India*, p. 86.
126. Williamson, *The East India Vade-Mecum*, I, p. 286.

But there is an interesting reference given by Lowrie that suggests that boatmen tried to complement their wages through this means.[127] As wages were given by the contracting agency, the *manjhee* had approached the missionary to lend him Rs 20. When this was denied, the missionary was approached by a dandy asking for Rs 1 as *dustoory* (customary). The fixity of wages, especially in the case of dandies who might have been experiencing precariousness due to the system of contract, perhaps forced them to invent or reinvent the practice of *dustoor*.

Barring caste-based criminal ethnographies, which anyway tell more about the colonial mindset than the precise historical reality, there is not enough evidence of caste- or community-based recruitment. Boatmen usually came from the Kaibarta and Mallah castes of eastern and northern India, but how far the colonial state relied on the traditional power structure of caste headmen or actively invented the authority of those headmen as service providers and recruiters is difficult to determine. Similarly, in the case of religion, boatmen were a mixed group of Hindus and Muslims. Social ties based on caste, village kinship, and religion that would have affected both the structure and world of work is a theme for further research.

The nature of work based upon mobility had an interesting characteristic and outcome. "Work" should therefore be regarded as an important category in writing the social and economic history of labour. According to one argument, because they were mobile boatmen needed advance payments, and this was seen both as a reason for and a cause of their mutinous behaviour. However, for a state that cherished the principles of sedentarization, mobility created its own set of anxieties. During early colonial rule, boatmen were gradually subjected to stringent forms of identification and regulation. One set of factors related to the nature of their work and their resistance in the form of desertion; another to the prevalence of crime in which they were seen as confidantes if not direct perpetrators. The colonial impetus to regulate and control was therefore a result of a mix of factors. The low wages and hard work that allegedly led to a "thievish" nature, the intrinsic nature of work based upon mobility, the "mutinous" solidarities formed during the journey, the variety of travel-based crime, and, not least, the state's obligation to protect both service providers and service consumers were the most important factors. Layered upon this mix was the gradual development of a caste-centric understanding that brought them further into the ambit of colonial control.[128]

---

127. Lowrie, *Travels in North India*, p. 65.
128. The further consolidation of caste identity as developing alongside strategies of the independent nation state has been traced by the anthropologist Assa Doron in his writings. Apart from his *Caste, Occupation and Politics* mentioned above, see also Assa Doron, "Caste Away? Subaltern Engagement with the Modern Indian State", *Modern Asian Studies*, 44 (2010), pp. 753–783.

IRSH 59 (2014), Special Issue, pp. 45–68 doi:10.1017/S0020859014000327
© 2014 Internationaal Instituut voor Sociale Geschiedenis

Getting Away with Murder: The Wrongful Deaths of Lascars Aboard the *Union* in 1802

JAMES W. FREY

Department of History, University of Wisconsin – Oshkosh
800 Algoma Blvd, Oshkosh, WI 54901, USA

E-mail: freyj@uwosh.edu

ABSTRACT: In 1802, several "country ships" arrived in London from Bengal, their lascar crews having suffered severe casualties due to fatigue, exposure, and starvation. Aboard the *Union*, the officers' treatment of the crew was so bad that the lascars and a sympathetic English sailor alerted the East India Company. Their testimony, recorded by the Company's Committee of Shipping, provides new insights into lascar living and working conditions – in particular the problem of undermanning ships – reminding us how the management–labour dynamic aboard a ship at sea always favoured owners and officers rather than workers.

THE "COUNTRY SHIP" *UNION*

On 28 February 1802, the *Union* reached Gravesend after a five-and-a-half-month voyage from Bengal under Captain John Luke. Unlike East Indiamen owned by the East India Company or leased for its Maritime Service, the *Union* was a "country ship". Its owners, William and Horsley Palmer, were established London shipping investors connected with their family's Calcutta agency house, Palmer & Company.[1] The *Union* was licensed to operate within the Company's exclusive economic zone, carrying non-monopoly cargoes and "gruff goods" for the East India Company. The officers and crews of such privately managed country ships were subject to laws and regulations laid down for and by the Company.[2]

---

1. Anthony Webster, "The Strategies and Limits of Gentlemanly Capitalism: The London East India Agency Houses, Provincial Commercial Interests, and the Evolution of British Economic Policy in South and South East Asia, 1800–50", *Economic History Review*, New Series, 59 (2006), pp. 743–764.
2. "Governor-General Wellesley to the Court of Directors, 30 September 1800", *Asiatic annual register, or, A view of the history of Hindustan, and of the politics, commerce and literature of Asia, For the Year 1801* (London, 1802), pp. 48–61.

When an official account of the ill-treatment of the *Union*'s mostly Indian or lascar crew was published in the widely circulated *Third Report of the Special Committee*, Captain Luke wrote to James Coggan, Master-Attendant of Shipping at East India House, defending his actions. The Company's Committee of Enquiries simultaneously investigated various charges brought against Luke and his officers by an aggrieved English sailor and several lascars. The present article is based on the 133-page proceedings of the Committee of Shipping, which regulated both the Company's shipping and licensed private trading vessels operating within the East India Company's monopoly zone.

The Company's investigation of the atrocities aboard the *Union* is significant because public exposure of these crimes tested the Committee of Shipping's resolve to act in its evolving role as regulator of labour conditions in the east India country trade. The testimony recorded by the Committee offers a glimpse of living and working conditions experienced by lascar crews in the late eighteenth and early nineteenth centuries, shedding light on undermanning, the practical handling of a large sailing ship, and discipline.[3] Exploration of the *Union* case also reveals the power dynamics inherent in management–labour relations aboard merchantmen making long voyages in the age of sail.[4]

Although subjected to extreme, often deadly, violence, the *Union*'s crew confronted their officers without resorting to mutiny. The lascars found an ally and advocate in John Moore, an English boatswain's mate, a low-ranking petty officer, who risked his career, and even his life, in trying to stop the assaults and neglect while the ship was at sea. Moore's attempt to organize his Indian shipmates speaks to the dangers and practical difficulties all maritime labourers faced even when *legally* questioning a captain's authority. Finally, the juxtaposition of the frenzied violence of Luke and his officers with Moore's humane concern and openness to the *Union*'s lascars uncovers the spectrum of attitudes regarding race and culture existing within the microcosm of a single ship.

I begin by situating my study within the framework of existing lascar research. I then consider the problem that first struck the Committee of Shipping – the small number of the *Union*'s crew, given the ship's size. As Moore and his Indian shipmates testified, undermanning was the prime cause of the *Union*'s problems, and such extreme undermanning indicates a callous, unrealistic view of maritime labour. The *Union*'s

---

3. Gopalan Balachandran, *Globalizing Labour? Indian Seafarers and World Shipping, c.1870–1945* (New Delhi, 2012).
4. Even at the beginning of the nineteenth century, "management" was used in its modern sense with regard to shipping, and I here use the term to refer not only to ships' officers, but also owners, bearing in mind that the authority of a ship's officer over subordinates, at sea, was absolute. The term "labour" was used in its modern sense in economic writings of the late eighteenth century, and entered common parlance in the early nineteenth century.

overworked crew were denied sheltered berths, time off duty, adequate provisions, appropriate clothing, and medical care, all while being terrorized and beaten constantly. The third section of this article examines the crew's testimony and resistance. Fourthly, I examine the opinions of the Company's attorneys, who, although convinced Moore and the *Union's* lascars were truthful, advised the Committee of Shipping *not* to charge Luke and his chief mate. In conclusion, I reflect upon the significance of the *Union* case with respect to the broader context of maritime labour history in the "Global South" during the age of sail.

PERSPECTIVES ON LASCAR LABOUR

"Lascar" was a term used by Europeans to refer to all Asian sailors, but in the British imagination lascars were usually "natives of India". The hiring of indigenous auxiliaries to complete depleted Western crews and bolster the ranks of dwindling military forces began with the Portuguese in the early sixteenth century. The practice of manning merchant ships with lascars spread and grew with the east India trade during the next two centuries, drawing mariners from nearly every population touched by Western commerce across the Indian Ocean, the archipelago of south-east Asia, and the China Sea.[5] Most of south Asia's Muslim seafaring communities contributed sailors to the European mercantilist companies, not to mention to a host of private traders. By the early eighteenth century several centres of lascar recruitment had emerged: Kachchh and the Gulf of Khambat, the Konkan, and Malabar – all on India's western coast – and Bengal-Bihar, specifically the districts of Sylhet, Noakhali, and Chittagong. Recruits from the districts around Patna usually worked as stewards and guards, not as second-class lascars (deckhands) or first-class lascars, who were able-bodied seamen working aloft on the masts and rigging.[6]

While some ships' officers were well-versed in Hindustani, most knew only key words and stock phrases. Because of this language barrier, and in conformity with pre-colonial patterns of labour procurement, lascars found work aboard European ships through intermediaries called *ghat-serangs*. Typically, a *ghat-serang* supplied an entire crew, embarking them already organized under their own petty officers, the most important being the *serang*, corresponding to a European boatswain, but also acting as the

---

5. Michael H. Fisher, "Working across the Seas: Indian Maritime Labourers in India, Britain, and in Between, 1600–1857", in Rana P. Behal and Marcel van der Linden (eds), "Coolies, Capital, and Colonialism: Studies in Indian Labour History", *International Review of Social History*, 51 (2006), Supplement 14, pp. 21–45.
6. Edward Simpson, *Muslim Society and the Indian Ocean: The Seafarers of Kachchh* (London, 2006); Franklin J.A. Broeze, "The Muscles of Empire – Indian Seamen and the Raj, 1919–1939", *Indian Economic and Social History Review*, 18 (1981), pp. 43–67; Michael H. Fisher, *Counterflows to Colonialism: Indian Travellers and Settlers in Britain, 1600–1857* (New Delhi, 2004), pp. 142–143.

ghat-serang's agent, being in charge of the men's pay. The *serang* was assisted by a number of mates, called *tindals*, while some lascars, such as "seacunnies", were experienced helmsmen able to take a turn at the ship's wheel, and thus had a status nearly equal to that of a *tindal*.[7]

Most recent research on lascars has focused on the well-documented period after 1870, when travel and trade between Britain and Asia was dominated by iron-hulled steamships. Steamers transformed shipping, especially in the Indian Ocean, where monsoons no longer dictated when and where ships could sail. Whether rusty tramps or crisply painted P&O passenger ships, steam-driven vessels were safer than sailing ships, especially in stormy weather. However, in the stokehold, where the sea was invisible, the working environment was more industrial than maritime.[8] Since seafaring skills were no longer in demand, any man could be a lascar. Those with brute strength and spirit enough to stand the long, punishing hours could find work as stokers in the fierce engine-room heat. Agile men with quick hands performed the dangerous task of manually applying lubricant to moving engine parts. Other men laboured aboard the new ships as cooks, stewards, and deckhands.[9]

Studies of the period after 1870 compare the lot of Indian seamen with the slave-like existence of south Asian coolies throughout the British Empire in the era of high imperialism. Like coolies, lascars were contract labourers recruited through middlemen. The very mobility of coolies and mariners trapped them in artificial, isolated settings – ships, plantations, mines, and construction sites – where they were a minority vis-à-vis indigenous populations, dependent on European employers for the necessities of life. Finally, like coolies, lascars had very little bargaining power due to their dependent, vulnerable condition.[10]

As Ravi Ahuja argues, contract labour systems in the late nineteenth- and early twentieth-century British Empire were racist institutions, their inequalities justified by appeals to Social Darwinist thinking. Racial categories, enshrined in law, were employed to limit opportunities and suppress

7. Fisher, "Working across the Seas"; Anne Bulley, *The Bombay Country Ships, 1790–1833* (Richmond, 2000), pp. 228–239.
8. Jonathan Hyslop, "'Ghostlike' Seafarers and Sailing Ship Nostalgia: The Figure of the Steamship Lascar in the British Imagination, c.1880–1960", paper presented at the Lascars Workshop, University of Southampton, 2011.
9. Ravi Ahuja, "Networks of Subordination – Networks of the Subordinated: The Ordered Spaces of South Asian Maritime Labour in an Age of Imperialism (c.1890–1947)", in Ashwini Tambe and Harald Fisher-Tiné (eds), *The Limits of British Colonial Control in South Asia: Spaces of Disorder in the Indian Ocean Region* (London, 2009), pp. 13–48.
10. Ravi Ahuja, "Mobility and Containment: The Voyages of South Asian Seamen, c.1900–1960", in Behal and Van der Linden, "Coolies, Capital, and Colonialism", pp. 111–141; Gopalan Balachandran, "Conflicts in the International Maritime Labour Market: British and Indian Seamen, Employers, and the State, 1890–1939", *Indian Economic and Social History Review*, 39 (2002), pp. 71–99.

wages for both coolies and lascars. Harder for capitalists, politicians, and not least white labour leaders to justify was the fact that Indian coolies and lascars, despite accusations of chronic weakness and malingering, worked long hours under difficult, even sub-standard conditions, performing work others considered tedious, degrading, or dangerous. Others did not bother with justifications, arguing instead that lascars were easier to manage (i.e. more amenable to exploitation) than British sailors.[11]

The lascar's world in the age of sail, however, seems different from the later periods in many respects, including the dynamic of racial difference: explicitly articulated in the late nineteenth-century archive, studies of later lascar history help to locate the racism of the pre-industrial lascar system, which must be understood not as crass, outright prejudice, but as a systematic fostering of inequality through dependency. The records of the late eighteenth and early nineteenth centuries were less obsessed with racial difference than those of the Victorian and Edwardian eras, although sometimes imbued with subtle racial tension. Instead of resorting to simplistic, pseudo-scientific arguments regarding racial difference, documents of the period under study in this article focus on perceived physical differences between European sailors and lascars, in particular the notion that Indian sailors could not function in "cold waters".[12]

However, overall, the documents dealing with the *Union* concern class more than race – class being an idea cutting across ethnic boundaries prior to the 1830s, as Michael Fisher has demonstrated in various publications. The primary "problem" with lascars, for most Britons at the time of the *Union* disaster, was not that they were Indian, but that they were not gentlemen, or – like *ayahs* and other Indian servants – clearly part of a gentleman's household.[13] One of the worries of Company officials was, e.g., that if "ordinary" Indians, like lascars, spent too much time in London with ordinary English men and women, they might carry home tales damaging to the Company's reputation in India.[14]

---

11. See Ahuja, "Networks of Subordination"; Gopalan Balachandran, "Searching for the Sardar: The State, Pre-Capitalist Institutions, and Human Agency in the Maritime Labour Market, Calcutta, 1880–1935", in Burton Stein and Sanjay Subrahmanyam (eds), *Institutions and Economic Change in South Asia* (Delhi, 1996), pp. 206–236.

12. David Macpherson, *The History of the European Commerce with India* (London, 1812), p. 235.

13. Michael H. Fisher *et al.*, *A South-Asian History of Britain: Four Centuries of Peoples from the Indian Subcontinent* (Oxford, 2007), pp. 23–70; Michael H. Fisher, "Excluding and Including 'Natives of India': Early-Nineteenth-Century British-Indian Race Relations in Britain", *Comparative Studies of South Asia, Africa and the Middle East*, 27 (2007), pp. 301–314; *idem*, *Counterflows to Colonialism*, pp. 8–13; Marika Sherwood, "Race, Nationality and Employment among Lascar Seamen, 1660–1945", *New Community*, 17 (1991), pp. 229–244.

14. "Report of the Special Committee to Henry Dundas", 27 February 1801, *Asiatic annual register* (1802), pp. 9–40. It is worth noting that this view was not uncontested, even within Company circles.

A lot of the research on the early period of lascar history (c.1750–1850) concerns the thousands of Indian sailors stranded in London by the anti-lascar clauses of the Navigation Acts. The work of Rozina Visram positions these early, rather hapless lascar migrants within a larger history of Asians and Indians in Britain, placing them alongside more socially visible or prestigious early "immigrants" – *ayahs*, envoys, scholars, merchants, princes, and eventually college students.[15] However, recent studies focus less on pioneering and more on the problems and prejudice encountered by lascars. Under late eighteenth-century British law, foreigners became British subjects after serving two years in the Royal Navy, but lascars were *never* considered British. Necessary but unwanted, possibly dangerous, aliens, lascars were both pitied and reviled. The British government forced the East India Company to take responsibility for all lascars, hospitalizing those who were ill while interning the rest in a barracks administered much like a debtor's prison. Here the lascars remained until they could be repatriated, for the protectionist Navigation Acts made it nearly impossible for them to find berths aboard ships returning to India.[16]

Norma Myers and Shompa Lahiri consider the limbo endured by lascars as part of the making of a non-white British working class.[17] Michael Fisher builds upon the work of Myers and Lahiri, bringing to it his nuanced understanding of the East India Company and the India from which lascars hailed. The research conducted by Myers, Lahiri, and Fisher uncovers hitherto unknown episodes of lascar resistance to what can only be termed semi-incarceration – resistance that occasionally took the form of rioting. Yet, there was more to the transitory world of the interned lascar than confinement, petty misbehaviour, and protest, as the Company's officials were aware. Lascars formed personal alliances with lower-class British women; they endured poverty and vagrancy; they appeared as victims and accused in criminal trials; and they suffered terribly during the cold winters of the period under study. The Company tried to help Indian sailors, but, as Fisher informs us, its sub-contracted system of lascar internment was exploitative, paternalistic, and – like so many Company endeavours – inadequate to the changing scope of a rapidly expanding task.[18]

Myers, Lahiri, and Fisher all mention the *Union* incident in passing. Indeed, for political purposes, the Committee of Shipping made sure their

15. Rozina Visram, *Asians in Britain: 400 Years of History* (London, 2002); and *idem, Ayahs, Lascars and Princes: Indians in Britain, 1700–1947* (London, 1984).
16. Fisher, *Counterflows to Colonialism*, pp. 137–161.
17. Norma Myers, "The Black Poor of London: Initiatives of Eastern Seamen in the Eighteenth and Nineteenth Centuries", in Diane Frost (ed.), *Ethnic Labour and British Imperial Trade: A History of Ethnic Seafarers in the UK* (London, 1995), pp. 7–21; Shompa Lahiri, "Contested Relations: The East India Company and Lascars in London", in H.V. Bowen, Margarette Lincoln, and Nigel Rigby (eds), *The Worlds of the East India Company* (Woodbridge, 2006), pp. 169–182.
18. Fisher, *Counterflows to Colonialism*, pp. 137–161.

printed description of conditions aboard the ship was widely distributed and reprinted before every debate about the relative merits of country ships and regular East Indiamen – the *Union*, therefore, is difficult to miss. However, this essay is the first to delve into the primary documents concerning the *Union* in detail, focusing specifically on lascar living and working conditions, and on management–labour relations aboard the ship. My purpose is to show why lascars often reached London at the point of death, and to critique the longstanding assumption that private shipping in the east India trade was more efficient and therefore "better" than East Indiamen. The private trader's short-sighted quest for rapid return on investment had an extremely high human cost.

THE UNDERMANNING OF COUNTRY SHIPS

The Committee of Shipping first became aware of the poor health of the *Union*'s lascars on 24 March 1802, twenty-five days after the ship's arrival at Gravesend. On that date, after visiting the ship, William Docker, the Company's Medical Superintendent for Lascars, wrote:

> [Nine] sick Lascars were ordered from on board the Union [...]. As they were removing them [...] one died – the rest appeared [...] exceedingly ill: three of these are dead. I waited on the captain to inform him in what manner the East India Company's men were attended, and offered my service to those on board. His answer was they were all well; and when any were taken ill, they should be sent on shore. I understand most of them were ill [...].[19]

As soon as the *Union* sailed up the Thames to London, its *serang*, Mir Jahan, was summoned to East India House. According to the *serang*, the *Union*'s crew initially consisted of fifty-five lascars and seven "sepoys" signed on at Calcutta.[20] Eight lascars were transferred aboard from the *Suffolk*, Luke's previous command, while both ships were anchored at Saugor, bringing the size of the *Union*'s crew up to seventy-four, of whom probably no more than sixty were seafarers. Of this number, twenty-eight had died at sea. James Coggan, himself a former merchant captain, was struck by the small size of the crew, remarking that the *Union* was a vessel of 750 tons. A regular East Indiaman of the same size would have been manned by a crew of 90 to 100 men, mostly British sailors.[21] In its assessment of Mir Jahan's testimony, the Committee of Shipping drew attention to the recent wreck of the *Suffolk*, grounded off Falmouth after her sails had been

19. William Docker to James Coggan, 24 March 1802, in East India Company, *Third Report of the Special Committee* (London, 1802), p. 114.
20. Here, "sepoys" refers not to Indian soldiers of the Company's army, but to mercenaries privately hired to repel pirates, guard stores, and protect the ship's officers.
21. British Library, London, Oriental and India Office Collections, India Office Records, /H/501, *Home Miscellaneous Series* [hereafter, HMS], fos 5–11, Testimony of Mir Jahan, Serang of the *Union*.

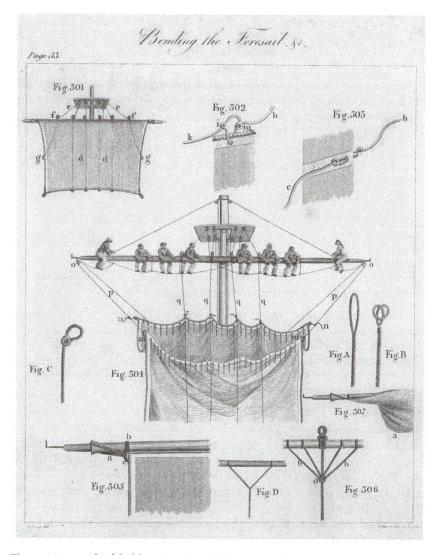

Figure 1. An example of the labour-intensive and dangerous working of a square-rigged ship which might also indicate why the persistent undermanning of country trade vessels was so dangerous. *From: Darcy Lever,* The Young Sea Officer's Sheet Anchor, or Key to the Leading of Rigging and to Practical Seamanship, *2nd edn (London, 1819), p. 53. Maritime Museum Rotterdam.*

blown away during a storm. This accident, attributed to the small size of the *Suffolk*'s crew, resulted in the death of a lascar trapped below decks.[22]

22. *Ibid.* For the wreck of the *Suffolk* (25 February 1802), see "Lloyd's Marine List", *Caledonian Mercury,* 6 March 1802.

In early October 1801, anticipating peace with France, the Company forbade bringing "Chinese, Lascars, or other natives of India" home as part of a ship's crew, "except in cases of absolute and unavoidable necessity". Due to the war with France, restrictions on lascar crews had been relaxed since 1793, especially for country ships, and the number of Indian mariners reaching London had increased six-fold. However, as *Bell's Weekly Messenger* smugly reminded readers, "[i]t has been ascertained that the labour of two Europeans is fully equal to the activity of three natives of India".[23] If lascars truly were unequal to English sailors, why were country ships with primarily lascar crews consistently undermanned?

In 1802, the average lascar earned about one-third less than a British sailor. For captains and shipowners, Indian sailors were cheap labour, especially as their provisions cost half as much as those provided to European mariners.[24] However, the East India Company – required by law to look after lascars arriving in Britain, even those not aboard Maritime Service vessels – charged captains £14 for the maintenance and eventual repatriation of each lascar delivered to its depot, adding significantly to the cost of hiring lascars. The *Union* incident reveals that many captains and owners of country ships pretended to be unaware of this requirement. Indeed, if we believe Luke's account, neither he nor the Palmer brothers, who had been involved in shipping for years, had ever heard of the Company's lascar depot in Shadwell.[25]

The most revealing statement in Luke's defence of his management of the *Union* is his remark that "I thought it an unnecessary expense to carry a Surgeon on board [...] when I had determined to remove every sick Person to Shore".[26] The memoirs of Robert Eastwick, another country ship captain, inform us that at the time of the *Union* events the country trade was a high-stakes, get-rich-quick business in which investors expected enormous profits from a single voyage, and accepted serious risks to life and property in order to maximize the return on their investment.[27] H.M. Elmore, writing around 1800, estimated that a rice ship making four runs annually across the Bay of Bengal could clear a profit of £9,500 after paying operating costs of Rs 2,000 a month.[28] Risk-taking and

23. "East India", *Bell's Weekly Messenger*, 4 October 1801, pp. 318–319.
24. Myers, "The Black Poor of London", pp. 7–21.
25. HMS, fos 1–5, Capt. John Luke to James Coggan, 6 April 1802; *ibid.*, fos 22–26, Nathaniel Dowrick to James Coggan, 8 April 1802.
26. *Ibid.*, fos 1–5, Capt. John Luke to James Coggan, 6 April 1802. Luke's voyage from Bengal to London was virtually non-stop, with only a brief pause at St Helena.
27. Robert William Eastwick, *A Master Mariner: Being the Life and Adventures of Captain Robert William Eastwick*, ed. by Herbert Compton (London, 1891), pp. 95, 252.
28. H.M. Elmore, *The British Mariner's Directory and Guide to the Trade and Navigation of the Indian and China Seas* (London, 1802), p. 291.

cost-cutting permeated the country trade, extending to crew management. At a time when water and provisions for one British seaman aboard an East Indiaman took up nearly a ton of cargo space, lascar provisions were cheaper and less bulky. Moreover, as Mir Jahan informed the Committee of Shipping, the *Union's* lascars were berthed "under the forecastle", exposing them to the elements, but freeing the lower-deck steerage for the stowage of extra cargo.[29]

In the age of sail, ships spent as long in port as they did at sea. In Asia, in particular, few ports had facilities for dockside loading and unloading. Weeks were needed to take on cargo and find a replacement crew. To trim costs, all non-essential crew were discharged from country ships, especially at Calcutta, where the interval between voyages was rarely less than six weeks.[30] *Ghat-serangs* knew European captains had to sail with the trade winds or risk a long, expensive delay due to the change of the monsoon. The commanders' urgency, of course, intensified competition for crews, especially in the 1780s and 1790s, when the number of country ships at Calcutta increased in both number and size. In 1783, the Government of Bengal, at the behest of country traders, had attempted to break the *ghat-serang* system by introducing a Marine Register Office, but the labour contractors had foiled this reform, supporting a general strike of lascars. European traders and captains continued to haggle with the *ghat-serangs* about the number and quality of the lascars they provided, demanding lower wages. Lascars, for their part, demanded larger advances, only to be accused of wanting to desert as soon as they were paid. After 1798, the struggle became desperate, with lascars accusing European captains of kidnapping stevedores, while Europeans believed every conflagration aboard a country ship was a ploy by lascars to abscond in the ensuing confusion.[31]

Mindful of the need to control costs, satisfy investors, and maintain reputations, country trade captains routinely put to sea with inadequate crews. However, whether undermanning was a cost-cutting measure or an expedient employed to gain a competitive edge in negotiations with *ghat-serangs*, it was always dangerous. In 1793, for instance, Robert Eastwick nearly died when the *Pesoutan*, an undermanned 450-ton ship on which he served as first mate, foundered in a storm off Burma. More than two-thirds of the crew, including the captain, and all of the ship's passengers drowned, while the ship itself was completely destroyed – a

29. HMS, fos 5–11, Testimony of Mir Jahan.
30. Elmore, *The British Mariner's Directory and Guide*, pp. 288–289.
31. Michael H. Fisher, "Finding Lascar 'Wilful Incendiarism': British Ship-Burning Panic and Indian Maritime Labour in the Indian Ocean", *South Asia: Journal of South Asian Studies*, 35 (2012), pp. 596–623; Jean Sutton, *The East India Company's Maritime Service, 1746–1834* (Woodbridge, 2010), pp. 237–238; Elmore, *The British Mariner's Directory and Guide*, p. 288.

disaster that might have been avoided if the lascar crew had not been over-extended and exhausted.[32]

The navigation of a three-masted sailing ship was a quest for balance. A ship's hull and everything in it was designed or stowed to return the vessel to an upright position. However, this steadiness also depended on the management of yards and sails, which provided both wind-driven propulsion and resistance, the latter being necessary to slow or halt the ship. Sails were the chief steering mechanism of a ship, wheels and rudders being used only for making minor adjustments. Depending on the manoeuvre, sails had to be raised and lowered, and yards braced about simultaneously, or in carefully timed succession, to avoid mishaps. The proper handling of yards and sails required a team of men aloft and on deck for each mast, with another team at the helm, all directed by competent officers and petty officers.

To sail a 450–800 ton ship safely, at least 30 men were needed at all times. Since (presumably) those men had to eat and sleep eventually, during a long voyage, a minimum of sixty sailors were needed to sail any distance, thus enabling a captain to form two watches. However, even this level of staffing left no margin for attrition, which is why regular East Indiamen carried enough men to provide three watches, several replacements, and a dozen officers and petty officers. Aboard undermanned ships, the watch system could not be maintained: this meant the men received no proper rest. Under such circumstances, when subject to prolonged stress, a crew's physical stamina, mental focus, and morale could degrade quickly, mistakes might be made, and these errors imperil sailors' lives and their ship. Unfortunately, in the sailing ship's struggle for balance, in the face of natural forces as swift and powerful as wind and sea, a moment's success or failure could mean life or death. Thus, as manuals of the time pointed out already, captains venturing out to sea in undermanned ships gambled with their men's lives.[33]

The loss of the *Pesoutan* illustrates the problem. When Captain Newton acquired the vessel, Eastwick recalled, the American-built bark was "a rotten craft, [...] in such bad and crazy condition, [...] we were delayed a month patching her up to cross the Bay [of Bengal]". Still, Newton and his partner, a Parsi speculator named Dorabjee Byramjee, tried to wring as much profit from the used-up vessel as possible. In August 1793, after loading timber at Rangoon, Newton set sail for Madras with a crew of approximately thirty lascars, several European officers and petty officers, and at least thirty-one passengers. Sailing at the height of the south-west

---

32. Eastwick, *A Master Mariner*, pp. 68–75.
33. Richard Hall Gower, *A Treatise on the Theory and Practice of Seamanship by an Officer in the Service of the India Company*, 3rd edn (London, 1808).

monsoon, they encountered a cyclone that battered the vessel for four
days, bearing it back toward the Burmese coast. Heavily loaded, the ship
wallowed, filling quickly after springing a leak. With only thirty men, all
suffering from exposure and fatigue, Newton could neither manage the
sails nor operate the pumps. He ordered Eastwick to cut away the masts,
leaving the stump of the foremast, but this merely bought the crew a
little time before, perhaps inevitably, the *Pesoutan* was overwhelmed.
While the dilapidated condition of the vessel and the manner of its lading
contributed to its loss, its undermanning could not be overlooked.[34]

BRUTALITY AND RESISTANCE ABOARD THE *UNION*

The connections between undermanning, deteriorating working conditions, and morale, discipline, and health are discernible in the testimonies
of *Union* crewmen who complained about the misconduct of Captain Luke
and his officers. Now, we will examine some of the evidence offered by those
who sailed aboard the ill-fated ship, both British sailors and lascars. Most of
these statements were offered and recorded at the Shadwell magistrate's
office, near the lascars' depot, in April and June 1802.

According to Mir Jahan, "no sooner had the ship left Bengal River than
the Mates began to flog the men till they fell sick, and while in that
situation they continued to exercise the same discipline until they became
totally unable to move".[35] John Thomas, an Indian Christian seacunny,
said, "I never beheld such cruelties [...] tho' I have sailed in two East
India ships before, *Henry Addington* and the *Coverdale*". Significantly,
Thomas contrasts his experiences aboard the *Union* with his treatment
aboard two regular East Indiamen, suggesting that Company ships were
better-managed. Like Mir Jahan, he also noticed officers flogging men as
soon as the voyage began, leading immediately to the deterioration of
their health, whereupon the lascars continued to be beaten for not
working. This brutality, Thomas asserts, caused almost all the deaths
aboard the ship.[36] Peter Bill, the captain's steward, also reported that
mariners who left Bengal in good health sickened due to the savage
discipline imposed by the ship's officers, adding, "I never beheld the like
before, tho' I have been two voyages to England in Country Ships".[37]

Mir Jahan noticed that men soon were sneaking below to hide, trying to
obtain a little rest and avoid being beaten. Responsible for discipline, the
serang himself was struck two dozen times for allowing lascars to shirk
their duties. Eventually, some men injured themselves hoping for a

---

34. Eastwick, *A Master Mariner*, pp. 68–69.
35. HMS, fos 15–17, Testimony of Mir Jahan, 16 April 1802.
36. *Ibid.*, fos 17–19, Testimony of John Thomas, Seacunny of the *Union*, 26 April 1802.
37. *Ibid.*, fos 19–21, Testimony of Peter Bill, Captain's Steward of the *Union*, 26 April 1802.

respite. However, the *Union*'s mates offered these lascars no medical treatment. Fit or ill, every lascar was required to remain on deck.[38] Peter Bill described how exposed the forecastle was to the elements, referring to it as perpetually wet. As the ship slowly approached the Cape of Good Hope, the lascars continued to be beaten despite "doing all they could".[39] A lascar named Abraham testified that he was beaten for falling asleep on duty in the main-top, while everyone round him suffered so much from poor rations they became feverish, with swollen bodies and legs. Abraham also reported that the men had neither bunks nor hammocks, merely "Bengal blankets", being forced to sleep on deck, splashed by water in rough weather.[40]

Most atrocities committed aboard the *Union* were attributed to the Chief Mate, Samuel Plumb. However, Captain Luke was said to have encouraged Plumb's behaviour, and his violent treatment of the men required the commander's complicity. As the *serang* stated, "the Captain Ordered the Chief Mate to flog the Men [...] till he should see their back bones".[41] John Thomas remembered Luke laughing, seeing the mates beat the lascars, telling them to use larger sticks.[42] Peter Bill testified that Luke ordered the mates to punish the lascars for complaining about their rations, remarking that he himself was struck by the captain when two chickens died in the coops off the Cape of Good Hope.[43]

Also testifying to the cruel behaviour of the *Union*'s officers was John Moore, a British boatswain who joined the ship at Saugor. We know nothing of Moore's antecedents except that he had met one of the *Union*'s lascars, Bakhshi, during a previous voyage aboard a different ship. Moore's experience aboard the *Union* offers insight into how the ship was managed. First, Moore was promised an advance of two months' pay, which he could not collect because the Chief Mate did not trust him to return to the ship from the agency house in Calcutta, where the money was held. Second, Moore was expected to participate in the mistreatment of the ship's crew, and help the officers conceal evidence of their assaults, which became necessary when lascars began to die. Moore, however, refused to be a party to these atrocities. As a result, he found his livelihood and his life in peril. Yet, instead of being a passive victim, Moore fought back, trying to organize both the ship's lascars and his fellow

38. *Ibid.*, fos 5–11, 15–17, Testimony of Mir Jahan.
39. *Ibid.*, fos 19–21, Testimony of Peter Bill.
40. *Ibid.*, fos 69–73, Testimony of Abraham, Sailor, 24 June 1802.
41. *Ibid.*, fos 5–11, Testimony of Mir Jahan.
42. *Ibid.*, fos 17–19, Testimony of John Thomas, 26 April 1802.
43. *Ibid.*, fos 19–21, 53–56, Testimony of Peter Bill, 26 April 1802. Chicken coops were usually located on the poop deck, and chickens often died from exposure in rough weather. As steward, Bill was apparently also poulterer.

European seamen to resist their tyrannical officers. However, he did not advocate mutiny.[44]

Even before the *Union* set sail, Plumb had marked Moore as a trouble-maker, employing accusations, threats, and physical attacks to reduce the new boatswain to compliance with his draconian style of discipline. With Captain Luke present, Moore was told he would be demoted to a mere "hand" before reaching England. His rations were withheld for three days, to break his will, and Plumb blamed him for all manner of infractions as a pretext for resorting to violence. Moore recalled being seized by Plumb, who "shook me against the ship's side till the Blood gushed out of my mouth and eyes [...] saying he would not strike me for fear of the law, but that he would shake me to pieces".[45] Significantly, this statement indicates that Plumb knew what the regulations protecting merchant seamen were, but had found or been shown ways to circumvent them.

Later, off the Cape of Good Hope, as the crew was setting a lower studding-sail, Plumb ordered Mir Jahan to beat the first *tindal* with a rope for taking too long roving the inner halyards. Moore, also ordered to beat the *tindal*, objected, arguing that the *tindal* "was an Officer of the Ship, as well as myself". This retort – recognizing the equality of a lascar, at least in Moore's mind – was intolerable to Plumb, who "threatened to throw me overboard", the boatswain testified, "if I did not obey his orders, be whatever they would". Seizing a rope, Plumb beat the *tindal* himself, leaving the man "for some time in a bruised state".[46]

The centrepiece of Moore's testimony, however, was his description of the fate of a *tindal* named Balla, injured so severely by Plumb he was no longer able to stand. Falling into despair, Balla told his shipmates he would not recover, and died, as Moore recalled, four days before the *Union* reached St Helena. According to John Thomas, the Chief Mate also beat another man, Bakhshi, so severely he, too, died within two or three days of being assaulted.[47]

At St Helena, the governor, Francis Robson, received a letter allegedly written by two of the *Union*'s European sailors, Thomas Harrison and Thomas Taylor. "I am sorry to trouble you", the document began, "but the usage on board the ship has been so bad that I hope your goodness will order it to be looked into, there has been two Men murdered, one thrown overboard, the other beat so as to survive but two days after".[48]

44. *Ibid.*, fos 10–15, Testimony of John Moore, 24 April 1802.
45. *Ibid.*
46. *Ibid.*
47. *Ibid.*, fos 17–19, Testimony of John Thomas.
48. *Ibid.*, fos 39–40, Thomas Harrison and Thomas Taylor to the Governor of St Helena, 4 January 1802.

Robson convened a court of enquiry consisting of the commanders of five East Indiamen which happened to be present in the anchorage, as well as Captain Brown of the country ship *Ganges*.[49] When called before the court, however, Harrison denied any connection with the letter, saying it had been written by Moore. Nevertheless, he told the assembled captains that a lascar "on the point of death" was placed in the *Union*'s fore-chains, and must have been heaved overboard after dying there.[50] Taylor said the *serang* had thrown a dead lascar into the sea, adding that this was the usual, unceremonious way of burying such men.[51]

Moore admitted to writing the letter to Governor Robson and signing Harrison's name to it. He also said he had not seen the *serang* pitch anyone overboard, but had heard about it from Harrison and a lascar named Jamal.[52] Jamal himself stated that an injured lascar, in a state of putrefaction, had been lashed into the fore-chains, being deemed a health risk. When he disappeared, all presumed he had been cut down and buried at sea by the *serang*. However, Jamal denied ever speaking to Moore, telling the court Moore had told him to say the lascar in the fore-chains had been thrown overboard.[53]

When questioned about the fatal beating of Bakhshi, the witnesses gave conflicting testimony. Harrison claimed to know nothing while Taylor said he saw Plumb knock the man down with a rope as he himself manned the wheel, although he later changed his story, remarking that Bakhshi merely became sick and died. Moore's story, meanwhile, was more elaborate. Plumb had ordered him to search below for a lascar who had quit the deck, and not to bring him back, but to "correct him" out of sight. Instead, aided by a *tindal*, Moore located the man and brought him topside, where the *tindal* and a sepoy "kick'd and beat the said Lascar so that he died three days after". Under cross-examination, however, Moore altered his account, stating that Plumb himself beat the lascar, who died fifteen days later.[54]

Unfortunately for Moore, Jamal denied Plumb ever beat the lascars "to do them injury". He contradicted Moore's revised statement, reminding the court the boatswain had told him what to say, before adding that Moore was plotting mutiny.[55] The Court of Enquiry instantly dismissed

---

49. *Ibid.*, fo. 39. The Maritime Service officers present were Richardson, Rymer, Eilbuk, Lamb, and Todd.

50. *Ibid.*, fos 40–41, Testimony of Thomas Harrison, St Helena, 5 January 1802.

51. *Ibid.*, fo. 41, Testimony of Thomas Taylor, St Helena, 5 January 1802.

52. *Ibid.*, fo. 41, Testimony of John Moore, St Helena, 5 January 1802.

53. *Ibid.*, fo. 42, Testimony of Jamal, Lascar, St Helena, 5 January 1802.

54. *Ibid.*, fos 43–44, Testimonies of Thomas Harrison, Thomas Taylor, and John Moore, St Helena, 5 January 1802.

55. *Ibid.*, fo. 44, Testimony of Jamal, Lascar. It must be noted that Jamal's testimony was given via a translator. In Hindustani, the words typically translated as "mutiny" in English are more suggestive of being faithless or fractious.

the charges against the *Union*'s officers, describing them as "injurious, malicious […] false accusations". Moore, meanwhile, was recorded as being of "mutinous and disaffected disposition".[56] As the court adjourned, the captains converged on Moore, one allegedly saying the boatswain should have been placed in the fore-chains, while another remarked that Moore ought to be hanged for accusing superiors of misconduct. Meanwhile, Captain Brown, of the country ship *Ganges*, merely suggested that lashing the rotting lascar into the fore-chains might have been for the best.[57]

In the aftermath of the court of enquiry at St Helena, Moore was demoted. However, as Moore later confessed to the Committee of Shipping, both Plumb and Luke suggested the former boatswain ought to help conceal what had happened aboard the *Union*.[58] Moore's shipmates avoided him after the enquiry at St Helena, but he persevered, despite continual harassment by Plumb. By the time the *Union* reached the Thames, the situation aboard the ship had deteriorated even further. More than two dozen men had died, and most of the crew was ready, finally, to rally behind Moore. As the Committee of Shipping reported, in addition to Mir Jahan, seven other lascars, sailors, and servants were clamouring to tell their stories.[59] Only one witness, a passenger aboard the *Union*, testified on Luke's behalf, informing the Company that the vessel's commander was "a remarkably mild tempered Man", adding that he had never seen Luke harm anyone, although Plumb he described as "a man of irritable temper", acknowledging that the Chief Mate beat the lascars with a rattan, although not "too severely".[60]

THE LIMITS OF LASCARS' LEGAL PROTECTION

Henry Smith, the East India Company's counsel, analysed the testimony provided to the Committee of Shipping on 27 June 1802, and was inclined to believe Moore and the lascar witnesses precisely because their stories were confused regarding details and dates.

> There are certainly […] material contradictions in the Evidence which make it necessary to weigh it with jealousy, but not withstanding such contradictions, I am convinced the whole of it is not founded in fiction, more especially as many of the apparent contradictions […] arise from the difficulty of making illiterate persons attend to the distinction of what they know of their own knowledge

56. *Ibid.*, fos 42–43, 45, Findings of a Court of Enquiry, St Helena, 5 January 1802.
57. *Ibid.*, fos 73–83, Testimony of John Moore before the Committee of Shipping.
58. *Ibid.*
59. *Ibid.*, fos 5–11, The Committee of Shipping's evaluation of the Testimony of Mir Jahan.
60. *Ibid.*, fos 87–89, Testimony of Captain Wright, Passenger aboard the *Union*. The other two passengers, a Lieutenant Murray and a Mrs Smith, could not be located by the Committee.

and what they have heard, and also from their imperfect acquaintance with our language and the imperfect manner in which their testimony can be taken by an interpreter.[61]

Seeking to corroborate some of the testimony they had heard, the Committee demanded Luke's logbook, which remains in the India Office archive to this day. Unlike the detailed log of a regular East Indiaman, Luke's journal was a vague record of navigational data – typical of the logs of private merchantmen. The only punishments recorded were those meted out to Thomas Harrison and George Andrews for theft, on 10 November 1801. Lascars' deaths were recorded, as they occurred, but no cause of death was ever mentioned.[62]

Aboard the *Union*, the distinction between formal, severe punishment (flogging) and "starting" (being struck with a rope) dissolved completely. The Chief Mate and other European officers resorted to corporal punishment to compel lascars to work beyond the normal limits of endurance – a desperate measure necessitated by undermanning the ship in the first place. Plumb emerges from the crews' testimonies as a violent sociopath, but the attitude of Captain Luke deserves close attention. The *Union* was not the only country ship arriving in London in 1802 with an incapacitated crew. Luke also was not the only commander feigning ignorance, using misleading arguments, and refusing to cooperate properly with the Committee of Shipping's investigation. Clearly, there was a pattern of brutality and obfuscation in the management of privately owned country ships.

Henry Smith noted, in his report, that the *Union*'s charter-party included three instructions. First, the vessel, being so large, was to be provided with a European or Indian "medical person", which presumes that the ship also was to be adequately manned. Second, the crew was to have "healthy and roomy births [*sic*] and lodging places". Third, the ship was to be inspected by the Master-Attendant at Saugor prior to departure.[63] As we have seen, during the *Union*'s voyage, the crew had neither medical care nor proper accommodation. However, for the sake of appearances, they might have slept below decks until the Master-Attendant had completed his inspection.

Smith's assessment of the evidence gathered during the Committee's investigation was that Plumb, although probably guilty of criminal assault, most likely would not be convicted of murder. In any event, by the time Smith drafted his report, Plumb had shipped out for India aboard

61. *Ibid.*, fos 95–123, Results of the Investigation into the Management of the *Union* and *Perseverance*.
62. British Library, London, Oriental and India Office Collections, India Office Records, L/MAR/B/117C, Logbook of the *Union*, Captain John Luke, 23 June 1801 to 2 April 1802.
63. HMS fos 95–123, Results of the Investigation.

another ship. Smith reckoned the Supreme Court of Bengal might prosecute Plumb, but there was little chance of organizing a trial with the witnesses so widely scattered.[64] Apparently, a warrant was issued for the apprehension of Captain Luke, but he, too, evaded the law, leaving the country at the first opportunity.[65]

William Adam, a barrister of Lincoln's Inn, also studied the *Union* case. He, too, felt that the testimony of Moore and the lascars was authentic, its inconsistencies proof they had not entered into a conspiracy. However, Adam believed only the testimony of a ship's surgeon could legally establish the cause of death of the lascars aboard the *Union*. Plumb might be convicted of a misdemeanour, but was unlikely to be found guilty of murder. In addition, it was uncertain, in 1802, whether Act 39, Geo. 3, ch. 37 (The Offences at Sea Act of 1799) permitted Indian courts to try cases involving misdemeanours at sea. Thus, Plumb could not be tried unless he returned to England. However, the crucial detail, for Adam, was the clearance of the *Union* by the Company's Master-Attendant at Calcutta. This official's stamp of approval provided Luke with a strong alibi. In the end, the only charge that could be laid at Luke's door was a mere violation of the charter-party owing to his failure to hire a surgeon.[66]

The system of lascar employment, designed to keep wages low and Indian sailors subservient, was in part the product of lascar acquiescence. However, as Mir Jahan told the Committee of Shipping, the *Union*'s crew eventually resisted en masse. After leaving St Helena, the crew practiced passive resistance, avoiding duty in various ways.[67] The fact that so many witnesses contrasted their experience aboard the *Union* with what they had seen on other ships indicates they did not consider how they were treated to be normal. Significantly, Peter Bill recalled how, en route from St Helena to England, the crew "remonstrated" with the officers regarding the treatment of the sick, whereupon the steward finally was allowed to provide men who were ill with some relief, although by then it was too late.[68]

The *Union*'s owners distanced themselves from the vessel's officers, who in turn tried to misdirect the Company's investigation. Ultimately, the Committee of Shipping did not prosecute the ship's officers, for practical reasons, but at the height of the *Union* inquiry the Company's will to secure justice was strong. Policy considerations overrode humanitarian concerns only when legal experts indicated the technical problems preventing successful prosecution of those responsible for the *Union* events.

---

64. *Ibid.*
65. *Ibid.*, fo. 49.
66. *Ibid.*, fos 127–134, Analysis of William Adam, 8 July 1802.
67. *Ibid.*, fos 15–17, Testimony of Mir Jahan.
68. *Ibid.*, fos 19–21, Testimony of Peter Bill.

We cannot attribute the decision not to prosecute to simple greed or racism, for other factors were taken into consideration, in particular practical legal problems concerning physical evidence and the possibility of obtaining convictions. Although they risked everything, even death – especially on the open sea – the *Union*'s crew made an impression on Company officials, reflected in later legislation. In future, captains were required to explain, in writing, why "missing" lascars had died at sea, and lascars' work, under the East India Company's aegis, became safer – at least theoretically.[69] In reality, since expedience always seemed to trump good intentions, lascar working conditions may have become worse, by the end of the Napoleonic Wars, than they were during the sailing season of 1801–1802.

Rather than focusing on their sadism, it is more useful to consider how Luke and Plumb employed violence to terrorize lascars as part of a system of labour management that included systematic, deliberate elimination of the evidence of brutality. Luke apparently understood that the weight of official documents was on his side, while the finding of the St Helena court of enquiry was probably a foregone conclusion. Few commanders of East Indiamen, at that time, would ever question a captain's absolute authority aboard his own vessel. In the face of such suppression and managerial control of information, it is remarkable that the story of the *Union*'s lascars was ever told at all.

CONCLUSION – THE *UNION*'S HISTORICAL SIGNIFICANCE

Fourteen years before the East India Company's counsel warned the Committee of Shipping that prosecuting Luke and Plumb would be impossible, anti-slavery activist Thomas Clarkson had noted that the conditions of a mariner's life generally denied him legal protection. Sailors engaged in long-distance trade were transients, without connections or resources, living in taverns while looking for work. Usually, it was impossible to find witnesses to corroborate a sailor's evidence, while the accused often left the country before they could be charged or prosecuted. In cities dependent on maritime trade, magistrates were usually local merchants who identified with ships' officers as fellow gentlemen. Magistrates and jurors viewed working-class plaintiffs as insubordinate employees rebelling against authority. Thus, Clarkson concluded, sailors faced nearly insurmountable obstacles in seeking redress for grievances.[70]

---

69. East India Company, *The Law Relating to India and the East-India Company* (2nd edn, London, 1841), p. 247.
70. Thomas Clarkson, *The Grievances of Our Mercantile Seamen: A National and Crying Evil* (London, 1845), pp. 13–17.

Clarkson's interviews with some sixty-three sailors, survivors of the Atlantic slave trade, garnered a wealth of information concerning the brutality of the Middle Passage, including the revelation that slave-trade sailors were systematically exploited and subjected to violent coercion. The narratives of shipboard labour practices gathered by Clarkson are identical, in nearly every detail, to the stories told by John Moore and the *Union's* lascars. Aboard slave ships, mariners were denied proper berths and medical care; they were kept constantly at work, harassed and threatened, beaten with handspikes, kicked when ill, given insufficient rations and water, and lashed to the shrouds if they claimed they were too injured or sick to work. Slave-trade veterans told Clarkson how men were driven to suicide, and others killed or maimed by officers concerned only with exerting authority, maximizing profits, and avoiding prosecution. One after another, Clarkson's informants described the "common system" of the "Guinea trade", consciously designed to wear men down, killing them or compelling them to desert their ships out of fear before they could be paid in full. In the West Indies, discarded and unwanted, diseased and injured English sailors literally piled up on the docks, forming communities of destitute whites in the plantation colonies, whose only friends, often, were the very slaves they had delivered into bondage. Reading Clarkson's report it becomes clear that, in fact, the situation of abandoned mariners in the West Indies was quite comparable to that of the lascars accumulating in London, to subsist as the objects of charity, unable to obtain passage home.[71]

There may be a connection between the specific brutality experienced aboard the *Union* and the institutionalized violence of the slave trade. We know little about Captain John Luke, but he may have been an American forced into the east India trade by the suppression of the slave trade and the wartime decline of trade with Europe. At least one American captain, Benjamin Stout of the country ship *Hercules*, shipped rice for the East India Company around the same time.[72] In 1802, Luke addressed his letters from the Virginia Coffee House, described in a contemporary guidebook as being "frequented by merchants [...] trading to those parts". Two other inns, within a few hundred feet of the Virginia, also specialized in entertaining officers involved in trade with the West Indies and Africa.[73] Because he resided in a tavern after a voyage from India, and not at home, Luke probably was not any of the men of the same name and social class known to have lived in England at the time.[74] However, he

71. *Idem, The Substance of the Evidence of Sundry Persons on the Slave-Trade, Collected in the Course of a Tour Made in the Autumn of the Year 1788* (London, 1789).
72. James Lindridge (ed.), *Tales of Shipwrecks and Adventures at Sea* (London, 1846), pp. 202–203.
73. John Feltham, *The Picture of London, for 1805* (London, 1805), p. 351.
74. The names and locations of all qualified electors are found in Great Britain, Parliament, *History of the Proceedings and Debates of the House of Commons* (London, 1802).

may be the John Luke mentioned in a Connecticut court case of 1796 as residing in Demarara, in Dutch Guiana, and named as co-executor of an estate.[75] It is impossible to say whether Luke and Plumb were former slavers, but comparison of the Company's documentation of the *Union* atrocities with the testimonies collected by Clarkson reveals that these men managed their ship exactly like a slaving vessel.

Violence played a part in labour–management interactions aboard almost all ships involved in long-distance trade during the age of sail, especially those employing contract labourers. Lascars, furthermore, were not the only contract labourers in maritime transport at this time. English sailors in the slave trade were often compelled to go aboard slavers by crimps, who colluded with ship owners and captains to swindle the men out of their pay.[76] In American whaling ports, contractors operating much like India's *ghat-serangs* helped "green" men and foreigners find ships, plunging would-be sailors into debt with heavy outfitting expenses and the cost of advances against meagre wages.[77] African-American sailors, representing 18 per cent of America's maritime labour force by 1803, found that their equal pay and integration into white crews frequently provoked violent backlashes, without breaking the racial barriers that prevented most black mariners from becoming officers even after decades of service.[78] Whaling voyages, lasting three to five years, taking ships to remote regions, were especially dangerous for both officers and men, as attested by the 1845 voyage of the *Archer*. Captain Moses Snell's carefully worded logbook, parts of which were fraudulently composed to conceal his violence, nevertheless could not hide the fact that his own brother led a mutiny against him.[79] In the South Pacific, meanwhile, Polynesian chieftains served as labour contractors, placing their countrymen aboard ships as maritime workers in exchange for trading privileges. Pacific islanders toiling aboard sandalwood-traders and whaling ships also endured the same violence meted out to lascars and European seamen, in addition to being cheated out of their pay and abandoned in foreign ports. The flogging of a Maori sailor, a chief's son, was one of the causes of the "Boyd Massacre" of December 1809, at Whangaroa in New Zealand.[80]

---

75. Jesse Root (ed.), *Reports of Cases Adjudged in the Superior Court and in the Supreme Court of Errors in the State of Connecticut*, vol. II (Hartford, CT, 1802), p. 364.
76. Clarkson, *Substance of the Evidence of Sundry Persons*, p. 16.
77. Kathryn Grover, *The Fugitive's Gibraltar: Escaping Slaves and Abolitionism in New Bedford, Massachusetts* (Boston, MA, 2009), p. 7.
78. W. Jeffrey Bolster, *Black Jacks: African American Seamen in the Age of Sail* (Cambridge, MA, 2009), pp. 2–6.
79. James C. Johnston, *The Yankee Fleet: Maritime New England in the Age of Sail* (Charleston, SC, 2007), pp. 114–116.
80. Robert McNab (ed.), *Historical Records of New Zealand*, vol. I (Wellington, 1908), pp. 306–308.

In branches of commerce in which contract labourers were rare, such as
the California hide trade of the 1830s, violence was still part of maritime
life, as attested by Richard Henry Dana in his first-hand account of an
ordinary sailor's life, *Two Years Before the Mast*, recording his voyage
aboard the American trading vessel *Pilgrim* in 1834–1836. Dana, a
Harvard undergraduate who went to sea to recover his health, clearly and
thoroughly analyses the working environment on board an isolated vessel
at sea. Dana explains the intricate power dynamic, based on scripted,
hierarchical roles, linking the captain, first mate, and subordinate officers
of a ship, as well as the subtle difference between the captain's servants
and the ship's crew – all matters brought vividly to life in the records
concerning the *Union*.[81]

Dana likens the sailor aboard a ship to a prisoner, writing, "in no
state prison are convicts more regularly set to work, and more closely
watched". Subject to constant surveillance, sailors were forbidden to talk
to each other and kept busy, as a matter of coercive policy, even when
there was nothing to do.[82] "Jack is a slave aboard ship", Dana remarks in
another passage, "but still he has many opportunities of thwarting and
balking his master". Working slowly, in a shoddy manner, was a common
resistance tactic adopted by sailors, but aboard the *Pilgrim* this "balking"
provoked a violent reaction from Captain Frank Thompson.[83] Dana
dramatically recounts how Thompson, desperate to retain control over his
men, flogged two of them while yelling that by doing this he was making
them "slaves", referring to himself as a "slave-driver". The racially
charged perception of violence, even aboard the *Pilgrim*, with its mostly
white crew, is impossible to ignore.

Dana makes it clear that Thompson employed violence not to punish
men, but to degrade and "break" them, furthering his control over every
aspect of their lives, taking advantage of their own prejudices.[84] As for the
first mate, he was not a man like Plumb, of the *Union*. Dana, significantly,
describes the *Pilgrim*'s mate as "too easy and amiable for the mate of a
merchantman. He was not the man to call a sailor a 'son of a bitch,' and
knock him down with a handspike".[85] Finally, Dana reminds us how
overt resistance by sailors, at sea, was legally construed as mutiny, while
seizing a ship, even for their own safety, was piracy. Well aware that the
peculiar nature of their work prevented them from obtaining justice
ashore, most sailors had little choice but to acquiesce. As for Dana, as

81. Richard Henry Dana, *Two Years before the Mast: A Personal Narrative of Life at Sea*
(Boston, MA, 1869), pp. 11–12.
82. *Ibid.*, pp. 15–17.
83. *Ibid.*, pp. 81–82.
84. *Ibid.*, pp. 113, 116–117.
85. *Ibid.*, pp. 103–104.

soon as Thompson realized he was educated and prepared to tell his companions' stories, he sent the young scholar home aboard another vessel, assuring he would arrive long after the *Pilgrim*, thus forestalling any legal proceedings.[86] Also, Clarkson had found, in his study of the slave trade, that owners and captains used their control over maritime labour to eliminate potential witnesses by placing them aboard departing ships.[87]

Viewed in a broader context, the *Union* events appear as an extreme case of violence in labour–management relations in the maritime transport sector, although – as I have demonstrated – deliberate and systematic violence was an integral part of "efficiency" in the shipping industry, together with officers' efforts to hide brutal aspects of maritime life by self-editing documents. Aboard Company vessels, several officers kept separate journals, which were examined by the Committee of Shipping after each voyage, making this sort of subterfuge far less likely. Thus, in a study of official records and private memoirs concerning more than twenty voyages of regular East Indiamen during the period 1768–1826, I have encountered nothing like the events aboard the *Union*, and few references to severe corporal punishment. Sailors aboard East Indiamen were well paid compared with seamen in other trades, and although lascars did not receive equal pay they were protected by enforced Company regulations and by the fact that regular East Indiamen carried numerous passengers, many of whom independently recorded events aboard these ships.

Most works on lascar history criticize the Maritime Service's treatment of lascars by emphasizing an uncharacteristic incident, the sinking of the *Elizabeth*, off Dunkirk, in 1810, in which 310 lascar passengers and 8 female servants being repatriated to India drowned after being driven from the lifeboats by European officers and passengers. It must be noted that the *Elizabeth* was not a regular Indiaman, but an "extra" ship, much like the *Union*. One of the only eyewitness accounts of the sinking we have was penned by country trade captain, Robert Eastwick, who disliked lascars.[88]

A much more accurate picture of the situation of lascars, however, can be gained when turning our attention away from regular East Indiamen and towards country ships. Aboard these, most sailors were lascars, yet they were considered incompetent and cowardly, hired only to reduce expenses, and because European mariners were scarce. John Hobart Caunter, a missionary sailing from Calcutta to Madras aboard a country ship manned by three European officers and forty lascars, noted how the Indian sailors fell into despair after encountering a gale, and how they

86. *Ibid.*, p. 114.
87. Clarkson, *Grievances of Our Mercantile Seamen*, p. 15.
88. Georgie Wemyss, *The Invisible Empire: White Discourse, Tolerance and Belonging* (London, 2012), p. 153.

were compelled to work, being struck with the ends of ropes.[89] A few years later, in November 1838, a British sailor voyaging from Moulmein to Madras aboard the country ship *Tenasserim* described the terror of the undermanned vessel's twenty lascars during a hurricane near the Andamans. Fleeing below decks, the men had to be "dragged from their hiding places and threatened with instant punishment".[90] One discerns in these anecdotes the everyday, humiliating maritime violence described by Dana, writing about the same period, but nothing like the atrocities committed aboard the *Union*, which were on a par with the worst outrages of the Atlantic slave trade.

---

89. John Hobart Caunter, *The Oriental Annual, or Scenes in India* (London, 1836), pp. 1–12.
90. Lindridge, *Tales of Shipwrecks*, pp. 278–279.

IRSH 59 (2014), Special Issue, pp. 69–88 doi:10.1017/S0020859014000406
© 2014 Internationaal Instituut voor Sociale Geschiedenis

Holy Rollers: Monasteries, Lamas, and the Unseen Transport of Chinese–Russian Trade, 1850–1911

DEVON DEAR

Department of History, University of Kansas
3650, Wescoe Hall,
1445 Jayhawk Blvd, Lawrence, KS 66045, USA

E-mail: dear@ku.edu

ABSTRACT: This article examines the roles of Mongolian monasteries and lamas in transportation between the Qing Chinese (1636–1911) and Russian Romanov (1613–1917) empires during the latter half of the nineteenth century. A series of treaties between 1858 and 1882 granted Russian subjects the right to trade in Mongolian territories under Qing sovereignty, and the resultant increase of Russian trade across Mongolia provided new wage-earning opportunities. Larger monasteries, with their access to pack animals and laborers, acted as brokers, while for poorer lamas haulage was one of the few sources of paid labor available in Mongolian territories, making working in transportation a strategy of survival for many Mongolian lamas. Mongolian porters provide a window on to how the broad processes of nineteenth-century imperialism in the Qing empire affected labor on the Sino–Russian frontier, and on to how imperialism was experienced in one of the most remote corners of the Qing empire.

INTRODUCTION

The influential American Sinologist Owen Lattimore wrote of his travels in Mongolia in the 1920s that "the caravan men and traders were not different in any important respect. Everything that I saw, felt and heard would have been seen, felt and heard, with little exception, by a stranger travelling two hundred or two thousand years ago".[1] Lattimore and other Western travelers in the early twentieth century promoted the trope of the Mongolian steppe as an unchanging region immune to global change: a living remnant of the ancient Silk Road.[2] As naturalized parts of a supposed

1. Owen Lattimore, "Caravan Routes of Inner Asia", *The Geographical Journal*, 72:6 (1928), reprinted in *idem, Studies in Frontier History: Collected Papers 1928–1958* (London, 1962), pp. 37–72, 38.
2. See, for example, Pavel Iakovlevich Piasetskii, *Puteshestvie po Kitaiu v 1874–1875 gg: cherez Sibir, Mongoliiu, vostochnoi-srednyi i severo-zapadnyi Kitai* (Moscow, 1882); Nikolai Przhevalsky,

age-old landscape, Mongolian porters have remained largely invisible as historical and economic actors. This myopia is further compounded by contemporary treatment of nomadic societies that often take nomadic production to be outside the sphere bounds of regular, quantifiable economic activity.[3]

Contrary to images of ancient porters traversing a pristine nomadic space, by the latter half of the nineteenth century a burgeoning labor market had developed in Mongolia, much of it centered on the transportation of goods between the Qing Chinese (1636–1911) and Russian Romanov (1613–1917) empires. Although Mongolian monasteries had been involved in trade before the mid-nineteenth century, a series of unequal treaties from 1858 to 1882 granted Russian subjects the legal right to move Chinese goods across Mongolia – then a part of the Qing empire – into Siberia, as well as to engage in trade within Mongolia itself. Although Russian trade missions had periodically crossed Mongolia through the seventeenth and eighteenth centuries, the nineteenth-century treaties facilitated the rapid growth of Russian and other foreign trade in and across the region.[4]

Working in transportation between the Russian and Qing empires became a strategy of survival for many Mongolian lamas in the nineteenth century. Mongolian porters provide a window on to how the broad processes of nineteenth-century imperialism in the Qing empire affected labor on the Sino–Russian frontier. The Opium Wars of the 1840s, the subsequent unequal treaties, and a series of large domestic rebellions taxed the coffers of the Qing state. This increased financial strain resulted in decreased subsidies to many parts of the empire, including to both monasteries and military installations in Mongolia.[5] As their stipends decreased, many turned to the informal economic sector,

Mongoliia i strana Tangutov: trekhletnee puteshestvie v vostochnoi nagornoi Azii (St Petersburg, 1875–1876); James Gilmour, *Among the Mongols* (New York, 1883); "*Vvedeniie*", in *Moskovskaia torgovaia ekspeditsiia v Mongoliiu* (Moscow, 1912), pp. 1–2.

3. Jörg Gertel and Richard Le Heron (eds), *Economic Spaces of Pastoral Production and Commodity Systems: Markets and Livelihoods* (Farnham, 2011), pp. 5–6.

4. For an overview of pre-nineteenth-century trade, see Mark Mancall, *Russia and China: Their Diplomatic Relations to 1728* (Cambridge, 1971). See Sarah M. Paine, *Imperial Rivals: China, Russia, and their Disputed Frontier* (Armonk, NY, 1996) for the diplomatic history of the Russian–Chinese border.

5. On how late-Qing financial crises affected provincial subsidies, see Kenneth Pomeranz, *The Making of a Hinterland: State, Society, and Economy in Inland North China, 1853–1937* (Berkeley, CA, 1993). In 1898, Aleksei Matveevich Pozdneev estimated that there were 1,076 state *gers* (portable dwellings) in the postal relay system, and that combined with those in required service at the *karauls* (guard posts), there were 6,000 Mongolian families in service by the late nineteenth century; Aleksei Matveevich Pozdneev, "Sovremennoe polozhenie i nuzhdy russkoi torgovli v Mongolii", *Baykal*, 15 (12 (24) April 1898), pp. 2–3.

Figure 1. Porters moving with camels through the Nankou Pass by the Great Wall, roughly 50 km from Beijing. The porters in this photograph were most likely Chinese men. Mongolian lamas rarely, if ever, took goods into Chinese cities, instead ending their contracts in towns along the Inner Mongolian frontier such as Hohhot and Kalgan.
US Library of Congress. Used with permission.

in which poor lamas and border soldiers traded requisite camels, oxen, and food.

The increase of Russian trade across Mongolia provided new wage-earning opportunities. Larger monasteries, with their access to pack animals and laborers, were able to act as brokers, while poorer lamas found portage to be one of the few sources of paid labor available in Mongolian territories. Portage, therefore, provides a lens on how imperialism was experienced in one of the most remote corners of the Qing empire: large monasteries

increased their wealth, while members of smaller monasteries and unattached lamas became part of a mobile labor force. Russian imperialism's
impact on the working lives of many Mongolian lamas highlights the
connection between the global and the local in late Qing Mongolia, while
the work of Mongolian porters underscores that rural borderlands, as much
as urban centers, were relational and interconnected places whose circumstances were shaped by their connections.[6] As Marcel van der Linden has
pointed out as well, global histories of labor can be told as micro-histories.[7]

Mongolians participated in trade and transportation on the fringes of
legality. Although Qing archives are prolific, they are the product of
bureaucratic and military elites.[8] Central Qing offices in Beijing conducted
no surveys and only rarely regulated Mongolian porters. It is therefore
difficult to obtain demographic data or original contracts between lamas and
Russian merchants and, with the exception of major cases of lost products,
one obtains only incomplete information about any given lama and his
cargo. Mongolian territories were specially administered regions of the Qing
empire: outside the regular provincial structure, Mongols' participation in
trade was highly circumscribed. Monasteries, however, had special regulations, and their economic practices were unregulated – neither permitted nor
condemned – by the Qing legal code. Although officials stationed in
Mongolia begrudgingly allowed Mongolian participation in trade, for those
in the imperial center it remained "unseen", and as such has remained
unexplored in the existing historiography.

This article utilizes previously unused documents from the National
Central Archive of Mongolia, as well as those from the office charged
with handling foreign affairs in the Qing dynasty, the Zongli Yamen. It
also draws from accounts by Russian travelers and economists in late
nineteenth- and early twentieth-century Mongolia, which provide some
information on labor brokering that is absent in Qing materials.

Qing ideas of proper governance were essential in shaping the contours
of labor in Mongolia. The Qing government based its economic policies
in Mongolia on the protection of a nomadic or Mongolian "way of life"
[Manchu: *banjire were*]. Official policies viewed nomadism as an economic and cultural mode that existed in isolation from markets and paid
labor outside the family. As policy developed through the seventeenth and
eighteenth centuries, Mongolians' participation in trade, mining, and even

6. Charlotta Hedberg and Renato Miguel de Carmo (eds), *Translocal Ruralism: Mobility and Connectivity in European Rural Spaces* (Heidelberg, 2011), pp. 3–4.
7. Marcel van der Linden, "The Promise and Challenges of Global Labor History", *International Labor and Working-Class History*, 82 (2012), pp. 57–76, 62.
8. Ottoman historians writing on labor have faced a very similar challenge. See Donald Quataert, "Labor History and the Ottoman Empire, c.1700–1922", *International Labor and Working-Class History*, 60 (2001), pp. 93–109, 95.

the use of specie was circumscribed, as Qing administrators argued that such participation would inherently corrupt nomads' "simple" natures and lead to societal unrest. Moreover, since Mongolia was regarded as a sensitive border zone between the Qing and Russian empires, the movement of people and goods there was much more strictly regulated than in the Chinese interior. Qing policies aimed at maintaining a fragile balance between granting Mongolian elites a degree of autonomy and maintaining Mongolian territories as subordinate parts of a wider Qing empire, a particular challenge after a series of large-scale wars and rebellions in the seventeenth and eighteenth centuries.[9] Within Mongolia's complex governmental matrix, culturalist justifications often buttressed strategic logic.

Some Chinese firms, often based in Shanxi province and known as "traveling Mongolian firms", were licensed by the Qing government to conduct limited trade in Mongolian territories.[10] Chinese firms acquired Mongolian raw materials, such as hides and furs, through exchanging products such as tea, tobacco, and sugar. The exchange rate between the commodities was manipulated in such a way that through each transaction, Mongolians became further indebted to the Chinese firms. In turn, the firms themselves profited by acquiring inexpensive goods and selling them at a significant mark-up in Chinese cities.[11] By the early twentieth century, large portions of the male population of Mongolia, including lamas, were indebted to Chinese merchants. Their indebtedness provided another incentive for working in transportation, and marked them as neither wholly free nor bonded.

In this restricted environment, rife with debt, monasteries after the treaties of the 1850s emerged as centers of Mongolian commercial life, and lamas provided the majority of transportation between the two empires. Lamas who worked or had trained in these monasteries were often literate and adept in contracting and conducting cross-border trade, and through monasteries had access to capital and labor. Legal regulations prohibited native firms in Mongolia, making monasteries the only corporate organizations with the requisite access to animals, labor, and relevant experience. As direct competitors with the Chinese for Mongolian raw materials, however, few Russian merchants were able to utilize the Chinese merchants' networks.

---

9. For an overview of the Zungar wars and the Qing solidification of power in inner Asia, see Peter Perdue, *China Marches West: The Qing Conquest of Central Eurasia* (Cambridge, MA, 2005), pp. 133–292.

10. On the origins of Chinese firms in Mongolia, see Ren Xiaofan, "Qianlong nian jian Lü Meng Shang piaozhao shenqing zhidu chutan", *Jinzhong Xueyuan Xuabao*, 29:2 (2012), pp. 79–81.

11. The classic account of Mongolian debt is M. Sanjdorj, *Manchu Chinese Colonial Rule in Northern Mongolia* (London, 1980).

This article begins with a brief overview of the social and political context of Mongolian transport workers, including the monasteries' corporate structure, and lamas' participation in cross-border trade before the treaties of the 1850s. It then examines how post-treaty trade with Russian merchants coincided with a retreat of state funding in Mongolia. Portage further exacerbated pre-existing wealth discrepancies among lamas, as it became a source of wealth for larger monasteries and a means of basic survival for others.[12] It concludes with a case study of lost cargo and a subsequent legal case between a Russian merchant and a group of Mongolian lamas. Reconstructed from archival documents from both Mongolia and Taiwan, this specific case reveals labor's connections to broader social and political contexts, and provides a rare opportunity to examine in detail how lamas drew upon their unique range of resources to attempt to manage risk while working without legal protections.

LAMAS AND COMMERCE BEFORE THE TREATIES

The variation in the size and resources of monasteries set the background for the different roles available to lamas in the nineteenth century. Men who had taken monastic vows comprised a significant proportion of the male population of Mongolian territories by the late nineteenth century, potentially as high as one in three.[13] The term "lama" itself designated both men who worked at large monasteries as well as those who had taken monastic vows but attached themselves to no particular temple. Some of these unattached lamas worked around *karauls* – the military border posts between the Russian and Qing empires – while others traveled, sometimes to Tibet.[14]

Religious connections between Mongolians on both sides of the Qing–Russian border facilitated the movement of goods and people before the international treaties of the 1850s, establishing ties that carried into the latter half of the nineteenth century.[15] Lamas had been engaged in cross-border trade between the Russian and Qing empires before the mid-nineteenth century.

12. Already Charles Bawden has pointed to this fact in his landmark general account of Mongolian history: Charles Bawden, *The Modern History of Mongolia* (New York, 1968), pp. 142–143.
13. Przhevalsky estimated that in the 1870s one in three Mongolian males were lamas; Nikolai Przhevalsky, *Mongolia, the Tangut Country, and the Solitudes of Northern Tibet: Being a Narrative of the Three Years' Travel in Eastern High Asia*, 2 vols (London, 1876), I, p. 11.
14. *Karauls* were guard posts located along both the Qing and Russian sides of the border. They housed up to several hundred soldiers. Listings of early twentieth-century Russian and Qing *karauls* can be found in Naitō Torajirō (ed.), *Kūron Mōga Karin taishōhyō* (Tokyo, 1920).
15. See, for example, Academia Sinica, Taiwan, Archive of the Zongli Geguo Shiwu Yamen [hereafter, ZLYM] 1–02–010–02–37, 01–02–011–02–066, 01–02–010–02–010, and 01–02–010–02–13; Mongol Ulsyn Undesnii Töv Arkhiv [National Central Archive of Mongolia,

Qing-subject Khalkh Mongolian lamas regularly traded livestock and other goods with Buriat Mongolians, the vast majority of whom were Russian subjects. Many Qing-subject lamas had established long-term relationships with Russian-subject Mongolians.[16] Lamas drew upon their cross-border ties to act as important facilitators between Russian subjects and Qing soldiers at the *karauls* along the border. Some trading parties were substantial. To take an example from an already later period (in which intra-Mongolian trade, however, continued), one trading party led by a Buriat Mongolian lama in 1895 deviated from the usual route between Kiakhta on the Russian–Qing border and Doloon Nuur in north-eastern Mongolia and was caught moving eastward towards the Huabaigt *karaul* with 59 pack horses, 5 rifles, and 4 carts loaded with goods valued in total at 1,200 rubles.[17]

Karauls' importance as sites of trade was further emphasized by the growth of nearby smaller monasteries. From 1820 to 1880, local elites established these smaller monasteries along the border, often replacing monasteries that had been previously funded by the central court but that had lost support as Beijing turned its attention towards other regions of the empire.[18] Most were located along roads and near to *karauls* and postal relay stations [Chinese: *yi zhan*] between the cities of Urga and Uliastai.[19] Although some were small outposts, others had permanent populations in the hundreds.[20]

Many lamas who worked in transport traded with the border posts that dotted the Qing–Russian borderlands. The decrease in stipends from Beijing forced soldiers in the borderlands' guard posts to earn money as providers of pack animals for nearby lamas. Soldiers were required to provide their own horses, tents to sleep in at the *karaul*, and provisions. By law, the commanding officer was required to provide a small living stipend, although there is archival evidence that these were rarely paid in full. One extant long deposition taken from a soldier at a border *karaul* provides a window into some border lamas' complicated ways of acquiring transportation animals.[21] In 1855, a Mongolian border soldier named Jamsaran had traveled to

hereafter, MUUTA] M1 [Office of the Amban at Ikh Khüree] Delo [hereafter, D] 1.4, doc. 6481.11, M1 D1.3 4780.1, M1 D1.1 2414.124a.

16. ZLYM 01–02–010–02–010.

17. ZLYM 1–17–049–04–001; ZLYM 1–20–014–02–40. In 1871, another small Buriat trading party of seven people had also tried to pass illegally through this *karaul*, as they were supposed to trade solely through Kiakhta and travel to Doloon Nuur through Urga. See ZLYM 1–20–019–01–093. See also ZLYM 1–20–013–04–008.

18. Lkham Purevjav, "Patterns of Monastic and Sangha Development in Khalkha Mongolia", in Bruce M. Knauft and Richard Taupier (eds), *Mongolians After Socialism: Politics, Economy, Religion* (Admon, 2012), pp. 249–268, 255.

19. Purevjav, "Patterns of Monastic and Sangha Development in Khalkha Mongolia", p. 258.

20. Torajirō, *Kūron Mōga Karin taishōhyō*.

21. MUUTA M1 D3 276.27, M1 D3 271.18.

another *karaul* to purchase items of daily use from a local lama. In his lengthy deposition, he recounted his deals with the lama, Gombu, who arranged to trade brick tea and cloth for animals from Jamsaran's herd. Underfunded by his official stipend as a soldier, Jamsaran traded with nearby local elites to obtain more animals. These animals were used for military purposes and as items of exchange to trade with lamas for necessary daily use items. Although Jamsaran and Gombu's dealings were illegal, they drew up letters of guarantee [Manchu: *akdulara bithe*] to record their transactions. As Jamsaran ran out of livestock and funds, he confessed that he raided the herds of several nearby members of the nobility in order to trade with the lama. For raiding the herds, Jamsaran was sentenced to eighty lashes with a whip, and, for trading without a license, ordered to pay a fine of five livestock. The primary lama involved in the case, Gombu, received sixty lashes and was fined two livestock.

The increased opportunities to work in transportation in turn sharpened pre-existing wealth discrepancies between different monasteries. Lamas from large monasteries with extensive landholdings and access to capital through their treasuries and storehouses profited more readily than their smaller counterparts. Monasteries in Mongolia were subject to three primary jurisdictions: the ecclesiastical estate under the leadership of the Jebtsundamba Khutuktu; monasteries under the jurisdictions of the four northern Mongolian administrative regions; and those established directly by the central Qing government. The wealthiest and most powerful was the ecclesiastical estate, whose considerable landholdings were distributed throughout northern Mongolia. The estate maintained vast herds, favorable grazing lands, and lay subjects, who provided essential manpower and served as envoys, porters, and labor in monastery construction and maintenance.[22] In the banners [*khoshuun*], i.e. the smaller administrative divisions interspersed with lands under the ecclesiastical estate's jurisdiction, head lamas determined both grazing areas and migration routes, and they often laid claim to the most fertile pasturelands, rich in streams and free from stony slopes.[23]

Large monasteries mobilized their considerable resources to take advantage of Russian–Chinese trade which ensued after the 1850s. The Jebtsundamba Khutuktu had protested the Russian consulate's establishment in an area already used frequently by pilgrims – a major source

22. Maria Fernández-Giménez, "Sustaining the Steppes: A Geographical History of Pastoral Land Use in Mongolia", *The Geographical Review*, 89 (1999), pp. 315–342, 320; Robert James Miller, *Monasteries and Culture Change in Inner Mongolia* (Wiesbaden, 1959). On the duties of the subjects of the monastic estate, see D. Tsedev, *Ikh Shav'* (Ulan Bator, 1964), pp. 33–54.
23. Andrei Dimitriyevich Simukov, "Materialy po kochevomy bytu naseleniia NMW", *Sovremennaia Mongoliia*, 2:15 (1936); S. Natsagdorj, "The Economic Basis of Feudalism in Mongolia", *Modern Asian Studies*, 1 (1967), pp. 265–281.

of revenue for the religious leader.[24] The ecclesiastical estate enhanced its generated wealth not only through its large herds and substantial treasury, but also through renting land to Chinese shops.[25] By the late nineteenth century, the ecclesiastical estate had expanded its business to supply camels even to Chinese shops. The Russian scholar and pundit Aleksei Pozdneev remarked about his 1876 travels through Mongolia that

> [...] it seems that in Khalkh [northern Mongolia] nowadays nobody is as rich in cattle as the monastery residents, and therefore if a Chinese needs a caravan of 50 or 60 camels, such a caravan is always supplied by the treasury of one or another monastery, or of one or another *khutukhtu* [incarnate lama].[26]

While exact statistics are not available, many lamas were attached neither to the ecclesiastical estate nor to larger monasteries. For these men, working as porters, guides, and livestock handlers were the only means of livelihood available. The lamas' financial difficulties were further compounded by widespread indebtedness to Chinese firms. As mentioned above, by the late nineteenth century a large segment of the adult Mongolian population was in some degree of debt to Chinese, and increasingly Russian, firms.[27] This combination of debt and the ecclesiastical estate's economy of scale led many living near Urga to work for the monasteries of the Jebtsundamba Khutuktu. To do so, they had to pay an up-front fee to the monastery; in Pozdneev's words "every disciple who wants to join the monastery caravan has to pay for permission to join, or in other words to pay for having been provided with profitable work".[28] He concluded that "the disciples' transportation business gives the *khutukhtus* great profit, and thanks to this the treasuries of *khutukhtu* monasteries are getting rich at no outlay, at the expense of their serfs".[29]

NEGOTIATING RUSSIAN MERCHANTS

Lacking Chinese firms' transportation and labor infrastructure, both individual Russian merchants and larger firms needed to recruit both

24. MUUTA M1 D1.3 4780.1.
25. Aleksei Matveevich Pozdneev, *Ocherki byta buddiiskikh monastyrei i buddiiskogo dukhovenstva v Mongolii v sviazi s otnosheniiami sego poslednego k narodu* (St Petersburg, 1887; repr. Elista, 1993). He reported that in the Erdeni Zuu monastery Chinese shops paid 20 *taels* per year for rental space, 25 *taels* at Zaya pandita, and 12 *taels* at Baruun Khüree; *ibid.*, p. 30. The *tael* was a unit of measurement of silver. Several measures of silver *tael* were in circulation during the Qing period.
26. *Ibid.*, p. 31. All translations are mine.
27. MUUTA M1 D1.1 2343 6b–7a.
28. Pozdneev, *Ocherki byta buddiiskikh monastyrei*, pp. 32–33.
29. Onerous charges at Urga's monasteries in the early twentieth century were also recorded by the lama Jambal in his memoirs; Jambal, *Tales of an Old Lama* (Tring, 1997), p. 11.

pack animals and porters to transport their goods in the post-treaty period after the 1850s. This was often exacerbated by their need to swap their oxen for camels upon leaving the taiga and wheat fields of northern Mongolia in preparation for the arid Gobi Desert en route to Beijing. Even if Russian merchants used their own horse-drawn carts to move goods from eastern Siberia through Kiakhta, the major port of entry on the Qing–Russian border, they often needed additional animals and local porters with knowledge of the difficult and harsh terrain.[30] Several routes connected the entrepôts of Kiakhta and Kosh-Agach with Beijing, but they were often dangerous and poorly marked.[31]

Although the treaties permitted Russian subjects to transport goods across Mongolian territories and to trade within Mongolia, Qing officials in Mongolia protested Russians' hiring of Mongolian porters. This issue arose immediately when a group of twenty men, the first group of treaty-permitted Russian traders, arrived in Kiakhta in 1861. Niktaev, a Russian official at Kiakhta had reported that "in addition to being unfamiliar with your local roads when they go and trade at the places before the capital [Beijing]", these merchants were unable to manage their large cargo over such a long distance. He therefore requested that local officials not interfere in their renting camels from Mongolians.[32] As the *amban* (the lead Qing official in Urga) pointed out, however, there was no specific treaty clause that allowed for such exchange between Russians and Mongolians. Niktaev argued that the auxiliary hiring of animals and labor fell within the parameters of Article VII, which stipulated that Russians "be free of vexations from local officials [...] they may sell and buy things both retail and wholesale. They make pay money or barter, deliver on credit, and receive credit, as confidence occasions". As such, he concluded, blocking these transactions was a hindrance of "free trade".[33] Qing officials in Urga could muster no legal argument for why such arrangements with Mongolians could not be allowed, and acquiesced.

Lamas' labor fell between two legal regimes: that of the international treaties, and that of pre-existing Qing codes on monastic behavior. The *amban* could not claim that Russian hiring of Mongolians was illegal, as no explicit statute in Qing legal codes existed to address this. Rather, he described an imagined scenario of a troublesome future,

30. MUUTA M1 D1.4 6481.31.

31. "Vvedeniie", in *Moskovskaia torgovaia ekspeditsiia v Mongoliiu*, pp. 4–7; Nina Evgen'evna Edinarkhova, *Russkie v Mongolii: osnovnye etapy i formy ekonomicheskoi deiatel'nosti (1861–1921 gg.)* (Irkutsk, 2003).

32. MUUTA M1 D1.3 4825.28.

33. *Sbornik dogovorov Rossii s Kitaem, 1689–1881 gg.* (St Petersburg, 1889), p. 164.

in which Mongolians' livelihood was stifled by an exploitative Russian presence:

> In the following days gradually many houses will be built, and this population will [make] many hindrances in Mongolian pastures. As for Mongolians, their innate nature is unrefined and simple-minded and their thoughts are too coarse. They seek broad grasslands in the empty spaces and make a living by herding the four types of animals. With everything, it is Russian nature to say "he would take only a finger, and take a rib", [so] how if Russian posts [*giyamun*] are set up in Mongol pastures [and] all low Mongols are coerced and find themselves in a difficult situation, being lorded over and oppressed, how can it be that issues don't arise?[34]

Qing ideals of Mongolian good governance are visible in the *amban*'s response to the Russian claims, as his primary objection to Mongolian participation in camel renting was grounded in his view of what constituted the basis of a Mongolian livelihood: open access to pastureland. This line of thinking relied upon vague understandings of pastoralism, which led to a line of reasoning that saw a proliferation of settlements as hindrances to Mongolians' access to pasturelands. His complaint did not acknowledge that many Mongolians were already engaged in activities other than herding.

The model of the recently signed international treaties provided the basis for the *amban*'s solution: just as China and Russia conducted trade according to the written terms and conditions of the 1860 Treaty of Beijing, written contracts should also be drawn up between Mongolians and Russians. The intended result of that would be that Mongolian camel renters and Russian merchants would be held to the same standards – in fact, the same Manchu-language term, *boji bithe*, was used for both. The *amban* hoped that written agreements would mitigate such future complications as fraud and theft, which would arise from Russians and Mongolians "mixing up" in Urga. Moreover, Mongolians' "inborn simplicity" made them more likely to be taken advantage of.[35]

Once both sides had agreed upon written contracts, the first official Russian trade caravan, headed by merchant Ivan Nerpik, his 18 porters, 170 rented camels, 14 boxes of silver, 337 bolts of fabric, and 15 boxes of equipment for the journey, was allowed to continue onwards.[36] Russian merchants of various guild levels quickly came from around eastern Siberia – Irkutsk, Chita, Verkhneudinsk (contemporary Ulan-Ude) – and

---

34. MUUTA M1 D1.3 4825.28.
35. *Ibid.* Large firms concerned Qing officials the least, because their members would be easier to track down in case of any subsequent malfeasance. Small firms and individual merchants, however, worried the *amban*, since "although small traders will trade a little, they may not engage in lending, [as] one cannot permit traders without shops to run away and hide".
36. MUUTA M1 D1.3 4825.29.

even the cities of western Siberia and European Russia to move goods legally across Mongolian lands to and from the Chinese capital. These initial trading parties rented camels and hired porters brokered through three lamas, all members of the Jebtsundamba Khutuktu's estate, who was the highest-ranking religious authority in Mongolia.[37] The porters' names, cargo, and dates of departure were all recorded bilingually in Mongolian and Russian. Thus, already the Mongolian lamas and Russian merchants who followed Nerpik through Kiakhta produced the types of written agreement that the Kiakhta official had requested. With the aid of Buriat translators, Russian officials at the Kiakhta Customs Authority [Kiakhtinskaia tamozhnaia] stamped the agreements written in both Russian and Mongolian, with amounts of goods, dates, and locations, and numbers of camels and laborers hired.[38]

Written agreements were not novel in Mongolian trade. Although not explicitly referenced in the communications between Russian and Qing officials in Kiakhta, Mongolians had already been employing written agreements, known in Manchu as "contracts" [*boji bithe*], and "promissory letters" [*akdulara bithe*]. Written agreements appeared in two major contexts: first, between Chinese firms, and second with the monasteries' own treasuries and storehouses. The written agreements reached by Chinese firms and their hired laborers, both Mongolian and Chinese, approximate to both contracts and trade licenses. They approximate to contracts insofar as both include the amounts of goods and employees and dates of the journey. They also attached an "itemized list" [Chinese: *ji kai*] of the names, ages, and occasionally places of origin for the workers.[39] These circulated to Mongolian elites as notifications that they should be expecting a certain Chinese trading party in their districts. This was not simply a courtesy; rather, the local government relied on the Mongolian nobility to aid in the expulsion of these trading parties when the duration of their licenses were up. The terms of labor, such as wages, were outside the scope of these codes, and were regulated internally by Chinese firms.[40] So while the Qing state did not regulate disputes about payments between hired laborer and firm, Qing officials referred to these documents when Chinese merchants violated the durations of their licenses, died, or committed another crime.

Monasteries also frequently used written agreements to manage their own commercial transactions. Stipends from the central government and

37. MUUTA Mi D1.3 4825.30.
38. MUUTA Mi D1.3 4869.28.
39. MUUTA Mi D1.3 4780.15, Mi D1.3 4780.16, Mi D1.3 4780.22, Mi D1.3 4780.30, Mi D1.3 4780.32, Mi D1.3 4780.33.
40. Imahori Seiji, *Chūgoku hōken shakai no kikō: Kisui (Fufuhoto) ni okeru Shakai shūdan no jittai chōsa* (Tokyo, 1955), pp. 336–365.

revenue generated from livestock were rarely sufficient to support a monastery. Lamas often conducted other business, such as money-lending, renting land, or selling manufactured goods, to support the monastery. Because monasteries were both corporation and bank, they provided lamas with both the incentive and means to profit from trade and transport. In order to facilitate these transactions, monasteries had storehouses, known in Mongolian as *jisa*, which were designed to provide permanent support for departments and schools within the monastery, as well as to fund special religious services.[41] These reserves of capital provided a modicum of stability for monasteries, which contrasted sharply with the nature of herding and animal husbandry, which were seasonally dependent and high risk.

As quasi-banks, monasteries occasioned opportunities for lamas to develop degrees of financial literacy: Treasuries and storehouses required lamas to maintain account books. Loans given from the *jisa* also required written agreements, which later became a valuable skill in working with foreign firms. Regional monasteries had particularly elaborate *jisa* systems, which made them well suited to the complexities of engaging in multiple industries, including providing pack animals and transportation.[42] Within a single monastery, each *jisa* was independent from the others and from the monastery as a whole. Working at a monastery did not guarantee an income: *jisa* had to be continually supported. Moreover, while a central account was held with the *tsogchin jisa*, the general assembly hall at the center of major monasteries, most funds remained individually allocated. This required lamas to supplement their incomes through trade in addition to reading scriptures or performing medical services, as they could not rely on monastery support to provide either for their own needs or for the monastery's as a whole. This need was only exacerbated as stipends continued to decrease throughout the nineteenth century.

GETTING BY TOGETHER? RUSSIAN MERCHANTS AND MONGOLIAN LABOR

As the nineteenth century drew to a close, increasing numbers of small-scale Russian peddlers, many impoverished themselves, were entering northern Mongolia. Although the specifics of the socio-economic composition of merchants in Qing Mongolia are still being debated among Russian historians, most were small traders with only limited

---

41. In practice, monastic funds were also held in a treasury [Mongolian: *sangai jisa*]. A small monastery had one or two *jisa*, while larger ones would have between 10 and 20 and sometimes over 100.
42. Purevjav, "Patterns of Monastic and Sangha Development in Khalkha Mongolia", p. 257.

access to capital.[43] Many Russian settlers were not much better off than their Mongolian counterparts, and some of these traders fueled the rental market away from major centers of trade. Those who could not afford the rates charged by larger monasteries looked to smaller monasteries or unattached lamas with lower rates.

Russian merchants adapted their hiring practices to the seasonal trading schedule used by Chinese merchants. They often contracted with Mongolian porters in December or January for work in the following autumn, providing them with a cash advance for the following nine months. The high cost of transport made finding the cheapest porters a priority for most Russian traders, and debt obligations to Chinese firms made many poorer lamas contract for lower rates. By 1910, one Russian economist reported that so many Mongolian men were arriving in the western Mongolian town of Uliastai in hopes of finding work as porters to the town of Ongudai, on the route to the Siberian cities of Biisk and Minusinsk, that there were too many porters, which drove down wages.[44] This coincided with increased financial troubles at one of the major Chinese firms, Da Sheng Kui, which had recently begun to demand debt repayment in silver. The economist reported that the pressures exerted by Da Sheng Kui further lowered the wages of many Mongolians, as they became increasingly desperate for any silver to repay their Chinese lenders.[45] Mongolian labor in transport was not immune to fluctuations in the global marketplace. As Chinese firms struggled to remain profitable in the early twentieth century,[46] their increased demands on their Mongolian debtors drove more Mongolians to work for lower wages.

Hardship in late nineteenth-century Mongolia extended beyond the border posts. The decrease in state subsidies coincided with increased pressure on natural resources such as wood and water, and led to increases in theft, homelessness, and uncontrolled outbreaks of epidemic disease.[47] The construction of the Trans-Siberian Railway in the 1890s increased the

43. Aleksandr Vladimirovich Startsev, "Russkie predprinimateli v Mongolii: sotsial'nyi oblik is obshchestvenno-kul'turnaia deiatel'nost", in *Vostokovednye issledovaniia na Altae* (Barnaul, 2004), IV, pp. 63–85, 64; Vladimir Vasil'evich Ptitsyn, *Selenginskaia Dauriia: ocherki Zabai-kal'skago kraia* (St Petersburg, 1896), p. 75; Ivan Mikhailovich Maiskij, *Sovremennaia Mongoliia* (Irkutsk, 1921), pp. 95, 203; Mikhail Ivanovich Bogolepov, *Ocherki russko-mongol'skoi torgovli; expeditsiia v Mongoliiu 1910 goda* (Tomsk, 1911), pp. 109, 172.
44. *Ibid.* Bogolepov, *Ocherki russko-mongol'skoi torgovli*, p. 370–371.
45. Shanxi Sheng zheng xie "Jinshang shiliao quanlan", bianji weiuan hui (eds), *Jinshang shiliao quanlan* (Taiwan, 2006), I, pp. 392–414.
46. Representative of this process is the decline of Shanxi banks. See Tang Zhenguo, "Shanxi piaohao shuaibai de zhidu xing yinsu fenxi" (MA, Fudan University, 2008).
47. Bawden, *The Modern History of Mongolia*, pp. 142–144; Elena Mrkovna Darevskaia, *Sibir i Mongoliia: ocherki russko-mongol'skikh sviazei v kontse XIX-nachalo XX vekov* (Irkutsk, 1994), pp. 99–113.

number of Russian settlers in eastern Siberia near the Mongolian border, which put further pressure on resources and increased demand for tea and other products from China. In the decades that followed the treaties, many conflicts arose between Russian merchants and Mongolian porters, and Russians reported stolen goods and lamas trading under false names.[48] Although there was no shortage of willing Mongolian porters, camels were often in short supply.[49] Solutions to the problems were twofold. First, Iakov Parfenievich Shishamrev, the Russian consul in Urga, declared in 1899 that the transportation of tea and other goods was such a "very important affair" that it needed to be increasingly regulated in order to diminish the frequency of theft, loss, and extortion. The number of shops engaging in the tea trade and its transport needed to be capped at the current figure. Secondly, regular written agreements between transporters, shops, and Russian merchants needed to be continued.[50]

LABOR AND LOSS: A CASE FROM DOLOON NUUR, 1885–1892

With the exception of high-ranking lamas of the wealthy ecclesiastical estate, most Mongolian porters worked in a precarious, high-risk environment. Their ambiguous legal position between the Qing code and the treaties offered few protections. Although local state officials encouraged written agreements, these had no clauses to establish limited liability.[51] And while some lamas went to banks in the early twentieth century, there was no option to purchase insurance. In short, there were no laws in place that established clear procedures when cargo was lost or destroyed. The case below explores how lamas made use of the resources available to them – monastery treasuries, loans from Chinese merchants, and extensive trans-local networks – to conduct business and cope when something went wrong.

The challenges lama porters faced are exemplified in a legal case that unfolded between 1885 and 1892 involving a Russian merchant named Sefetov, who lost 588 boxes of tea while in transit, and a group of lamas from the Shanyin monastery in Doloon Nuur.[52] This case involved lamas from a relatively large monastery who were transporting a considerable volume of Russian tea, and it therefore produced a sufficient body of documentation, including depositions from many of the lamas and other

48. MUUTA M1 D1.1 2343.5a–5b, M1 D1.1 2343 6b, M1 D1.1 2414.142a–152a.
49. MUUTA M1 D1.4 7001.4, M1 D1.4 7001.5.
50. MUUTA M1 D1.4 7001.11.
51. The lack of corporate law in late imperial China is explored in William C. Kirby, "China Unincorporated: Company Law and Business Enterprise in Twentieth-Century China", *Journal of Asian Studies*, 54 (1995), pp. 43–63.
52. MUUTA M1 D1.4 6481.18; ZLYM 01–20–002–04.

hired laborers, that one may reconstruct its details.[53] The case came to light because of Sefetov's subsequent demands for repayment to the Zongli Yamen, the Qing foreign affairs office, which then conducted a thorough investigation into the circumstances that led to the tea's disappearance. This specific case study provides insight into how lamas attempted to mobilize all available resources to conduct business and manage risk, as well as a rare glimpse into the networks of lama porters.

The Russian merchant Sefetov had entrusted lama Tudebubašar, a resident and representative of the Shanyin temple in Doloon Nuur, to oversee the transport. Following the requests of the *amban* at Ikh Khüree and officials in Kiakhta, the initial agreements between Sefetov and the lamas from the Shanyin temple were settled by a written, Chinese-language contract. Tudebubašar was an experienced porter, and first contracted with Sefetov in Kalgan seven years prior to 1885.[54] Tudebubašar's first step was to send a team of lamas with oxcarts to Kalgan, where they made arrangements to transport the goods through Khalkh territory to Urga. The lamas organized by Tudebubašar lamas affiliated with the Shanyin temple, both from his home region and from the neighboring Tumot banner.

Details of Sefetov's loss of tea during transit came through in multiple depositions taken by Qing officials. One lama, Baoma, reported in his deposition that he had been following his teacher Tudebubašar to a place called Darhan Cegelen in the Cecen Han *aimag* [province]. Anticipating an overnight stop, plans changed when it became clear that some of the porter-provided pack animals were becoming ill, with some dying near the planned stopping point. The party was unable to continue towards the Russian border and therefore stopped, and some members of the party returned to Doloon Nuur for more pack animals. The problems of the porters were further aggravated by natural conditions, since it had been a poor year for rain, and the grasses throughout the region were dry, leaving the remaining animals weakened and in need of rest. Sefetov's tea was put up in the storehouse of a man named Bašar, who was a "black man", a colloquial term for a Mongolian who had not taken monastic vows.[55] The lamas' connection with Bašar underscores the socially embedded networks many monasteries maintained: monasteries in Doloon Nuur, like those

---

53. These documents are held both in the National Central Archive of Mongolia in Ulan Bator and the Academia Sinica in Taipei. Although cases of loss were not rare, losses were often partial. For example, in 1871 two Russian traders' six boxes of otter pelts, tanned leather, and silver goods were lost when pack animals panicked and scattered somewhere between Kiakhta and Kalgan; ZLYM 01–20–001–04–001.

54. ZLYM 1–20–02–04–15:01.

55. "Black men" living on lands under the jurisdiction of the Ikh Shav' were often viewed by the Qing government as potential thieves and accomplices in tax evasion. See, for example, *Veritable Records of the Jiaqing Emperor* 24.1, *juan* 353, p. 652.

throughout Mongolia, housed not only lamas but also homeless and unmarried people, many of whom made a scant living as hired workmen at the monasteries, providing lamas with access to potential lay partners.[56] Tudebubašar had also hired Chinese laborers to help transport Sefetov's cargo. More detailed information about the subsequent prairie fire came from one of the Chinese men, Zhang Yuxi from Zhili. Zhang and the other hired laborers were all from the Zhili area, and had gone to the Shanyin temple in Doloon Nuur to find work.[57] Zhang had been instructed to stand guard by Bašar's storehouse. A Mongolian hired worker was also left behind at the site. This man left before the fire, however, to sell the skins of the dead cattle in Urga, leaving nothing to waste. After a day had passed, Zhang sat watch during sunset when he saw a fire arise among men who were picking up piles of animal droppings to later be dried and used as fuel. As the fire "came slanting" across the prairie, it engulfed the storehouse, and Zhang was able to extract only eleven boxes of the tea before the rest burned, along with Bašar's home.

Tudebubašar was then faced with repaying Sefetov the value of the lost tea. Tudebubašar's attempts demonstrate how he drew upon all available resources, both within his monastery and from local Chinese merchants, in an attempt to repay the loss. The burden of repaying both the value of the lost tea and an indemnity to cover expected profits fell upon Tudebubašar and the other lamas from the Shanyin temple involved in the case. The *demci* lama – a lama charged with overseeing monastery finances – reported that he was unable to repay any more than a fraction of the calculated cost. In principle, the *demci* lama's position made resources from the temple's *jisa* and central treasury [*sang*] available to him to repay the debt.[58] In his deposition, he recounted how, following the fire, he had attempted the recoup the lost funds for the tea. He estimated the losses at 1,000 *taels*, although the amount was significantly higher in other accounts.[59] He had gone to the acting head of his monastery, Kambu Gokcukrasai, to leverage *sang* property towards the debt. This fell far short, however, producing only 200 *taels* – hardly sufficient to cover a significant portion of such a major loss.[60] With the monastery unable to help, he took out a loan from a local Chinese, putting up his oxcarts as collateral. In the end, the *demci* lama explained, he had tried everything. "My temple, the lamas of this temple are completely

56. Pozdneev, *Ocherki byta buddiiskikh monastyrei*, p. 30.
57. ZLYM 1–20–02–04–15:02b.
58. Isabelle Charleux, "Padmasambhava's Travel to the North", *Central Asiatic Journal*, 46 (2002), pp. 168–232.
59. As already mentioned, several measures of silver *tael* were in circulation during the Qing period; in this case, the specific type of *tael* is not given.
60. MUUTA M1 D1.4 6481.23: 2b.

unconnected", he pleaded. "Having arrived at the extreme of destitution", he simply could not muster the interest, let alone the required principal.

The struggles of Doloon Nuur's monasteries encapsulated the problems of the empire as a whole, and show how the conditions of lamas' labor were shaped by the weakening of the Qing state in the late nineteenth century. Even allowing for hyperbole in the *demci* lama's account, 1,000 *taels* was an extreme sum of money for a lama in an impoverished town on the edge of the steppe. Moreover, Tudebubašar's situation was not unique: lamas in other cases of loss went to both monastery treasuries and Chinese merchants to obtain capital.[61] At the time of their eighteenth-century founding, lamas were guaranteed rations of grain and stipends for tea, paid out by the county.[62] By the late eighteenth century, however, the central government enforced stipends for only the lamas situated permanently at Doloon Noor, and not for those who had been sent as representatives of their home districts. As in the case of the border soldier Jamsaran discussed above, with the support of the central state receding, these men relied on their home regions, increasingly afflicted by the dual burdens of debt to Chinese firms and declining central stipends to support their imperial service.

Not all individual lamas within these monasteries fared equally well, and they struggled to earn enough to keep themselves sufficiently clothed and fed in the harsh climate. Although the temple exteriors and main halls were well-maintained, filled with bronze statues [*burkhan*] and even a pair of stuffed tigers and human skulls mounted in silver, the housing of the lamas was rarely luxurious; Pozdneev described their dilapidated state, with some so decrepit that monks erected their own *gers* (portable dwellings) rather than live in the ruined structures.[63] Once centers of bronze statue production for the Tibetan Buddhist world, Doloon Nuur's monasteries had been transformed into scrapyards of empire: ruined structures around which lamas and poor men vied to make a living from the Russian imperial presence.[64]

The Shanyin temple lamas' vulnerability was further intensified by poor communication between the Qing authorities in Doloon Nuur and the Russian consulate. The Russian consul accused both Doloon Nuur's

61. MUUTA M1 D1.4 7110.32: 2a.

62. Lai Huimin, "Qingdai Guihua cheng de Zang fu fo si yu jingji", *Neimenggu Shifan Daxue Xuebao*, 39:3 (2010), pp. 88–101, 93.

63. Aleksei Matveevich Pozdneev, *Mongoliia i Mongoly: Rezul'taty poiezdki v Mongoliiu, ispolnennoi v 1892–1893 gg.* (St Petersburg, 1896–1898), p. 298; see also "Account of a Journey in Mongolia by Mr. Kidston and Mr. Flaherty in September–November 1903", in *China: A Collection of Correspondence and Papers Relating to Chinese Affairs*, Great Britain, Foreign Office, China No. 3 (London, 1904), p. 10.

64. Pozdneev, *Mongoliia i Mongoly*, pp. 277–279, 282.

sub-prefect and the monastery of theft and of profiting from the loss of Russian tea.[65] By 1892, seven years after the prairie fire itself, Sefetov settled on a compensation amount of no less than 12,000 *taels*, which included both the value of the tea lost as well as lost expected profits. Sefetov calculated that each of his 588 boxes was worth 21 *taels*. As for transportation costs, the lamas received 1 silver *tael* and 8 copper coins for each box, giving a rough total of 1,000 *taels* – the amount that the *demci* lama thought he was initially responsible for repaying. Sefetov also reported paying an additional 570 *taels* to the lamas. While the addition is not exact, through these combined costs Sefetov arrived at the sum of 12,000 *taels*, which he communicated through the Russian consul to both the Zongli Yamen and to the famous statesman Li Hongzhang, then the Commissioner for Military and Foreign Affairs in the North.

Li's final decision recognized the differences between wealthy lamas as brokers and poorer lamas as porters. "Mongolian porters are all connected to being hired laborers", he wrote, "and most are impoverished".[66] Wealth discrepancies at the Shanyin temple were obvious to Li, who explained that the "camel proprietors are all (of) powerful families". Li's aim was to find a way to obtain compensation for Sefetov's lost tea while not allowing the more powerful lamas to "shift the burden" onto the porters themselves.[67] Unfortunately, as with many cases between lamas and Russian merchants, the documentary record is incomplete, and the final outcome of the case is not known.

CONCLUSION

Contrary to Lattimore's descriptions of Mongolian porters as living embodiments of the ancient past, labor in Mongolian transportation was not ahistorical. Rather, it was deeply embedded in social and political contexts that changed over time. The decline in imperial support and monastic living conditions pushed many impoverished lamas into low-paying jobs in caravan transportation, while simultaneously drawing wealthier monasteries into the burgeoning trade. Lamas possessed a set of unique resources that enabled them to participate, and occasionally thrive, in transport: familiarity with numeracy and contracts, access to monastery treasuries that provided reserve capital in a high-risk environment, prior experience in cross-border trade, and widespread social networks.

The growth of the transportation industry was closely tied to the spread of the Russian empire and the retreat of the Qing state. As state subsidies declined, Mongolians faced increased financial burdens, forcing many to

---

65. MUUTA M1 D1.4 7110.32.
66. ZLYM 01–20–002–04–25:1.
67. ZLYM 01–20–002–04–25:2.

seek additional sources of income. Russian traders – the motors of Russian imperialism in Qing Mongolia – made use of Mongolian lamas' need for paid labor. Although Qing Mongolia lacked plantations, large-scale mines, or other, more recognizable sites of labor, transport in Mongolian territories draws attention to the importance of wage labor in reshaping the livelihoods and social worlds of many Mongolian men in the region.

IRSH 59 (2014), Special Issue, pp. 89–112 doi:10.1017/S0020859014000170
© 2014 Internationaal Instituut voor Sociale Geschiedenis

Empire on their Backs: Coolies in the Eastern Borderlands of the British Raj*

Lipokmar Dzüvichü

North East India Studies Programme, Jawaharlal Nehru University New Delhi 110067, India

E-mail: postlipok@gmail.com

ABSTRACT: In the nineteenth century, colonial officials relied heavily on coercion to recruit "coolie" labour for "public works" and to provide various support services in the North-East Frontier of British India. "Treaties" with defeated chiefs and the subsequent population enumeration and taxation were strongly oriented to the mobilization of labour for road building and porterage. Forced labour provided the colonial officials with a steady supply of coolies to work on the roads as well as carriers for military expeditions. In mobilizing labour resources, however, colonial officials had to create and draw upon native agents such as the headmen and interpreters who came to play a crucial role in the colonial order of things. Focusing on the Naga Hills, this article will examine the efforts of the colonial state to secure a large circulating labour force, the forms of labour relations that emerged from the need to build colonial infrastructure and the demand for coolies in military expeditions, the response of the hill people to labour conscription and its impact on the hill "tribes".

Besides his dao the Naga carried a spear, iron-spiked at both ends. On his back, he carried his personal property in a commodious conical basket. On the top of that came the sixty-pound load, which he was carrying for the Maharani.[1]
Powell Millington, 1912

The colonial labour regime on the Assam tea plantations has been an important field of study for historians researching the eastern borderlands of British India. Focusing on the complex relationship between questions of labour, capital, and colonial policy, these studies have drawn our attention to the various forms of recruitment, the modes of exploitation, and changing

---

* I would like to thank Radhika Singha for her critical advice and valuable comments on earlier drafts of this article, as well as Joy L.K. Pachuau and Manjeet Baruah for reading and commenting on an earlier draft.
1. Powell Millington, *On the Track of the Abor* (London, 1912), p. 22.

labour relations on the tea plantations.[2] This body of research has broadened our conceptual understanding of colonial labour on the plantations and the interactions between planters, recruiters, labourers, and colonial government at varying levels. In contrast to these significant studies on the labour regime on the Assam plantations, the story of large numbers of circulating hill "coolies" in the eastern borderlands of the British Raj has remained strikingly neglected. Furthermore, the manpower resources generated through colonial "public works" on the frontier are often seen as "normal", self-evident effects of colonial rule and so are not discussed in historical works.

Focusing on the Naga Hills,[3] this article examines colonial efforts to secure a large circulating workforce which could provide a steady supply of porters and labourers for road building. Colonial infrastructure improvements demanded heavy and continuous labour. In fact, studies on colonial "public works" in Orissa by Ravi Ahuja have shown how the construction of infrastructural road projects relied on "the widespread utilisation of forced and unpaid labour". They in turn instituted new forms of labour regime.[4] As Ian Kerr shows in the context of railway construction, colonial infrastructural projects could also stimulate the flow of labour between different regions even as opportunities for wage labour multiplied and labour markets expanded.[5] In another significant work, Shekhar Pathak draws our attention to pre-colonial labour practices in the Kumaun hills and how the colonial state mobilized labour resources by appropriating the existing system of *begar* or unpaid forced labour in British Kumaun.[6] In the Kumaun hills, as Pathak points out, the

2. Some important works on colonial labour systems in British Assam are Jayeeta Sharma, "'Lazy' Natives, Coolie Labour, and the Assam Tea Industry", *Modern Asian Studies*, 43 (2009), pp. 1287–1324; Rana P. Behal, "Coolie Drivers or Benevolent Paternalists? British Tea Planters in Assam and the Indenture Labour System", *Modern Asian Studies*, 44 (2010), pp. 29–51; *idem*, "Power Structure, Discipline and Labour in Assam Tea Plantations Under Colonial Rule", *International Review of Social History*, 51 (2006), pp. 143–172; *idem* and Prabhu P. Mohapatra, "'Tea and Money versus Human Life': The Rise and Fall of the Indenture System in the Assam Tea Plantations 1840–1908", *Journal of Peasant Studies*, 19:3–4 (1992), pp. 142–172.
3. In the nineteenth century, as the British expanded into the North-East Frontier, certain groups of people were classified under the generic category "Naga" such as Ao, Angami, Chang, Lotha, Sema, Konyak etc. These categories are products of colonial encounter and therefore problematic. The various Naga groups who inhabited the geographical space named after them, i.e. the "Naga Hills", are the focus of this paper. For an important work on the processes of knowledge production on the "Nagas" see Andrew West, "Writing the Nagas: A British Officer's Ethnographic Tradition", *History and Anthropology*, 8:1–4 (1994), pp. 55–88.
4. Ravi Ahuja, *Pathways of Empire: Circulation, "Public Works" and Social Space in Colonial Orissa (c.1780–1914)* (Hyderabad, 2009), p. 290.
5. Ian J. Kerr, *Engines of Change: The Railroads that Made India* (London, 2007), p. 39.
6. Following the occupation of the hill district of Kumaun, the British continued the existing *begar* system, which originated under its earlier rulers, and subjected the hill population to forced unpaid labour. See Shekhar Pathak, "The *Begar* Abolition Movements in British

British not only "regularized" the system of *begar* but also intensified its "oppressive effects", leading to popular mass movements against the system.[7] This analysis of the system of *begar* reveals how subject populations in the hill district of Kumaun were constantly ensnared in the web of colonial labour requirements. The present article resonates with this literature by analysing the mechanisms through which colonial officials mobilized labour resources in the hills, and how the local population in the Naga Hills came to be subordinated as "coolies" in the imperial enterprise of road building.

In the nineteenth century north-east, an expanding frontier in the hill tracts generated a demand for a flexible and mobile labour corps. Annual tours by frontier political officials meant that coolies had to be found to carry their baggage and supplies. A steady supply of labour was also needed to develop colonial infrastructures such as roads in the hills. While roads enabled the British to extend their reach into the hills, they also enhanced the ability of the colonial state to extract labour resources from the hill communities. If, in the words of James Scott, the hills constituted ungoverned spaces of refuge,[8] this did not necessarily imply that the state was incapable of extracting resources such as labour from the hills. In fact, the notion of scattered areas and communities provided the colonial state with a legitimating factor in converting the local population into pliable labouring subjects. In the process, colonial officials relied heavily on coercion to recruit "coolie" labour for "public works" and to provide various support services in the region. "Treaties" with defeated chiefs and the subsequent population enumeration and taxation were strongly oriented to the mobilization of labour for road building and porterage. This was a process of labour impressment, intimately related to the expansion of the wage-labour market, which would turn the "primitive tribes" into "coolies". Moving across colonial boundaries these coolies sustained the supply lines of the imperial army, and built infrastructures such as roads and military outposts.

Colonial officials could not, though, simply mobilize the huge manpower from the hills by imposing it from above. They had to engage with

Kumaun", *Indian Economic and Social History Review*, 28 (1991), pp. 261–279; for a discussion of the link between the *begar* system, the expansion of the reserved forests, and the demand to abolish this "feudal" system by the nationalist leaders in the Kumaun hills, see Richard P. Tucker, *A Forest History of India* (Delhi, 2012), pp. 99–103.

7. *Ibid.*
8. James C. Scott, *The Art of Not Being Governed: An Anarchist History of Upland Southeast Asia* (Hyderabad, 2010). However, given the importance of settled agriculture, especially among the Angami Nagas, the idea that hill societies and their practices were constantly engaged in the act of escaping the state may perhaps not be applicable in all cases. In fact, one factor that attracted the British to the Angami hills was the existence of a settled agrarian system, and it was from this agrarian-based society that the British sought to mobilize resources to meet their imperial needs in the hills.

the "traditional" structures and institutions. In their effort to tap into the labour resources, the colonial state had to create and draw upon native agents such as headmen and interpreters. However, coolie work was much resented by the Nagas, who countered it by developing tactics to avoid work or, at least, to minimize their labour. This article will study the mechanisms employed by the colonial state in the recruitment of labour, the reactions of hill peoples to labour demands, and the changing role of the hill "tribes" in the imperial enterprise.

"EXCELLENT MEN FOR MOUNTAIN WORK"

In 1873, Alexander Mackenzie, Junior Secretary in the Government of India, in his letter to the Secretary of the Foreign Department, remarked that "the want of carriage", especially for hill works, was "the great[est] difficulty" confronted by British officials in the North-East Frontier.[9] In fact, requisitioning labour was a constant colonial anxiety since concern for crops and families often compelled local labourers engaged in road works to return to their homes and villages when needed. For instance, in 1873, an official working on the Golaghat–Samaguting road reported: "Beginning of December and end of February [...] work on the roads came to a standstill as coolies left to their homes to cut and store their rice crops."[10]

As an alternative to the labour requirements in the Naga Hills, colonial officials often drew upon the Nepali coolies who had been brought in to work in the Assam tea gardens. These Nepali coolies, mostly recruited from Darjeeling and Jalpaiguri, were primarily employed in working on the hill roads and as porters in the episodic military campaigns against the "wild hill tribes". The diversion of coolies from the tea plantations, however, resulted in vehement opposition from the tea planters as it created "a considerable scarcity of this labour" seriously impeding "the prospect of many gardens".[11] "Sudden call for their services", wrote Mackenzie, "places the planters in an unfair position and leads to much grumbling". Moreover, requisitioning these coolies suddenly and marching them "hurriedly to field service" resulted in sickness and much loss of life.[12]

To meet the labour exigencies, in 1873 Alexander Mackenzie proposed to form a permanent labour corps for the North-East Frontier. Such a labour corps was essential, Mackenzie argued, since campaigns on the North-East Frontier "depend[ed] more on the efficiency of the coolies than of the soldiers". And besides, "We have yet very much to do in

9. National Archives of India, Foreign and Political Department, New Delhi [hereafter, F&PD] – A, October 1873, nos 277–293A.
10. F&PD – A, September 1873, nos 219–229.
11. F&PD – A, October 1873, nos 277–293A.
12. *Ibid.*

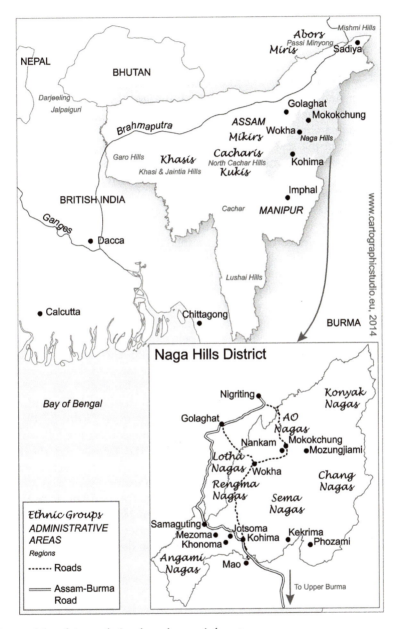

Figure 1. Map of Assam during the early twentieth century.

opening out our hill tracts by proper roads."[13] Mackenzie hoped to enlist the Nepali coolies, whom he considered to be "excellent men for mountain work".[14] He argued that there was more than enough work in "opening hill roads" to justify a permanent workforce. Mackenzie knew that such a labour corps would be indispensable to the government as the empire expanded on the North-East Frontier: "In the Garo and Naga Hills, and on the south frontier of Cachar, there is work enough to occupy such a corps for years to come."[15]

However, in the scheme of colonialism, policies were also often framed upon contingent circumstances. With the introduction of the Inner Line Regulation in 1873, mobility between the "hills" and the "plains" was placed under stricter restrictions and movement of people became more regulated.[16] In this respect, having a more organized coolie corps became essential. A large labour force could now move across the hills only under the supervision of colonial officials. Thus, in 1876 under the supervision of the Political Agent of the Naga Hills, Nepali coolies recruited from Darjeeling reportedly carried out most of the hill work on the Wokha road.[17] In 1879, another group of 150 Nepali coolies from the Garo Hills, along with 50 Mikir coolies, were employed on the Samaguting–Kohima road by Guybon Henry Damant, the Deputy Commissioner of Naga Hills.[18]

Even as "imported" coolies were being increasingly employed in the Naga Hills, contradictory elements seep into the official narratives. Colonial officials or "men-on-the-spot" soon expressed their reservations about the practicability of engaging the "plainsmen" in the hills. Expressing his discomfort about the Punjabi coolies, John Butler, the Political Agent of the Naga Hills, remarked in 1875: "I do not consider the Punjabi plainsmen, as a rule, make the best coolies for hill work."[19] On the contrary, he found hill people like the Khasis and the Kukis "cheerful and jolly". In his evaluation, their work was "such a marked contrast to the sad and weary manner of the Punjabi that it was a matter of general remark".[20] In another striking instance, in 1876, Jack Francis Needham, the Assistant Political Agent in the Naga Hills, ridiculed the plains Assamese coolies and the Gurkha coolies (enlisted mostly from Darjeeling and Jalpaiguri), who were employed on the Golaghat–Wokha road.

13. *Ibid.*
14. *Ibid.*
15. *Ibid.*
16. The Inner Line Regulation was introduced in 1873 and restricted all British subjects, including the people in the hills, from crossing the inner line without a pass or permit.
17. F&PD – B, March 1876, nos 163–167.
18. F&PD – A, January 1880, nos 495–497.
19. F&PD – A, December 1875, nos 91–99.
20. *Ibid.*

Dismissing them as "useless for road making", he preferred to replace them with 100–200 Cacharis.[21]

Such apprehensions about the "plainsmen's" competence for hill works provided grounds for colonial authorities like Colonel James Johnstone, the Officiating Political Agent of Naga Hills, to advocate strongly the tapping of "local" labour from within the hills. Writing in 1878 Johnstone declared that:

> Government should not have been burdened with a heavy expense annually for coolies from the plains, when local labours was at hand, nor should the disgraceful spectacle have been seen of coolies forced up from the plains to work on the Hills Roads, because we were afraid to make the lazy hillmen perform their share of necessary work.[22]

Arguing against the government policy of importing coolies, Colonel Johnstone thus pressed for more aggressive measures to obtain labour from within the hills. Such a policy was deemed crucial both for political and financial reasons. Extraction of labour from the Naga Hills was to be a more forceful process. At a particular juncture, the Anglo-Naga war of 1879–1880 provided a crucial context for this enterprise.

REBELLION AND PACIFICATION

In October 1879 G.H. Damant, the Deputy Commissioner of Naga Hills, had called on the Angami villages of Khonoma, Mezoma, and Jotsoma to comply with the government's revenue demand and to supply coolie labour.[23] The Angamis were targeted because they were the most outspoken opponents of forced labour. Besides, Damant remarked, these Angami villages were used to levying contributions on their weaker neighbours. Thus, once large villages such as Khonoma and Jotsoma were compelled to pay revenue, weaker villages would "follow their lead".[24] The Angamis, however, refused to comply with the colonial demand. To push forward the colonial policy, Damant proceeded to Khonoma with a detachment of fifty-four sepoys. As the military column advanced into Khonoma, the entire force was wiped out and the Angamis laid siege to the military base in Kohima.[25] It took almost a year and a massive

21. F&PD – A, September 1876, nos 142–145.
22. F&PD – A, October 1878, nos 7–51.
23. F&PD – A, March 1880, nos 331–395D.
24. In 1879, G.H. Damant, the DC of Naga Hills, wrote to the Chief Commissioner of Assam stating that, "the larger villages in the Angami community have been for generations past in the habit of levying contributions from all their weaker neighbours whether of their own or different tribes, and they will not readily pay revenue in place of receiving it". See F&PD – A, January 1880, nos 498–511.
25. F&PD – A, March 1880, nos 331–395D.

mobilization of resources to suppress what has been described as "the last Angami rebellion".[26]

A treaty imposed after pacification included an obligation to provide labour, and an annual house tax of Rs 2. In what would become a familiar argument, the imposition of state *corvée* was justified on the grounds that it was the only way of "making the Nagas pay something for their administration".[27] In addition, the figures of the headman or *lambardar* and the interpreter or *dobhashi* were introduced to simplify, facilitate, and systematize revenue and labour demands.

Under the new politico-economic regime, the Nagas were required to work for 15 days a year at a rate of 4 annas a day. To distribute the burden of building a particular road, colonial officials also developed the idea of rotating *corvée* labour from different villages.[28] However, in calculating the labour resources, the agricultural cycle of the hill people also had to be taken into account to ensure that enough stocks of food, particularly rice, were available locally. Thus, in 1882, Charles Alfred Elliott, the Chief Commissioner of Assam, directed the district officials to draw upon the "contributed labour" only when the Nagas were not engaged in agricultural work:[29] "Among the Lhotas, part of March was occupied in sowing and from May to November, in working and reaping the crop; the month [*sic*] from December to February and April are those in which labour may safely be demanded."[30] Such a caution against disturbing the "traditional" pattern of cultivation was also because "we want them to cultivate enough rice for themselves and for us too":[31]

> When the regular roster of Naga labour is made out, there will be no difficulty in calling on the men whose time it is to work to come in, and until that time much can be done to prevent hardship to individuals by distributing the corvee as widely as possible.[32]

---

26. A force of 1,135 of all ranks along with two mountain guns (from Calcutta) was mobilized under the command of General Nation, from Shillong. This was in addition to Colonel James Johnstone's force of 2,000 Manipur troops, including his own personal escort of 30 men as well as a frontier force of 50 men; F&PD – A, February 1880, nos 275–289. The transport train organized during the expedition, for transport and supply, comprised 700 boats, 200 carts, 305 elephants, 227 ponies, and 405 coolies. See V.J. Moharir, "Operations on the Eastern Frontier", in B.N. Majumdar (ed.), *History of the Army Service Corps*, II: *1858–1913* (New Delhi, 1984), p. 306.

27. F&PD – A, February 1880, nos 291–305.

28. National Archives of India, Home and Political Department [hereafter, H&PD] Judicial, March 1882, nos 58–67.

29. F&PD – A, June 1882, nos 134–137.

30. *Ibid.*

31. F&PD – A, August 1882, nos 70–77.

32. F&PD – A, January 1882, nos 134–137. In working out the labour contribution, Elliott argued that ensuring a steady supply of labour was only possible by expanding *corvée* labour in the hills. In other words, *corvée* labour would continue to be indispensable for the colonial state to maintain a continuous supply of labour in the hills.

Since the rhythm of agricultural cycle and the demand for labour often clashed with the need for continuous labour on the road, it was through such strategies that the British hoped to secure a steady supply of labour as well as a crucial supply of rice for themselves in the hills.

RATIONALIZING LABOUR IMPRESSMENT

The efforts of the colonial officials to get the Nagas to turn up to labour on "public works" or for portering requirements were not, however, readily or easily complied with.[33] The kind of force which had to be used to extract labour continuously for public works and frontier portering is illustrated in Major Thomas Bernard Michell's acknowledgement that if he needed coolies, "to go a day or two's journey from Kohima, almost the only means I have of getting them is to send a party of police to the village from which they are requisitioned, seize the headmen, and confine them in the quarter-guard at Kohima until the coolies are forthcoming".[34] In effect, the system of forced labour was then considered by colonial authorities as "a necessary step towards linking these savages into the first rudiments of civilized life".[35]

In the logic of colonialism, coercion was justified since, as Major William Ewbank Chambers categorically remarked, "no rate of pay will induce any man to work as coolly and the only means was by impressments of labour".[36] Impressing labour also became more forceful especially in a context in which the creation of a district capital at Kohima in 1881 pushed the government to structure grand plans of "public works" to consolidate its rule in the newly established territory. The Naga Hills Administration Report for the year 1882–1883 thus recorded 20,000 coolies as employed "voluntarily" on the local roads in the headquarter subdivision Kohima. Another 30,000 coolies were reportedly engaged in roadworks and the carriage of rice in the Wokha subdivision.[37]

In an environment where opposition to labour impressment began to circulate in the Assam plains, the need for and legitimacy of forced labour

---

33. "Some months ago", Major T.B. Michell wrote, in May 1881, "I sent constables with orders to the headmen of Jampi and other villages in its neighbourhood to furnish their quota of labour. The order was not obeyed and we have not received a single coolie from any of those villages." Faced with such hostility, Michell sought to send out a strong detachment of troops so as "to enforce obedience"; Proceedings of the Chief Commissioner of Assam, Foreign Department, July 1882, Assam State Archive, Guwahati [hereafter, PCCOA, FD, ASA].
34. *Ibid.*
35. F&PD – A, February 1880, nos 291–305.
36. F&PD – A, August 1880, no. 175.
37. *Report on the Administration of the Province of Assam for the Year 1882–1883* (Shillong, 1884).

had to be constantly reiterated and demonstrated.[38] For instance, Robert Cunliffe Low, Commandant on the Eastern Frontier, stated that: "No impressment of any description is being resorted [...] in procuring labour. If labour is required, a requisition is made to the civil authorities with whom it rests to obtain voluntary labour or in difficulty to impress the labour required."[39] The argument here was that "voluntary" labour was "traditional" and therefore could continue to be treated as a resource at the disposal of district officials. Moreover, impressment, in the language of colonial authorities, operated only to sustain the continuity of the "civilizing" work in which they were engaged, which occasioned the need to maintain a stable labour force.

Impressments were, as is to be expected, much resented by the local inhabitants, who would often adopt drastic strategies to evade the oppressive colonial labour regime. In one instance, a certain Captain Williamson starkly expressed his uneasiness to the Chief Commissioner of Assam: "The demand for Naga labour naturally falls on those villages near [...] Kohima [and] unless relief is afforded, it may result in the people abandoning their homes and dispersing among distant villages in the East which would place us in an awkward predicament."[40] Williamson's cautious note to the Chief Commissioner came at a time when a "heavy and disproportionate degree" of forced labour coupled with "unsystematic and spasmodic" methods had reportedly put pressure on a large number of inhabitants to leave Samaguting to avoid these exactions.[41]

To bring the "disproportionate" labour demands under "some system and order", colonial authorities subsequently initiated a systematization of local labour in the Naga Hills.[42] This involved measures such as setting up a register. In 1881 Charles A. Elliott, the Chief Commissioner of Assam, thus proposed to maintain "a register [...] showing the number of adult males in each village, whether near or far". Explaining the usefulness of such a register Elliott wrote:

> Whenever labour is required, this register should be consulted and the Lambardar should be ordered to send in so many men for so many days work to such a place.

38. What seemed to be occurring was that British orders stipulating the supply of labour for the repair of roads, etc. often glossed over and therefore blurred the social class/caste distinctions in the Assam plains, much to the displeasure of the social elite. To meet their objections, in 1882 the Assam administration under Charles A. Elliott, Chief Commissioner of Assam, initiated a series of consultations with the various district officials in the plains during which details of the existing operation of labour impressments was discussed. The general conclusion was that impressment of labour could not be done away with, but that ways had to be found to keep it within more acceptable limits and to allocate the burden more systematically and equitably; H&PD Judicial, March 1882, nos 58–67.
39. F&PD Secret – E, May 1885, nos 139–178.
40. F&PD – A, August 1880, nos 70–77.
41. F&PD – A, April 1880, nos 264–265; F&PD – A, January 1882, kept with nos 134–137.
42. "Memorandum on the Administration of the Naga Hills District", in PCCOA, FD, May 1881.

When the next demand is made, the villages, which supplied the first indent, should be excused, and application should be made to the next in order; and in this way the whole of the villages on the register should be laid under contribution before a second demand is made on the first village.[43]

While instructing the district officials to ensure early implementation of this "important reform", Charles James Lyall, Officiating Secretary to the Chief Commissioner, expressed the hope "that when he [Chief Commissioner] visits the hills next spring he may find such a roster in force at least in Kohima and the villages adjoining it and the route down to the plains".[44] By creating a more organized and finely tuned system of labour conscription, colonial authorities thus saw in the register a means to solve the great need for labour in the hills.

The aim of the register was to distribute the demand for labour more equitably between the households and villages, and hence simplify and systematize tax and labour conscription lists in the Naga Hills. Yet, this mechanism clearly did not end the prevailing system of forcible recruitment of supposedly voluntary labour.[45] In fact, it was not intended to bring an end to such a system but, as we shall see later, only to take the responsibility for forcible recruitment from the shoulders of British officers and transfer it to those of the chiefs and headmen.

THE POLITICS OF HOUSE TAX

Closely linked with the labour conscription was the gradual evolution of a rationalized and standardized tax assessment in the Naga Hills. In 1882, the house tax was fixed at the rate of Rs 2 for the Angamis and Rs 1 for the Rengmas and the Lothas.[46] The argument was that the Angamis practised terrace cultivation and engaged in trade, and so were "much richer" than those "who practise[d] the system of cultivation called *jhumming*".[47] Taxation thus placed each household under the direct control of a centralized authority for the first time.[48] Paying revenue was also cast as a "rite of passage": "A savage who pays revenue considers himself a

---

43. *Ibid.*
44. PCCOA, FD, July 1882.
45. Well into the early half of the twentieth century, incidents of impressment in the Naga Hills are found in colonial records. For instance, the tour diary of H.C. Barnes, the DC of Naga Hills, for 1916 includes this entry: "the Sibsagar local boards have not yet made the road from Santok Hat to Naginimara passable for carts. So 135 coolies had to be impressed from a distance and sent to Nazira"; "Tour Diary of H.C. Barnes, D.C., Naga Hills, 1916", Government Record Cell, Nagaland Secretariat, Kohima [hereafter, GRC].
46. F&PD – A, January 1882, nos 134–137.
47. PCCOA, FD, July 1882.
48. Julian Jacobs, *The Nagas: Hill Peoples of Northeast India: Society, Culture and the Colonial Encounter* (London, 1990), p. 23.

British subject bound to carry out all orders given him, while a savage who does not pay revenue considers himself independent and free to obey orders or not as [he] chooses."[49]

The imposition of a house tax in the Naga Hills also fell in with the imperial project of introducing the "primitive tribes" to the disciplining power of wage labour capitalism. While taxes were gradually increased, those persons unable to raise money through the sale of their agricultural or pastoral surpluses were often forced into the labour market in search of wages. In fact, large numbers of Nagas were pushed into "public works" in the region by the need to pay the house tax.[50] That this was the desired effect is also evident from cases in which road-building projects were cited as a reason for enhancing the house tax on nearby villages. Thus in 1900 the Commissioner of Assam ordered an increase in the house tax in the Angami hills from Rs 2 to Rs 3, arguing that wages earned by working on the Assam–Burma road had privileged the Angami "tribe" who lived along this route.[51] From the Naga perspective, the imposition of taxation was a turning point in their history.[52] A Sangtam Naga villager in the early twentieth century complained that "when we were administered we had to sell our buffaloes to pay the tax".[53] While some Nagas worked as coolies on colonial "public works" sites, there were others who were often driven to work as transport carriers for the colonial officials in addition to providing various support services at the frontier, as we shall see below.

CARRYING LOADS

The period after the Anglo–Naga War of 1879–1880 was followed up by the practice of long regular tours in the interior areas. These tours often resulted in episodic punitive expeditions against recalcitrant villages. In 1882 Charles A. Elliott, the new Chief Commissioner of Assam, decided that the District Commissioner (DC) should spend a full one-third of the

49. F&PD, March 1880, nos 331–395D; see also Piketo Sema, *British Policy and Administration in Nagaland, 1881–1947* (New Delhi, 1992), pp. 115–125.

50. Jacobs, *The Nagas: Hill Peoples of Northeast India*, pp. 38–40. Also see J.P. Mills, "Notes on the Effect on Some Primitive Tribes of Assam of Contacts with Civilization", in *Census of India, 1931* (Delhi, 1933), I, pt IIIB, p. 147.

51. An estimated Rs 18,15,643 *lakhs* was reportedly spent in the Naga Hills section of this Assam–Burma route. In 1895, a large number of Naga labour gangs had been employed on this road project. "This tribe", the Commissioner of Assam thus remarked, "has gained more than any other tribe by the money, which has recently been spent in these hills on public works of considerable magnitude, more especially in the villages in close proximity to the main lie of road". See F&PD External – B, October 1895, nos 152–154, and, F&PD External – A, December 1900, nos. 24–26.

52. Jacobs, *The Nagas: Hill Peoples of Northeast India*, p. 23.

53. Cited in *ibid.*

year on district tours.[54] Covering every village in his jurisdiction, the DC was instructed to "enquire into their revenue assessment [and] their supply of contributed labour".[55] To give one example of this practice, in 1881–1882 the district tour undertaken by Thomas Bernard Michell, the Political Officer of Naga Hills, and Robert Blair McCabe, Deputy Commissioner of Naga Hills, took 102 days.[56] On these tours, almost all transportation was on foot, in the absence of carts, boats, or "roads", and the Naga coolies emerged as an irreplaceable means of transport in the hills.

In conjunction with the tours, the British also set in motion a series of "military promenades" to consolidate their control over the people and territory in the interior hill areas. These "military promenades", as one British official explained, were "expeditions made by the Deputy Commissioner with an armed escort among the Frontier tribes". In December 1884, Robert B. McCabe, the Deputy Commissioner of Naga Hills, thus inaugurated one of the earliest "military promenades" to the eastern Angami villages along the Manipur border to the east of Kohima.[57] Announcing the intent of the expedition, McCabe remarked:

> [...] this is the first occasion on which a party has proceeded into these hills trusting to obtain carriage from village to village, and I considered that the success or failure of this attempt would enable me better than any other condition to gauge the real attitudes of these tribes towards our government.[58]

On 25 December, reaching the trans-frontier village of Razami, McCabe requisitioned thirty-five coolies from the headmen. However, early next morning, only twenty coolies turned up to transport the baggage and supplies of McCabe's column. To ensure that the village fully met the stipulated labour requirement, an exasperated McCabe took ten sepoys into the village and "demonstrated forcibly that orders were meant

---

54. One major function of this colonial regulation was the administrative division and organization of space. In 1905, the *Imperial Gazetteer* records show two subdivisions, Kohima and Mokokchung, in the Naga Hills district, along with a chain of territory being annexed into "the empire's geography". For some early instances, Samaguting in 1866, Wokha in 1878, Kohima in 1881, the Ao Naga country in 1889, the Semas and the Eastern Angamis (now Chakesang) in 1906, etc., see *Imperial Gazetteer of India* (Delhi, 1905), XVIII, p. 287.
55. F&PD – A, January 1882, nos 134–137; F&PD – A, January 1882, no. 35. Charles A. Elliott declared in his memoir of 1882: "I attach the greatest importance to constant and free personal intercourse between district officers and their assistants on the one hand, and that this intercourse is best secured when the officers are as little at their headquarters and as much possible on tours in the district."
56. F&PD – A, January 1882, no. 35.
57. According to McCabe, the proposed expedition would march through "Razami, Thecholumi, Khizobami, and Losemi, to Lozaphehomi where I could call in the Melomi men and return *via* Khromi and Purabami, to the Nummuh spur on the eastern frontier of the Naga Hills district"; PCCOA, FD, November 1885.
58. *Ibid.* See also F&PD External – A, May 1885, nos 175–181.

to be obeyed". This punitive action seemed to have had the desired effect, as McCabe remarked that "[i]n less than five minutes over 70 coolies turned out, and [...] we were enabled to make a very quick march to Thecholumi."[59] As a result of this intervention, McCabe claimed to have faced no difficulty in obtaining carriage throughout the whole expedition. In the ensuing years, with tours and expeditions becoming an important feature of the colonial administration, district officials would often resort to coercive measures to get men to transport supplies as well as to make roads in the hills.

Coolies accompanying the punitive expeditions were issued with meagre rations or none. Instead they were often made to live off the land or otherwise to forage for food in the villages deserted by the populace, who often fled when such expeditions approached. "No special supplies were taken for the coolies", noted Alexander Porteus, the Officiating DC of Naga Hills, in 1889, during a punitive expedition against trans-Dikhu Naga villages.[60] This, as Porteus explains, was because "in a deserted village ample supplies of pigs and rice are usually forthcoming".[61] At other times, where travelling required covering longer distances with fewer habitations, additional coolies were added to accompany each detachment to carry a few days' supply of food and *zu* (local fermented liquor) for the marching column. They also supplemented the men who fell sick or were wounded. These measures, as Porteus claims, were based on "experiences in these short expeditions".[62]

In the Naga Hills, coolies accompanying troops were sometimes also required to travel on long journeys over distant areas. This was rather unpopular as it not only took the coolies away from their homes and fields for extended periods,[63] but also often placed them in danger as the expeditions involved passing through hostile areas. "Their [the Ao coolies from Nunkum] alarm at hearing that they were to be taken into the Sema country was so great that, not withstanding they were under guard, almost the whole number succeeded in escaping, without demanding their pay during the night", wrote Porteus in 1887.[64] Desertion, however, could convey different meanings in different frontier contexts. It could mean a sense of the coolie's notion of a boundary. Crossing beyond a

59. *Ibid.*
60. F&PD External – A, May 1889, nos 209–212.
61. *Ibid.*
62. *Ibid.*
63. For instance, J.E. Webster, DC of Naga Hills, wrote how Naga coolies employed during the trans-Dikhu tour loathed being away from home for a long time, but, more importantly, disliked "most missing the sowing season – March, April". See "Report on the Trans-Dikhu Tour", PCCOA, Political Department [hereafter, PD], Political – A, August 1913.
64. F&PD External – A, November 1887, nos 64–66.

certain point could also mean putting oneself in danger by entering a rival's territory or unsafe area.[65] In response to these actions, colonial officials developed counter-strategies. Coolies were forced to do double marches, especially from those villages that refused to provide coolie service.[66] Fines were imposed on villages for any delay in furnishing coolies to the district officials. For instance, Albert E. Woods, the Officiating DC of Naga Hills, wrote in 1893 that "One *khel* of Nerhema delayed in giving coolies and I fined them Rs. 100."[67] Unwillingness to carry on with their loads was further met with harsh treatment, as was the case with the Angamis employed in the Abor expedition of 1911–1912.[68] It was through such penalizing measures that colonial officials sought to turn the supposedly "wild tribes" into a compliant labour force.

CARRIER WORK IN FAR-FLUNG AREAS

By the first decade of the twentieth century, Nagas began to be used as carriers in far-flung areas of the frontier. In fact, a series of tours and expeditions were planned in the Abor, Miri, and Mishmi areas by the British. An important purpose of these expeditions was to check on any possible Chinese influence in these areas.[69] In January 1911 Lieutenant-Colonel Philip Richard Thornhagh Gurdon, while arranging coolies for a

65. For instance, in his study on porterage in colonial Tanzania Stephen Rockel has shown how desertion among porters was often linked to the issue of security. See Stephen Rockel, "Wage Labor and the Culture of Porterage in Nineteenth Century Tanzania: The Central Caravan Routes", *Comparative Studies of South Asia, Africa and the Middle East*, 15:2 (1995), pp. 15–24.
66. "Tour Diary of K. Cantlie, officiating D.C., Naga Hills, 1919", GRC. Tours or expeditions in the hills were usually organized into stages. Depending on the location of the villages, a stage would normally mean covering a particular village by the marching column. The distance travelled by a tour party on a regular day (which normally involved covering one village or stage) could vary from 7 to 30 miles. In this sense "double marches" (which were usually carried out under compulsion) would mean making the coolies cover two stages or more in a day with their loads over steep and difficult country. In one instance, the Kekrima villagers were made to do a "double march" to Khezabama (Chizami) without halting at Tekhubama (Pfutsero) on the way.
67. "Tour Diary of Captain A.E. Woods, Officiating DC of the Naga Hills" for the month of April 1893, Sl. No. 434 (S), Kohima State Archive, Kohima [hereafter, KSA]. In another instance, finding that no coolies had arrived to carry their baggage, Keith Cantlie, the DC, fined the Khozama village a sum of Rs 50. See "Tour Diary of K. Cantlie, officiating D.C., Naga Hills, 1919", GRC.
68. A. Bentinck, the Assistant Political Officer in the Abor expedition of 1911–1912 wrote: "We tried to make an early start, but [...] the coolies particularly the Angamis gave any amount of trouble and over an hour was lost in getting clear the camp [...] throughout the day they continued putting down their loads on every possible occasion." Nevertheless, "the correction administered to the principal offenders last evening had an excellent effect on the Nagas and we got off in good time"; F&PD Secret – E, November 1912, nos 599–690.
69. For instance see "Report of Mr. N. Williamson, Assistant Political Officer, Sadiya and his tour in the Mishmi Hills", Government of East Bengal and Assam [hereafter, GEB&A], PD, Political – A, September 1910.

"THE UNSOPHISTICATED NAGA IS THE CHILD OF NATURE."

Figure 2. As the caption for this picture in the original source from 1912 makes clear, obtaining coolie labour was accompanied by a typically exoticizing and racist view of the Naga by the British.
Photograph: Angus Hamilton, from In Abor Jungles, Being an Account of the Abor Expedition, the Mishmi Mission and the Miri Mission *(London, 1912), p. 158.*

tour of Abor country, preferred to employ 400 Ao, Lotha, and Sema Naga coolies since "these have been found the most useful for tours of this nature".[70] In 1913, around 700 Semas and 100 Lothas were further employed by John Edward Webster, the DC of Naga Hills, for a trans-Dikhu tour.[71] Relying on Naga coolies placed frontier officials "in the enviable position of being independent of local transport".[72] This was especially so as Naga coolies were considered more skilled and efficient when out in camp. During a tour of Passi Minyong country in March 1908, Noel Williamson, Assistant Political Officer at Sadiya, thus remarked, "Some of the Aos have

70. "Tour by the Assistant Political Officer, Sadiya, in the Abor country", GEB&A, PD, Political – A, January 1911.
71. "Report on the Trans-Dikhu Tour", PCCOA, PD, Political – A, August 1913.
72. "Diary of a Tour of the Assistant Political Officer Sadiya", GEB&A, PD, Political – A, March 1909.

been out in camp several times in the Naga hills [...] and are quite proficient in putting up a tent and helping generally."[73]

Prior to embarking on an expedition, the stores and supplies for the military column were packed into loads of fifty or sixty pounds for the coolies. Angus Hamilton gives one such description during the Abor expedition in 1911: "As all stores had to be portered by the Naga coolies through the jungle, careful packing was an important feature of the transport arrangements. Everything was put up, therefore, in loads of fifty or sixty pounds' weight."[74] It was these crucial assortments of supplies, transported by the coolies on their backs, which largely enabled the British officials and sepoys to travel to the interior areas and enforce their rule.[75] For their labour service the Naga coolies were paid "4 annas a day and free rations" for the duration of these expeditions.[76] Apart from carrying provisions and military equipment, the Naga coolies also performed tasks such as building roads when not on the march. In 1909, during a tour of the Mishmi Hills, Noel Williamson, the Assistant Political Officer at Sadiya, engaged fifty Lotha Nagas to construct a bridle path from the Tiju river to Sati in the Mishmi Hills, covering a distance of about ninety-two miles.[77] Earlier, in February 1908, Williamson had employed thirty Ao Nagas from Nankam in clearing jungles and cutting roads in and round Sadiya. After completing their work at Sadiya, the Ao coolies were employed as transport carriers for a tour of the Abor villages.[78] By using these same coolies for various other tasks, colonial officials sought not only to ensure the presence of a steady workforce but also to keep costs low during the expeditions.

In the first few decades of the twentieth century, the colonial authorities began to distinguish certain communities in the Naga Hills as ideal for transport carriers. They were assessed and praised for their physical capacity to carry heavy loads. For instance, in 1923 John Henry Hutton, the DC of Naga Hills, wrote:

> The physical powers of the Angami are considerable, for though he is not athletic in a gymnastic way, he has great powers of endurance, being able to do forced marches of thirty to forty miles on successive days over exceedingly steep

73. *Ibid.*
74. Hamilton, *In Abor Jungles*, p. 130.
75. For instance, the rations carried by the coolies for the sepoys and followers during the Chinglong expedition included items such as, tea, salt, Dhal, rice, ghi, chillies, turmeric, ginger, garlic, gur, rum, as well as medical kits, etc. See "Chinglong Expedition", PCCOA, PD, Political – A, March 1913.
76. "Report on the Trans-Dikhu Tour", PCCOA, PD, Political – A, August 1913.
77. "Report of Mr. N. Williamson, Assistant Political Officer, Sadiya and his Tour in the Mishmi Hills", GEB&A, PD, Political – A, September 1910.
78. "Diary of a Tour of Mr. N. Williamson, Assistant Political Officer, Sadiya", GEB&A, PD, Political – A, March 1909.

country. He can stand exposure well [...] and is also able to carry very considerable burdens, the standard load being 60 lb. The women can also carry loads, but with less endurance.[79]

Such descriptions of the endurance and physical capacity of the Naga coolies, however, tended to conceal the harsh and unpleasant conditions under which coolies operated; besides, coolies accompanying military columns were often caught in skirmishes resulting in injury or death.[80]

COOLIE WORK AND LOCAL RESPONSE

While some Nagas turned out to work as transport coolies, there were others who began to seek out wage labour in the hills. This was often linked to the payment of house tax or the opportunity to earn money for their own personal wants. Drawn into wage labour by *corvée* and the house tax, subsequently Nagas also began to ask for and bargain over wages. In fact, the early twentieth century witnessed the different communities competing in an emergent labour market, especially in and around the district headquarters, Kohima. For instance, in November 1917 John Henry Hutton, the DC of Naga Hills, was confronted by a group of labourers from Kekrima demanding a rise in the coolie rate from the then current 6 annas. In pressing their case, the labourers argued that since other neighbouring villages were being paid 8 annas by the government, they should therefore be allowed the same equivalent rate.[81] This incident reveals how, with their gradual integration into a wage-labour market, Nagas were now aware of the prevailing wage rates and could draw on this knowledge to bargain over wages with the district officials while making available their labour services.

The growing availability of labour in the wage market also meant that contractors involved in state projects could choose to keep wages low and turn to those labourers willing to work at a lower wage. In doing so, other Naga villages that relied on colonial public works sites to earn cash could find themselves in a difficult position, with no work to fund their tax payments. For instance, in June 1938, the *gaonburha* (Assamese village leader) of Khabvuma village complained to Eric Thomas Drummond Lambert, the DC of Naga Hills, that "they cannot get any money to pay house tax" because "the contractor will not employ them". This was despite them living "close to the [road] slip". Instead, much to the annoyance of

---

79. J.H. Hutton, *The Angami Nagas* (London, 1921), p. 20. See also, *Frontier and Overseas Expeditions from India* (Calcutta, 1911), VII, p. 133.
80. For instance, during the Chinglong expedition in 1913 the casualties among the coolie corps included nine killed, five badly wounded, and twenty with slight wounds. See "Chinglong Expedition", Assam Secretariat Proceedings, PD, Political – A, March 1913.
81. "Tour Diary of J.H. Hutton, D.C. of Naga Hills, for the Month of November 1917", GRC.

WOUNDED NAGA COOLIE.

Figure 3. Coolie work could also include carrying other people, a load still heavier than the standard sixty pounds.
Photograph: Angus Hamilton, from In Abor Jungles, *p. 243.*

the Khabvumas, the contractor employed the "Mao coolies", who were reported to be "cheaper".[82]

While some Nagas began to engage slowly in the emerging wage labour economy, others at the same time resisted the demands of the colonial state in various ways. For instance, flight was a potent means of defence and protest in the Nagas' strategy of resistance to tax, *corvée*, and forcible impressment for military expeditions.[83] Another tactic was migration, with many individuals and families leaving their homes in order to escape taxation and forced labour. In January 1921, while passing through Ayenbung village, Hutton interviewed "one Goanbura of a village of Betes [who] admitted that he had settled in Diger to avoid being impressed with other inhabitants of the North Cachar Hills for a Lushai Expedition".[84] Another "Thado admitted that he and his fellow villagers had migrated from the Naga Hills to the North Cachar Hills but had come back because it was possible to sit in Diger without being called on to work on bridle path or to carry load or to supply rice."[85] Further, "an old Kuki gaonburra [...] admitted having moved to Diger to escape work on the Henima Bridle path".[86] Hutton goes on to add, "The story is everywhere the same, and is frankly admitted by these immigrants."[87] By resorting to such acts some of the hill populace refused to give in to the demands imposed by the colonial state. And yet, there was also a group in the Naga Hills which came to have an important stake in the colonial order of things, to which we now turn.

COLONIAL CHIEFS

It was in 1882, in the aftermath of the pacification campaign in the Angami country, that Charles A. Elliott, the Chief Commissioner of Assam, established a two-layered agency in the Naga Hills, i.e. the headman or *lambardar* and the interpreter or *dobhashi*. Elliott described the measure as one which would inaugurate a change, "from the democratic and independent habits [...] into one of subordination to a council of

82. "Tour Diary of E.T.D. Lambert, D.C. Naga Hills for the Month of June 1938", GRC.
83. Michael Adas, *State, Market and Peasant in Colonial South and Southeast Asia* (London, 1998), p. 233. For instance, coolies employed by Albert E. Woods in 1900 "bolted leaving the load" at Lemhama. In another instance, in 1923, while touring the Konyak country, John H. Hutton wrote that "eight of his coolies ran away" after passing through Longphong. See F&PD, External – A, May 1900, nos 152–153; J.H. Hutton, "Diaries of Two Tours in the Unadministered Area East of the Naga Hills", *Memoirs of the Asiatic Society of Bengal* (1929), p. 41.
84. "Tour Diary of J.H. Hutton, D.C. Naga Hills during the Month of January 1921", GRC. These stories were extracted by Hutton during a visit to the Ayenbung village, which was mostly a "mixed village of Thado and Bete Kukis".
85. *Ibid.*
86. *Ibid.*
87. *Ibid.*

elders under a village headman".[88] Apart from assessing revenue for the state, the headman was required to allocate or distribute labour demand among the households of a village. For his services, the headman was to receive 20 per cent of the revenue collection.[89]

These headmen proved very useful to the government in labour conscription for road works. During one of his tours in 1917, H.C. Barnes, the Deputy Commissioner, was quite impressed with the headmen of Phozanagwemi and Phozanasami, who reportedly brought ninety coolies for working the village path.[90] The service of the *gaonburhas* was also crucial in locating and counting houses and subjects. This was especially so since the government had little or no information on the number of houses in the Naga villages.[91] The headmen could also be held responsible for delays in supplying labour to the district officials. In one instance, having failed to bring in any coolies for the tour party of John Henry Hutton, the DC of Naga Hills, "the gaonbura ate stick"[92] [i.e. he was flogged]. Further, the carrier corps accompanying the punitive columns in the frontier was often organized and placed under the supervision of the headmen.

The supply of labour to the colonial administrators and the threat of retribution further came to shape the relationship between the different village *khels*.[93] Communities were often divided into factions, with rivals refusing to go out on labour levies. Thus at Mozungjiami village a conflict arose between the various *khels* on the question of supplying labour. "The upper khels mildly suggested that I should burn the lower khel, and then they themselves would supply my coolies", recorded Albert E. Woods in his tour diary.[94] On another occasion, while requisitioning coolies for a proposed visit to Furkating, Hutton observed some trouble between the village of Imbarasa and Lisio over the allocation and "proper shares" of coolie labour.[95] This then shaped new distinctions and conflicts between the *khels* and communities in the Naga villages.

In the facilitation and consolidation of colonial rule the *dobhashis* or interpreters constituted another important institution. They operated as

88. F&PD – A, January 1882, nos 134–137. Following Elliott's proposal, Major Michell, the Political Officer in the Naga Hills, appointed twenty headmen in the Naga Hills.
89. *Ibid.*
90. "Tour Diary of H.C. Barnes, D.C., Naga Hills, 1916", GRC.
91. See Peter Robb, "The Colonial State and Constructions of Indian Identity: An Example on the Northeast Frontier in the 1880s", *Modern Asian Studies*, 31 (1997), pp. 245–283, 261; see also "Tour Diary of K. Cantlie, officiating D.C., Naga Hills, 1919", GRC.
92. "Tour Diary of J.H. Hutton, D.C., Naga Hills, 1921", GRC.
93. A *khel* comprised several clans and each *khel* inhabited a designated area within the village.
94. "Tour Diary of A.E. Woods, D.C., Naga Hills, 1900", GRC.
95. "Tour Diary of J.H. Hutton, D.C., Naga Hills, 1921", GRC.

interpreters in road works and escorts during military campaigns.[96] The *dobhashis* were also assigned the task of communicating to the villages the government labour demand for road works. For instance, during the construction of a new road between Cheswejuma and Yarabama, Captain Albert E. Woods sent his "Dobhashas to call in thirty Chajubama coolies and thirty Yarabam coolies to work tomorrow cutting the road. I hope", Woods wrote, "to get about 200 men working daily".[97] In addition to these tasks, they also furnished district officials with news and intelligence.[98] However, owing to their position in the colonial system, the *dobhashis* could also misuse their power and oppress people by extorting money from the coolies as well as the villages.[99] At other times, they could also enhance their social standing. For instance, Charles Ridley Pawsey, the DC of Naga Hills, writes about Imlong, the Chang *dobhashi*, who had set up a shop in Mokokchung from which he issued rations to the carriers on the march. He also accompanied Pawsey as guide in punitive expeditions and was the head interpreter in camp.[100] By 1930, the number of *dobhashis* in the Mokokchung subdivision stood as follows: ten Aos, four Lothas, four Semas, three Changs, and one Konyak.[101] Increasingly emerging as dominant brokers between society and the state, *dobhashis* continued to hold a considerable stake in the colonial administration in the Naga Hills.

CONCLUSION

In the nineteenth century and the first half of the twentieth century an expanding frontier meant that colonial officials relied heavily on coercion to recruit "coolie" labour for "public works" and to provide various

96. F&PD – A, May 1873, nos 271–274; "Tour Diary of Captain A.E. Woods, Officiating D.C. of the Naga Hills for the Month of May 1893", GRC.

97. "Tour Diary of Captain A.E. Woods, Officiating D.C. of the Naga Hills for the Month of March 1893", Sl. No. 434 (S), KSA.

98. "The first thing in the morning", wrote Lt C.R. Macgregor, Detachment Commander, 44th Regiment, Sylhet Light Infantry at Kohima, "a Dobhashi of Kohima came in [...] and reported that the road was *panjied* and obstructed, and resistance intended"; F&PD – A, January 1880, nos 498–511.

99. In 1893, Albert E. Woods, the DC of Naga Hills, received complaints against five Ao *dobhashis*, who were accused of "having extorted money from the coolies, and also from some villages". See "Tour Diary of Captain A.E. Woods, Officiating D.C. of the Naga Hills for the Month of March 1893", Sl. No. 434 (S), KSA.

100. Pawsey further writes that Imlong "has far more influence than Sittobung who always was thick headed but who now owing to age and drink is worse than ever"; "Tour Diary of C.R. Pawsey, D.C., Naga Hills, 1938", GRC.

101. Piketo Sema has argued that with the gradual incorporation of the Naga "tribes" into the fold of administration, the appointment of new *dobhashis* for representing tribes having different linguistic groups and regions became increasingly necessary; see Sema, *British Policy and Administration in Nagaland*, pp. 34, 35.

support services in the region. Roads which were laid out in the hills soon came to replace what Penny Edwards has referred to as the "tyranny of distance" with a new "tyranny of proximity", which extended the reach of the state in a myriad ways, from colonial armies dispatched along routes to crush dissent to mobilizing *corvée* labour to lay new roads.[102] Furthermore, to borrow Edwards's words, the "liberating road" taking the hill people to markets also took tax collectors to the hill people, besides taking people away from their homes to serve as porters and carriers in the various frontier wars.[103]

This article has focused on the intimate connection between the need to ensure adequate supplies of labour and the push to pacify and conquer. "Coolie" labour on the frontier was "political labour". Coolie work was, however, much resented, and the Nagas often countered this by developing tactics to avoid work and minimize their labour.[104] While some Naga villagers deserted their households to evade a much-resented colonial imposition, others, such as the headmen and *dobhashis*, came to play a crucial role in collecting the resources demanded by the state. These intermediaries then became a striking feature of authority in the hill society. In the course of time, some of these individuals also emerged as "men of status" within their communities. In 1924, Surendra Nath Majumdar, the Medical Officer at Mokokchung, gave a description of one such person. Imna Meren, an Ao chief and chief interpreter at Mokok-chung, had built "a large house roofed with corrugated sheets", and was the owner of "150 'mithans', the price of each being on average rupees hundred".[105] In addition he was the only Ao practising wet cultivation or "panikhets", an indication that he also owned the better cultivable lands in the area.[106] This example shows how, through their position in the colonial system, individuals like Imna Meren could enhance their social standing in the Naga Hills.

---

102. Penny Edwards, "The Tyranny of Proximity: Power and Mobility in Colonial Cambodia, 1863–1954", *Journal of Southeast Asian Studies*, 37 (2006), pp. 421–443, 427.

103. *Ibid.* For an important work on the impact of labour recruitment on peasant societies in Africa, see David Killingray, "Labour Exploitation for Military Campaigns in British Colonial Africa 1870–1945", *Journal of Contemporary History*, 24 (1989), pp. 483–501.

104. Douglas Haynes and Gyan Prakash, "Introduction: The Entanglement of Power and Resistance", in *idem* (eds), *Contesting Power: Resistance and Everyday Social Relations in South Asia* (Delhi, 1991), p. 2.

105. Surendra Nath Majumdar, "The Ao Nagas", *Man in India*, 41 (1924), p. 43. Imna Meren was the head *dobhashi* in Mokokchung from 1 June 1914 to 21 October 1917. See Purtongzuk Longchar, *Historical Development of the Ao Nagas in Nagaland* (Dimapur, 2002), p. 374. The "mithan" (*Bos frontalis*), a semi-wild bison, is a highly valued animal among the hill "tribes" and is a symbol of wealth and status.

106. *Ibid.* "Panikhets" is a form of farming where terraces are built on steep hillsides for wet rice cultivation.

Labour conscripted from the Naga Hills continued to be extensively used in colonial pacification campaigns in the North-East Frontier. Moving across colonial boundaries, these coolies were employed largely for transport in frontier expeditions and to build colonial infrastructures such as roads and military outposts. What is more, the use of coolies to carry supplies was to be only the first step in the conscription of Nagas by the colonial authorities – later, they would also be used to serve the British Raj in global wars. This was particularly evident during World War I, when more than 2,000 Nagas served as part of the Indian labour corps in the trenches of north-eastern France.[107] In addition, a large number of Nagas would again be conscripted for building roads, carrying loads, and as guides, interpreters, and soldiers, etc., for the allied troops during World War II, especially in the India–Burma–China theatre of war. The history of these war services – to be explored in further detail in future studies – can only be understood, however, as a continuation of the practice of forced labour extraction which reaches back into the 1880s.

107. See, for instance, Henry Balfour, "Foreword", in J.H. Hutton, *The Sema Nagas* (Bombay, 1921).

IRSH 59 (2014), Special Issue, pp. 113–132 doi:10.1017/S0020859014000376
© 2014 Internationaal Instituut voor Sociale Geschiedenis

Free and Unfree Labour and Ethnic Conflicts in the Brazilian Transport Industry: Rio de Janeiro in the Nineteenth Century*

PAULO CRUZ TERRA

History Department of Campos, Federal University Fluminense
Campos dos Goytacazes Campus, Rua José do Patrocínio 77,
Centro CEP 28.010-385, Campos/RJ, Brazil

E-mail: p003256@yahoo.com.br

ABSTRACT: Over the course of the nineteenth century, major changes transformed the transport of people and freight in Rio de Janeiro, the capital of Brazil during this period. These transformations involved both technological change, as transport evolved first from carriages and carts to horse-drawn trams and then to electric trams, as well as economic developments, such as the establishment of the first tram companies, many of which became important vehicles for foreign capital to enter Brazil. Although there has been extensive research from various angles into the changes undergone by the city's transport sector, there remains, however, a significant lacuna in the existing literature: the workers involved in that sector. The aim of this article is to analyse the workforce of the urban transport sector in Rio de Janeiro in the nineteenth century, and to understand the labour that these workers provided, how they were affected by the transformations in the sector, and, at the same time, how they responded to those transformations. During this period, issues such as the connections between free and unfree labour, ethnic conflicts, and work regulation were very important in transport work in Rio de Janeiro, and they are explored in the text.

For at least the first half of the nineteenth century, black porters were key figures in the transport of people and freight in Rio de Janeiro. According to contemporary reports from travellers in Brazil, porters were responsible for providing various basic services in the *carioca* society of the time, including the transport of water, food, the sick and the dead, and the collection of waste, as well as for carrying out removals. They also played an important role in moving freight through the Customs House.

---

* This article is based on the doctoral research I conducted at Universidade Federal Fluminense, Brazil up until March 2012.

Jean-Baptiste Debret, who lived in Rio de Janeiro between 1816 and 1831, reported that to transport coffee there was a porter for each sack, with a foreman motivating the workforce with songs.[1] As well as carrying freight on their shoulders and on their heads, when transporting large volumes of freight the porters would also use equipment such as wheelbarrows. However, the motive power provided for this equipment still came from human beings.

Foreigners were particularly struck by the use of blacks for transporting people and freight. Thomas Ewbank, who lived in Brazil from 1845 to 1846, said that "The whole business part of Rio is singularly well adapted for railways, and if the people determine to continue blacks as beasts of draught, it would be to their interest to have them."[2]

The widespread use of these porters was generally seen as a consequence of the fact that most of them were *escravos ao ganho*, i.e. wage-earning slaves who had to pay a fixed income to their owners at the end of the day or the week. Debret believed that the opposition to the introduction of new means of transport was directly connected to the importance of wage-earning slaves in Rio de Janeiro in the first half of the nineteenth century.[3] To maintain the predominance of porterage was in the interest of the slave-owners as it meant an opportunity for economic return.

To understand the widespread use of slave labour in the Brazilian transport sector, it also helps to bear in mind the tradition of porters in Africa. In the main regions from which slaves were brought to Brazil – western Africa, central western Africa, and eastern Africa – porters played a fundamental part in enabling trade between villages and cities. Europeans who traded with Africans in the interior of the continent entered into contact with these porters regularly when transporting goods.[4] In Brazil, slave-owners were able to use to their own advantage a tradition that existed in Africa, by using their slaves as wage-earning porters.

As well as noting the significant economic benefits that the service provided by the porters generated for their owners, it should also be

1. Jean-Baptiste Debret, *Viagem pitoresca e histórica ao Brasil* [1834–1839] (Belo Horizonte [etc.], 1978), p. 321.
2. Thomas Ewbank, *Life in Brazil; or, a journal of a visit to the land of the cocoa and the palm. With an appendix, containing illustrations of ancient South American arts in recently discovered implements and products of domestic industry, and works in stone, pottery, gold, silver, bronze, etc.* (New York, 1856), p. 85.
3. Debret, *Viagem pitoresca e histórica ao Brasil*, p. 234.
4. On the African porters, see Paulo Cruz Terra, "Relações étnicas no setor de transporte: carregadores, cocheiros e carroceiros no Rio de Janeiro (1824–1870)", *Revista do Arquivo Geral da Cidade do Rio de Janeiro*, 3 (2009), pp. 27–40; Toyin Falola, "The Yoruba Caravan System of the Nineteenth Century", *International Journal of African Historical Studies*, 24 (1991), pp. 111–132; Roquinaldo A. Ferreira, "Dos sertões ao Atlântico: Tráfico ilegal de escravos e comercio lícito em Angola, 1830–1860" (M.A., Universidade Federal do Rio de Janeiro, 1997).

noted that this work highly suited these slaves, even though it had been forced on to them. According to Mary Karasch, the role of porter was the favourite role of the *escravos ao ganho*.[5] Travellers' reports explain that this was because the activity allowed the slaves themselves to organize their collective labour. The members of the groups of porters, always with a leader chosen from amongst them, negotiated the tasks to be carried out and decided how large a team would be required, depending on the volume and weight of the goods.[6]

On occasions, the porters would also unite to buy their freedom. According to the testimony provided by J.B. Moore, Chairman of the Brazilian Association of Liverpool, to the Select Committee on the Slave Trade, porters of coffee from the Mina ethnic group would advance money to buy the emancipation of a member, and would then be paid back in monthly instalments.[7] Charles Ribeyrolles, another traveller, claimed that members of this ethnic group in Rio de Janeiro constituted a corporation among themselves which put money aside to buy freedom and each year sent freed slaves back to Africa.[8] It should be noted here that although these urban slaves enjoyed a certain freedom of movement, as they often carried out their activities far removed from the direct control of their owners, one of the main reasons for the creation of the police in Rio de Janeiro as early as 1808 was precisely to monitor and control the city's slave population.[9]

FROM BLACK PORTERS TO THE FIRST VEHICLES

Despite the major role played by black porters, mainly slaves, in the daily life of the city, there is also evidence of the existence of vehicles in Rio de Janeiro at this time.[10] A survey of applications for vehicle licences from

5. Mary C. Karasch, "From Porterage to Proprietorship: African Occupations in Rio de Janeiro, 1808–1850", in Stanley L. Engerman and Eugene D. Genovese (eds), *Race and Slavery in the Western Hemisphere: Quantitative Studies* (Princeton, NJ, 1975), pp. 369–393, 377–378.
6. See, for example, John Luccock, *Notas sobre o Rio de Janeiro e partes meridionais do Brasil. Tomadas durante uma estada de dez anos nesse país, de 1808 a 1818* (São Paulo, 1942), p. 74; Debret, *Viagem pitoresca e histórica ao Brasil*, p. 238.
7. See his testimony cited in Manuela Carneiro da Cunha, *Negros estrangeiros* (São Paulo, 1985), p. 34.
8. Charles Ribeyrolles, *Brasil Pitoresco* (Belo Horizonte [etc.], 1975), pp. 208–209. Porterage had, of course, its hideous side too. Travellers' accounts give graphic descriptions of bodily deformities among black porters caused by the excessive weight carried.
9. On the formation of the police at the beginning of the nineteenth century, see Leila Mezan Algranti, *O feitor ausente – estudo sobre a escravidão urbana no Rio de Janeiro* (Petrópolis, 1988); Thomas Holloway, *Policing Rio de Janeiro: Repression and Resistance in a Nineteenth-Century City* (Stanford, CA, 1993).
10. For the transport history of Rio de Janeiro see Francisco Agenor de Noronha Santos, *Meios de transporte no Rio de Janeiro (história e legislação)*, 2 vols (Rio de Janeiro, 1934); Charles

the city authorities shows that 621 such licences were requested in the first half of the nineteenth century.[11] In my research of the documentation, I found requests for licences for tilburies, luxury carriages, and four-wheeled carriages. However, the great majority of submissions for licences were for carts, which accounted for 83.89 per cent of the licences granted.

In many of the requests for licences made to the City Council, the uses of the carts concerned were indicated. These included the transport of firewood and furniture, the provision of removal services, and the delivery of agricultural produce to markets. A large proportion of the carts were used to provide basic urban services such as the delivery of barrels of water and the transport of waste water, basically sewage. There were also carts used to transport waste from individual residences to designated sites for disposal.

It is important to note here that the functions carried out by means of these carts were practically the same as those carried out by the black porters. However, the methods of transport were very different. The carts were pulled by animals, whereas the porters generally transported their goods on their shoulders or even on their heads. There was another major difference referring to the workforce behind the two modes of transport: while the porters were mainly slaves, with a minority of free men among them, the cart drivers were nearly all free men, many of them immigrants from Portugal.[12]

The presence of these vehicles in the transport of freight and people in the first half of the nineteenth century provides us with evidence for the beginning of a process of segmentation and the establishment of a hierarchy in the transport sector, a process that was also developing on a wider scale in the general labour market in Rio de Janeiro. Slaves and free men, Brazilians and immigrants, shared working spaces every day – factories, shops, and streets – and often disputed work positions. Free men secured the best positions for themselves, and in the transport sector this meant that they represented the clear majority of the drivers of vehicles. Meanwhile, the manual transport of freight and people was

Julius Dunlop, *Os meios de transporte do Rio antigo* (Rio de Janeiro, 1973); and Maria Laís Pereira da Silva, *Os transportes coletivos na Cidade do Rio de Janeiro: tensões e conflitos* (Rio de Janeiro, 1992).

11. Vehicle owners were required to apply for a licence from the city authorities. The licences issued from 1837 to 1870 were consulted in the Arquivo Geral da Cidade do Rio de Janeiro (AGCRJ), Códices 51.1.17, 57.4.10, 57.4.13, 57.4.15, 57.4.17, and 57.4.20.

12. For the period between 1824 and 1870, the analysis of licences to work *ao ganho*, licences for vehicles, and the House of Detention's documentation show that for the porter function only 1.1 per cent consisted of free workers, while 98.9 per cent were enslaved. In relation to the coachmen and carters, free workers accounted for the overwhelming majority (95.4 per cent). Among those identified as coachmen and carters, the Portuguese represented 56.2 per cent of all free workers.

carried out mainly by slaves, the black porters. This process of segmentation and increased hierarchy became more accentuated in the second half of the nineteenth century. There was a sharp rise in the number of vehicle licences awarded from 1851 to 1870, reaching a total of 2,477 licences. Free workers, including Portuguese immigrants, continued to represent the majority of the drivers of these vehicles. Carts assumed an even greater role in the transport of freight in the streets of Rio de Janeiro and in the daily life of the city.

The number of Portuguese in the transport sector is related, firstly, to the large number of immigrants who came from Portugal, which was already considerable in the first half of the century and grew further after 1850. The Portuguese comprised about 10 per cent of the inhabitants of Rio de Janeiro in 1849, a figure that reached 20 per cent of the total population in 1872, making up 66 per cent of foreigners.[13] Secondly, the strong presence of Portuguese immigrants among transport workers can be related to the fact that they already had contact with the same vehicles in their homeland.[14] In the Rio de Janeiro context, driving vehicles was one way that these Portuguese immigrants found to differentiate themselves from slave workers, with which the figure of the black porter was commonly associated. For those who came with some savings, or who acquired them in Brazil, the low initial cost of buying a cart and animals meant that the transport sector was an attractive option for "immigrants who came here and had little money to start a small business".[15]

Although carts had taken over much of the activities previously performed by porters, the porters had by no means disappeared. For part of the second half of the century, cart drivers and porters would continue to coexist. According to Karasch, the porters protested when tradespeople began to replace them by horses and carts, depriving them of the income opportunities mentioned above.[16] As the records show, the introduction of new means of transport was generally not an automatic or natural process. On the contrary, it led to competition, disputes, and open conflict between the workers. Over the course of the second half of the

---

13. Luiz Felipe de Alencastro, "Proletários e escravos: imigrantes portugueses e cativos africanos no Rio de Janeiro, 1850–1872", *Novos Estudos*, 21 (1988), pp. 30–56, 54.

14. On transport in Portugal, see Terra, "Relações étnicas no setor de transporte"; Artur Teodoro de Matos, *Transportes e comunicações em Portugal, Açores e Madeira (1750–1850)* (Ponta Delgada, 1980); Fernando Galhano, *O carro de bois em Portugal* (Lisbon, 1973); Guido de Monterey, *O Porto. Origem, evolução e transportes* (Porto, 1972).

15. Elciene Azevedo, "A metrópole às avessas: cocheiros e carroceiros no processo de invenção da 'raça paulista'", in *idem et al.* (eds), *Trabalhadores na cidade: cotidiano e cultura no Rio de Janeiro e em São Paulo, séculos XIX e XX* (Campinas, 2009), p. 91. The author's considerations regarding the São Paulo context are also valid for analysing the decision of Portuguese immigrants to opt for the transport sector in the case of Rio de Janeiro. All translations from Portuguese into English are my own.

16. Karasch, "From Porterage to Proprietorship", pp. 377–378.

century, the black porters would witness how their operations were gradually restricted to the transport of freight within the port area. Moreover, although they continued to form the major part of the workforce in the port, they also had to face increasing competition from free workers, many of whom, again, were Portuguese immigrants.[17]

In May 1872, a group of black porters who worked at Praça das Marinhas and were *escravos ao ganho* demanded a pay rise from the service contractors. These contractors called on white workers, probably Portuguese, who agreed to provide the service for a lower price. However, the group of black porters got together and physically abused the white workers, throwing some of them in the water.[18] This case is but one example of how free and unfree work was closely connected in Rio de Janeiro in the nineteenth century. The fact that *escravos ao ganho* were paid, as Marcel van der Linden has noted, shows that the boundaries between concepts such as "slavery" and "wage labour" could be extremely confusing. Further, "the wage laborers are often less 'free' than the classic view suggests".[19] In this sense, as Alessandro Stanziani has shown, for the majority of European countries between the sixteenth and the end of the nineteenth century "the barrier between freedom and bondage was not only moveable and negotiable, it [was] also thought of differently from how we are used to thinking of it today". This author noted that "labour was submitted to serious legal constraints, usually justified by reference to the 'debt' or the 'deed' the worker, or the peasant, had contracted with both master and community".[20]

In the case of Brazil in the nineteenth century, things were not very different, and it was possible to find former slaves who had signed service contracts promising to repay through years of work the loan of a certain amount which had usually been used to buy their own manumission. Although they were no longer slaves, they promised to serve their employer with obedience.[21] However, it was not only former slaves who

---

17. Compared to other areas of Rio de Janeiro, the proportion of blacks found among those labouring in the port was higher. Yet the proportion of whites, including many Portuguese, was significant. According to Erika Bastos Arantes, among longshoremen in the House of Detention between 1901 and 1910 29 per cent were white, 32.6 per cent were black, and 28.5 per cent mulatto; Erika Bastos Arantes, "O Porto Negro: cultura e associativismo dos trabalhadores portuários no Rio de Janeiro na virada do XIX para o XX" (Ph.D., Universidade Federal Fluminense, 2010), p. 76.

18. *Jornal do Commercio*, 5 March 1872.

19. Marcel van der Linden, *Workers of the World: Essays Toward a Global Labor History* (Leiden [etc.], 2008), p. 23.

20. Alessandro Stanziani, "The Legal Status of Labour from the Seventeenth to the Nineteenth Century: Russia in a Comparative European Perspective", *International Review of Social History*, 54 (2009), pp. 359–389, 388.

21. Henrique Espada Lima, "Sob o domínio da precariedade: escravidão e os significados da liberdade de trabalho no século XIX", *Topoi*, 6:11 (2005), pp. 289–326, 305.

were subjected to such situations. Many Portuguese came to Brazil as *engajados*, a condition similar to that of the indentured servants who arrived in the eighteenth century in the West Indies and North America.[22] In return for the costs of transport by sea, the *engajados* were charged twice the regular fare. They could land in Brazil only with the permission of the boats' captains. In Brazilian ports genuine auctions of men and women took place, very similar to the auctions of African slaves. Local recruiters paid the ticket and those who desired to contract the services of immigrants were charged a higher sum then paid by the recruiters.[23] Then, a service contract was drawn up which subjected the *engajados* to payments lower than those received by other workers, such as the amount paid to rent a slave. It was possible to find in the newspapers advertisements concerning *engajados* who had run away from their place of work before the end of the contract period, very similar to the runaway slave advertisements.[24]

The changes that took place in the transport sector in Rio de Janeiro, which went from being a city in which freight was carried by black porters to one in which carts predominated and then to a city of trams, have often been seen as a consequence of urban growth. For example, according to Ana Maria da Silva Moura, the increase in the city's population and production from 1849 to 1856 led to a larger market for the carts and also to a greater need to distribute both imported and domestically produced goods.[25] However, this process of transformation cannot be reduced to a direct equation between population growth and the growth in the number of carts without taking into account several other key variables that were at work at this time. Although the demographic data for Rio are problematic, they do show that the city's total population grew only slightly between 1849 and 1872, from 266,466 inhabitants to 274,972, a growth of just over 3 per cent. In the same period, the number of vehicles increased by almost 300 per cent. Clearly, population growth by itself cannot explain this increase.

The main difference between the census of 1849 and that of 1872 was in the number of slaves, which fell dramatically in the capital in this period. From representing 41.5 per cent of the city's total population in 1849, when Rio de Janeiro had the largest population of slaves of any city in the Americas, by 1872 the slave population had fallen to just 17.8 per cent of

22. Alencastro, "Proletários e escravos", p. 36.
23. Miriam Halpern Pereira, *A política portuguesa de imigração* (Lisbon, 2002), p. 37.
24. Artur José Renda Vitorino, "Mercado de Trabalho e Conflitos Étnicos em Meio à Escravidão: portugueses e africanos no Rio de Janeiro, 1850–1870", *Cadernos Arquivo Edgard Leuenroth*, 27 (2009), pp. 11–57, 29.
25. Ana Maria da Silva Moura, *Cocheiros e carroceiros: homens livres no Rio de senhores e escravos* (São Paulo, 1988), p. 42.

the inhabitants.[26] According to Karasch, the reasons for this decrease included high mortality rates in the early 1850s and an increase in the price of slaves (because of the prohibition of the slave trade in 1850 and the demand for labour from coffee plantations), both of which led many slave-owners either to rent or sell their slaves to rural areas.[27]

The opposition to the introduction of other means of transport came mainly from the slave-owners, who were concerned by the impact on the economic opportunities of their wage-earning slaves who were working as porters. The relative decline in the slave population surely contributed towards rendering this kind of opposition obsolete.

1850 is also considered to have been a watershed year for the Brazilian economy in general. The end of slave trading in that year released capital that had previously been employed in this activity. This enabled an "increase in the liquidity of the economy, a diversification of investments, and the start of financial activities to be deployed in the service sector and the nascent industrial sector".[28] If before 1850 Brazil had barely responded to the rise of international capitalism, Maria Bárbara Levy has shown that following that year the country was able to draw up its own legal framework for a company law, enabling the establishment of the *sociedade anônima* or the limited liability company.[29] The freight and passenger transport companies that sprung up after 1850 were hence clearly related to this process of the wider transformation of the Brazilian economy, which supported the establishment of new forms of companies.

Several companies were established specifically in the freight transport sector, which promised very high profits. The importance of this sector is related to some of the basic characteristics of Rio de Janeiro in the nineteenth century, when it was both the capital of the country and the main port for exporting coffee, the most important product of the Brazilian economy.[30] As a result, the port of Rio de Janeiro generated enormous demand for freight transport services.

Commercial and industrial facilities also began to develop their own fleets of vehicles and to hire workers to drive them. Many advertisements for drivers can be found in newspapers of the time, such as that placed by a timber warehouse in Rua da Saúde, which in 1873 advertised for a driver

26. Sidney Chalhoub, *Visões da liberdade: uma história das últimas décadas da escravidão na corte* (São Paulo, 1990), p. 199.
27. Mary C. Karasch, *A vida dos escravos no Rio de Janeiro (1808–1850)*, (São Paulo, 2000), p. 28.
28. Elisabeth von der Weid, "A cidade, os bondes e a Light: caminhos da expansão do Rio de Janeiro (1850–1914)" (Ph.D., Universidade Federal Fluminense, 2010), p. 49.
29. Maria Bárbara Levy, *A indústria do Rio de Janeiro através de suas Sociedades Anônimas. Esboços de história empresarial* (Rio de Janeiro, 1994), p. 52.
30. Eulália Maria Lahmeyer Lobo, *História do Rio de Janeiro (do capital comercial ao capital industrial e financeiro)*, 2 vols (Rio de Janeiro, 1978), II, p. 47.

and offered to "pay a good wage".[31] Carts and their drivers had a presence in almost all the city's businesses, from breweries such as Brahma to laundries, textile companies, mills, factories for soap and sails, brickmakers, and others.[32] Cart drivers were responsible for transporting nearly all the goods produced and sold within the city.

In the area of passenger transport, since the beginning of the nineteenth century the city had been home to establishments that rented out carriages and chaises. In 1859, donkey-drawn trams were introduced in Rio de Janeiro, which was the first city in South America to have this type of transport. By the end of the century, there were four main companies in Rio de Janeiro providing tram transport on rails: Companhia Jardim Botânico, in the southern zone of the city; Companhia Carris Urbanos, in the centre; and Companhia Vila Isabel and Companhia de Carris da Tijuca, both in the north.

In this period, the tram became the main means of transport for passengers in Rio de Janeiro. From 1870 to 1905, the number of users increased by over 1,680 per cent, rising to more than 100 million passengers in 1905. The number of passengers using the trams was significantly higher than the number of passengers for other forms of transport. For example, from 1886 to 1896 the Estrada de Ferro Central do Brasil, a railway company which connected the centre of the city with the suburbs, transported 30 million people in total, while in 1896 alone the number of tram passengers reached almost 73 million people.

WORK AND DISCIPLINE IN THE TRAM COMPANIES

As we have discussed, the establishment of the first tram companies was closely associated with the economic transformations taking place in Brazil. But what did the creation of these companies mean for the workers involved, and what was it like to work for them? There was a clear division of labour at the tram companies: the coachmen were responsible for driving the trams, while the conductors collected the fares. As the conductors received part of the companies' earnings, the transport companies created a network to monitor their employees. There was constant suspicion on the part of employers that the conductors were pocketing the fares. For example, the *Gazeta de Notícias*, a newspaper of general circulation, of 27 August 1898 stated that employees who stole these sums were disloyal as the fares represented "remuneration for the work and for the capital of the company", and were also the source of investment in improving the tram service.[33]

---

31. *Jornal do Commercio*, 23 May 1873, p. 7.
32. De Noronha Santos, *Meios de transporte no Rio de Janeiro*, II, p. 26.
33. *Gazeta de Notícias*, 27 August 1898, p. 1.

The companies were also worried that they were losing money because of conductors not collecting the fares in all cases. An employee of Jardim Botânico received a letter of dismissal from the company's chairman telling him that he had already been warned that he was taking too many non-paying passengers and, as the company could not carry all these people for free, that the employee had become "too expensive for the Company as a conductor".[34] The letter illustrates how the company tried to control the revenues from the vehicles. It also demonstrates that despite the company's best efforts to monitor the service the workers had found ways to avoid these controls and to take passengers without collecting fares.

The monitoring of the conductors was carried out by inspectors, who were the companies' eyes on the ground. On 1 August 1903, the workers' journal *A greve* argued that the employees of the transport companies were being victimized by capitalism, and "persecuted by these vandals and exploiters of their sweat". The newspaper said that the inspections formed a key part of the policy of the company owners, and that the inspectors were robbing the conductors of their daily bread in order to earn the good graces of the bosses.[35] In 1898, the generalized suspicion against conductors and the concern of the transport companies to maximize their profits led one transport company, Companhia Carris Urbanos, to install a system in its trams designed to ensure that fares were paid correctly. The system was based on calculating the average passenger traffic of a particular line. If this level was not reached, conductors were obliged to make up the difference from their wages.[36]

Over time, the monitoring of conductors and of transport workers in general intensified and company owners introduced secret inspections. These took place when there were suspicions about a particular employee. To catch the suspect in the act, the inspections were carried out by unidentified inspectors who were not known to the employees. However, the employees were given no right of defence and were only alerted when they received letters fining them or dismissing them from the company.[37] Relations between inspectors and conductors were tense, as the former had the power to reduce the salaries of the conductors by recording any misdemeanours and even to have them dismissed. According to *A greve*, in its 1 August 1903 edition, the inspectors' director of the Companhia Jardim Botânico required conductors, through his assistants, to provide him with valuable gifts, such as cases of port wine, and threatened conductors who refused with dismissal.[38]

34. Charles Julius Dunlop, *Apontamentos para a história dos bondes no Rio de Janeiro*, 2 vols (Rio de Janeiro, 1953), II, p. 31.
35. *A greve*, 1 August 1903, p. 1.
36. *Gazeta de Notícias*, 16 March 1898, p. 1.
37. *A greve*, 1 August 1903, p. 1.
38. *Ibid.*

Coachmen had to comply with schedules of working hours and shifts. The inspectors were responsible for verifying the coachmen's compliance with the working hours established by the employers. The coachmen worked in shifts, with the first shift starting at 3.30 in the morning. The workers' journal *Gazeta Operária*, in its edition of 8 February 1903, said that employees of the tram companies had wages that were "negligible considering they worked twelve, fourteen, or even more hours per day".[39] By way of comparison, in Berlin in 1902 coachmen and conductors generally worked eleven hours a day, and a maximum of twelve hours.[40] A manifesto from the coachmen of Lisbon, dated 1910, says that "by day they work from seven in the morning to seven at night, and by night from eight until the morning, in the cold and the rain".[41] Average working hours for employees of tram companies in Rio de Janeiro were generally the same as in other cities around the world, although they could be extended. Coachmen and cart drivers who worked for other transport companies outside the tram sector might work even longer hours. In 1906, the working day in the transport sector was "fourteen, sixteen, or more hours per day, beginning in the morning and going on until late at night". In December that year, transport workers went on strike, demanding a working day of twelve hours.[42]

The companies imposed a range of regulations on their employees. These established the respective punishments that could be inflicted, including fines, suspension, and dismissal. These rules were mandated by the employers, who were also responsible for ruling on each case. According to Carlos da Fonseca, such fines have to be regarded, in general, as "the everyday expression of employer justice, and a sort of purgatory of small offences".[43] These regulations were common not only in transport companies in Rio de Janeiro but also in other countries, including Portugal. By the end of the nineteenth century such regulations had become common practice in different types of Brazilian companies. According to Robério Santos Souza, company regulations "were established as an increasingly wide-reaching set of rules and norms, which covered areas ranging from moral teaching for employees to information about wages, fines, suspensions, and the management of conflicts".[44]

39. *Gazeta Operária*, 8 February 1903, p. 3.
40. John P. McKay, *Tramways and Trolleys: The Rise of Urban Mass Transport in Europe* (Princeton, NJ, 1976), p. 233.
41. *O Sindicalista*, 27 November 1910, p. 3.
42. *Gazeta de Notícias*, 17 December 1906, p. 1.
43. Carlos da Fonseca, *História do movimento operário e das ideias socialistas em Portugal*, 4 vols (Lisbon, 1980), IV, p. 6.
44. Robério Santos Souza, "Organização e disciplina do trabalho ferroviário baiano no pós-abolição", *Revista mundos do trabalho*, 2:3 (2010), pp. 76–98, 76.

Company regulations also constituted disciplinary mechanisms in which employers established their expectations for the performance and behaviour of their workforce.

From 1903 the rules of the Companhia Jardim Botânico required conductors and tram drivers to buy uniforms from a related company. The journal *A greve* said that at this company each uniform cost 50,000 *réis* "from a very ordinary factory", "while other companies" provided them to their employees for just 37,000 *réis*.[45] Complaints about companies forcing their employees to benefit related parties can also be found in letters from the coachmen of Companhia São Christovão to the journal *A Reforma* in 1873. According to the coachmen, company management required employees to use a metal badge on their caps. Although the coachmen had repeatedly called for this to be "replaced by any other form of emblem, the management paid no attention, perhaps because they were afraid of damaging the interests of the metal manufacturer, which are looked after by a well-known director at the company".[46] We should also note that one of the reasons for the workers' rejection of the metal might have been that metal insignia were used by wage-earning slaves. Most employees of the tram companies were free men, and in Rio de Janeiro in the second half of the nineteenth century their refusal to use the metal could well have been connected with their unwillingness to be identified with slave workers. The coachmen of São Christovão also complained that company employees had to pay 1,000 *réis* a month to a doctor, although most of them already had doctors and mutual societies for medical treatment. The workers warned that if their demands were not met, the company would end up with no employees, as many of them were determined to leave the firm.[47]

The obligation on workers to buy their uniforms and badges from specific providers, or to pay for a medical service they did not want, suggests that relations between employers and employees were not limited only to the simple remuneration of their labour. Marcel van der Linden argues that ties were possible "between both parties outside the circulation process", and that the employers had ways of binding their employees to them.[48] As mentioned before, wage labour was often less "free" than has been assumed.

It can be seen from this survey that the hours worked by employees and their earnings were subject to intense controls by the transport companies,

---

45. *Ibid.* In 1910 motormen and conductors of the Light Company in São Paulo complained that they, too, were forced to buy their uniforms for twice the normal price; João Marcelo Pereira dos Santos, "Os trabalhadores da Light São Paulo, 1900–1935" (Ph.D., Universidade Estadual de Campinas, 2009), p. 146.
46. *A Reforma*, 22 January 1873.
47. *Ibid.*
48. Van der Linden, *Workers of the World*, p. 29.

and that strategies for these controls evolved over time. In addition, systems for fines, suspensions, and dismissals aimed to punish employees and to establish rules and hierarchies, as well as to maximize exploitation of the workers.

CONFLICTS AND THE REGULATION OF THE TRANSPORT WORK

In addition to the inspection practices at the companies themselves, which became more sophisticated over time, transport workers were also governed by an extensive system of laws and rules designed to control them. This was related to some of the inherent characteristics of the profession: coachmen and conductors worked far from the eyes of their employer, they were much more mobile than any other group of industrial workers, and they had direct and daily contact with the population.[49] Another important point is that, despite the importance of companies in the transport sector, there were still self-employed workers engaged in transporting people and freight, such as waste. In this sense, the laws and regulations also aimed to control workers who were not subject to company rules and punishments.

In 1853, the City Council of Rio de Janeiro passed the first specific laws aimed at the drivers of vehicles. These laws required all coachmen to register with the police and to take an examination to prove their vehicle-driving skills. Later, in December 1872, the City Council signed a contract with Nunes de Souza & Cia, according to which the company would collect waste from residences, replacing around 120 cart drivers who had provided this service independently. Over the course of 1873, this contract became highly controversial, with opposition to it led by Luiz Fortunato Filho, the lawyer representing those workers who had provided the service before the contract was announced. In various letters to newspapers and in submissions to the relevant authorities, he alleged that the company would have, in fact, a monopoly over the service, in breach both of the freedom of trade and the freedom of the residents themselves to choose people that they trusted to provide the service.[50]

As a way of making their decisions effective, the local authorities then halted the provision of licences to the waste collectors and seized the vehicles of those cart drivers who continued to work. Faced with the quantities of waste piling up in the streets – partly because the licensed company could not cope with demand and partly because some residents refused to use the company's services – the city authorities subsequently

---

49. Anton Rosenthal, "Streetcar Workers and the Transformation of Montevideo: The General Strike of May 1911", *The Americas*, 51 (1995), pp. 471–494, 479.
50. See, for example, *Jornal do Commercio*, 22 February 1873, p. 2.

decided to hand out licences to the cart drivers again. The cart drivers then refused to go back to work, on the grounds that the licences were conditional and could be withdrawn at any time. A strike was organized with the aim of forcing the authorities to guarantee them their right to work.[51] The Ministry of Business of the Brazilian Empire then issued a ruling indicating that, as the company did not have the materials necessary to carry out the contract, the licences to the cart drivers should be maintained.[52] The cart drivers decided to return to work.

Ultimately, the company could not comply with the terms of the contract, and the cart drivers continued with their trade. However, in 1875 the city authorities approved a series of rules for carts which collected waste from the city's streets and houses to tighten controls on the workers involved. These rules included establishing sites where the cart drivers could dispose of the waste and the model of cart that could be used; they also stated that the service could be carried out "only until 9 o'clock in the morning, in the months of October to March, and until 10 o'clock, from April to September". The penalty for breaking any of these rules was a fine of 30,000 *réis* and "eight days in prison, to be doubled for repeat offenders".[53]

In February 1876 the authorities also published a decree that required rigorous compliance with the times it had stipulated for collecting waste. The workers considered this attitude and the fines to be excessively harsh, and also noted that their carts could be confiscated and impounded without there apparently being any legal basis for this. These grievances, combined with the decision to restrict the waste collection service to the morning, resulted in a second strike by the cart drivers. Luiz Fortunato Filho argued that the right to work was at stake in this new dispute. The cart drivers who carried out waste collection services were mainly self-employed workers, and the press emphasized this fact in their support of the workers. The *Gazeta de Notícias* of 15 February 1876 asked:

> Does the City Council have any contract with the cart drivers who collect the waste from individual residences? Does it provide them with any guarantees? No, it forces them to pay for a licence [...] with taxes, fines, prison, and the pound. How can it expect to impose laws on free men, who have to be able to work if they want? How can it impose a duty on those workers to whom it gives no rights?[54]

For the workers, the service they provided would not have been advantageous under the conditions imposed by the City Council. The workers said that they were not responsible for ensuring the health and hygiene of the city

---

51. *Ibid.*, 27 November 1873, p. 4.
52. *Ibid.*, 29 November 1873, p. 4.
53. *Código de Posturas, leis, editais e resoluções da Intendência Municipal do Distrito Federal* (Rio de Janeiro, 1894), pp. 231–232.
54. *Gazeta de Notícias*, 15 February 1876, p. 3.

and that they worked to earn their daily bread: "[I]f they want us to continue to work as we have in the past, we will: if not, we will not return to work."[55] The strike was reported widely in the press, as the waste left uncollected at residences was associated with concerns over the rising number of deaths from yellow fever. At this time, the waste accumulation was considered one of the causes of the outbreaks of yellow fever in 1873 and 1876, which claimed 3,659 and 3,476 lives respectively.[56] In both years, the workers responsible for waste collection had considerable bargaining power.

The clear support of the press, the waste that was piling up in the streets, and the spike in yellow fever cases led to yet another victory for the workers. According to the *Revista Illustrada* of 19 February 1876, "finally the City Council, the Police, and the Ministry had to respond to the noble class of cart drivers" and the contested rulings were overturned.[57] Not surprisingly, just after the end of the strike, the defeated City Council again discussed the possibility of giving a company a monopoly over the collection of domestic waste. It was more important than ever for the authorities that the service should not remain in the hands of the cart drivers who had repeatedly defeated them, and who had been able to block the City Council's attempts to control and even abolish their work.

With regard to the carters who collected waste, the 1873 strike was an attempt by workers to stop the increasingly aggressive process in the city whereby workers would no longer own their instruments of production. In 1897, the city government, finally, signed another contract with a company and carters were no longer allowed to carry out their traditional work. Although the company acquired a monopoly of domestic waste collection, it is possible to identify the enduring persistence of the self-employed in other spheres of the transport sector, albeit in small numbers.

Transport workers also saw themselves affected by (and acted against) the introduction of certain more general laws. In 1890, following the Proclamation of the Republic in 1889, workers in the urban transport sector went on strike to protest against the Penal Code of 11 October 1890. Most of Rio de Janeiro's newspapers claimed that the coach drivers and cart drivers were complaining about provisions that were not, in fact, included in this new Code. For example, the *Jornal do Commercio*, a newspaper of general circulation, claimed that the workers' allegations were not founded on facts and must have been maliciously invented by "wretched speculators who thrive on the simplicity of the workers", and who manipulated the "placid spirits of these poor coachmen".[58]

55. *Ibid.*
56. Sidney Chalhoub, *Cidade febril: cortiços e epidemias na Corte imperial* (São Paulo, 1996), p. 86.
57. *Revista Illustrada*, 19 February 1876.
58. *Jornal do Commercio*, 2 December 1890, p. 1.

One dissenting voice, however, was that of the *Gazeta da Tarde*, in its 2 December 1890 edition. The newspaper said that a commission formed by transport workers had gone to the newspaper to explain that their protest was not as unjustified "as is generally believed[;] even if the item that was discussed at such length yesterday does not in fact exist, there are in the legislative reform of Mr Campos Salles some draconian proposals and it is against these proposals that the cart drivers are protesting".[59] The commission from the workers cited in particular two of the articles in the Code, addressing the issue of punishment for accidents.

The evidence that the workers sent a commission to the newspaper casts them in a new light, not as helpless and simple souls manipulated by forces that were using them for their own purposes, but as people with clear, conscious demands, who knew exactly what they were fighting for and who they were fighting against. By specifically citing the articles in the Code that they were opposing, the workers were able to rebut the accusation made by the *Diário de Notícias* newspaper that they were not really protesting against the Penal Code, "mainly because the Code is almost unknown, even to educated people in the country".[60]

Although various newspapers argued that the offending article in the Penal Code relating to accidents did not apply only to coachmen and cart drivers, these workers understood that it did directly affect them. There were constant accidents involving their vehicles, and these accidents were one of the major points of conflict between drivers and passengers, with drivers widely caricatured and attacked in the press. In 1890 a child had been run over, leading to significant tension and protests from the population.[61] In this context, the vehicle drivers were well-advised to be concerned about any new law on accidents that would also apply to them.

As well as claiming that workers were being manipulated in the strike, some of the press also questioned the reasons for the walkout. According to the *Diário de Notícias*, "in every corner of the world the criminal code contains punishments for all kinds of crimes and there were never strikes against the law upheld by their governments".[62] The *Jornal do Commercio* argued that "a workers' strike aims either to right a wrong or to achieve an increase in pay. However, in this strike, the cart and coach drivers have no determined goal at all."[63] The line of argument in these newspapers was, thus, that opposition to a particular law or ruling generally was neither a normal nor a sufficient ground for a strike.

59. *Gazeta da Tarde*, 2 December 1890, p. 2.
60. *Diário de Notícias*, 3 December 1890, p. 1.
61. *Ibid.*, 14 July 1890, p. 1.
62. *Ibid.*, 2 December 1890, p. 1.
63. *Jornal do Commercio*, 4 December 1890, p. 1.

However, some newspapers provided their readers with a different version of events. The *Gazeta da Tarde* explained why the coachmen had gone on strike in the following way, offering an interesting interpretation of the relationship between the strikes and the law:

> Since the right of law was replaced by the right of force; since at every moment the law and administrative procedures are disparaged; since the people are represented by a congress full of appointees, without the authority to carry out justice or to right wrongs; since the people are convinced that the laws imposed on them do not reflect the will of the people but that of a cabal that keeps itself in power by force alone, and that these decrees and rules serve only to support interests that cannot always be disclosed, the one brake on popular unrest that exists along with religion, has disappeared – respect for the law has disappeared.[64]

In 1899, new rules were established for inspecting vehicles. These consisted of the most detailed document ever produced at that time for controlling transport workers. These rules proved to be the trigger for the strike that started on 15 January 1900. The *Gazeta de Notícias* noted that the walkout was a consequence of a lack of clarity on the part of the police concerning the technical details of these new regulations. According to the newspaper, it was, for instance, incomprehensible that the police had made no statement about the rumours circulating that the coach drivers would have to be photographed.[65] Although the government said that the mandatory photograph requirement was only a rumour, the *Jornal do Brasil*, a newspaper of general circulation known to be concerned with workers' conditions, then found out that for the coach drivers it was, in fact, a real obligation, even though it did not appear in the new regulations. The workers alleged that several companies, such as São Christovão, had published rules requiring a photograph of the worker to be taken, and that vehicle inspectors were also requiring photographs.

But why did the workers protest so strongly against being photographed by the police? As all the newspapers of the time explained, until then it was only thieves whose photographs were taken by the police. A member of the police anthropometry service wrote that the photographs were used for purposes of identification, so that the suspects could not use any name they desired.[66] When they learned that they would be photographed compulsorily, the drivers believed they were being equated with common thieves. Their demand for the requirement to be dropped was closely connected to the symbolic aspects of the requirement for a police photograph, which represented the tightening of police control over the workers.

---

64. *Gazeta da Tarde*, 10 December 1890, p. 1.
65. *Gazeta de Notícias*, 16 January 1900, p. 1.
66. *Jornal do Brasil*, 16 January 1900, p. 1.

Following the end of the transport workers' strike, on 17 January the Beneficial Society for the Protection of Coachmen delivered a document to the Ministry of Justice containing the demands of its members. This document also protested that coachmen were being charged fees for licences that were higher than the amounts that had been set. In addition, the coachmen complained about certain provisions of the rules, such as Article 36, which covered the impounding of vehicles. The document alleged that it was unfair that coachmen and cart drivers were to be doubly punished: in addition to having their licences confiscated the seizure of their vehicles would lead to further expenses for recovering them from the pound.[67] The workers were successful. On 20 January, the Minister of Justice, Epitácio Pessoa, issued a decree that accepted all the amendments requested in the submissions lodged by the Beneficial Society for the Protection of Coachmen.[68]

The laws and regulations cited in this article indicate the concern of the institutions of the state with controlling transport workers, workers who, as mentioned above, formed a constant presence in the public space and had direct and daily contact with the population. The relationship between passengers and transport workers could be very contentious, especially with regard to the frequent vehicular accidents. The causes of such accidents were widely discussed in the press, impunity being considered the major contributor to the large number of cases. The population demanded that the government act vigorously, and the regulations and laws reflected this demand too.[69] The forms of control were tightened over time in Rio de Janeiro, with increasingly detailed regulations, while at the same time they were adapted to the technological transformations of the sector, such as the specific regulation created to cover electric trams, which arrived in the city in 1892.

It was not only in Rio de Janeiro that transport workers were the subject of extensive laws and that these measures constituted an important trigger in their strikes. In Lisbon, two out of three stoppages organized by transport workers in the nineteenth century were linked to laws approved by the City Council. In turn, in April 1899, the coachmen of Buenos Aires went on strike to protest against the City Council's decision to require them to have a photograph taken in order to get a driver's licence.[70]

---

67. *Jornal do Commercio*, 19 January 1900, p. 1.

68. *Relatório apresentado ao Presidente da República dos Estados Unidos do Brasil pelo Dr Epitácio Pessôa, Ministro de Estado da Justiça e Negócios Interiores em Março de 1900* (Rio de Janeiro, 1900), p. 163.

69. *Diário de Notícias*, 7 July 1890, p. 1.

70. Mercedes García Ferrari, "'Una marca peor que el fuego'. Los cocheros de la ciudad de Buenos Aires y la resistencia al retrato de identificación", in Lila Caimari (ed.), *La ley de los profanos: delito, justicia y cultura en Buenos Aires: 1870–1940* (Buenos Aires, 2007), p. 126.

For their part, the transport workers had their own readings and interpretations of these measures and demonstrated their response in actions such as the series of strikes that have been analysed in this article. In their reactions, the workers challenged "the law as an instrument of power of dominant groups", and made use of the "legal resources available to defend their rights and subvert the original purpose of the legal codes, which was to serve the interests of the ruling elites".[71] Their struggles against new laws also show just how well the coachmen and cart drivers understood that strikes represented an effective means of restricting the actions of the dominant classes.[72]

CONCLUSIONS

Over the course of this article it has been shown how the urban transport sector in Rio de Janeiro underwent major changes in the nineteenth century. Many scholars have analysed these transformations in terms of the various technologies involved. Here, however, I have tried to present a different perspective, focusing on the direct impact of the changes on the workers involved, most notably on how those changes transformed the city from one that relied mainly on slave porters for its freight transport to one that used vehicles driven largely by free workers. The introduction of new means of transport and the transformation of the workforce caused competition and ethnic conflict. Further, in Rio de Janeiro in the nineteenth century the barrier between free and unfree labour was very diffuse and confusing.

The establishment of the first major transport companies in the city was directly connected to the transformation of the Brazilian economy in general. Labour in these companies was subject to strict controls, regulations, and inspections, as this was a sector in which workers travelled all over the city and spent much of their working day far from the eyes of their employers. Coach drivers and cart drivers, company employees and self-employed workers alike, were also subject to various laws and regulations emanating from the City Council and the police.

Faced with these transformations in their sector, transport workers were by no means passive. Indeed, they were much more active than is supposed in the only study to date on Rio de Janeiro's coach drivers and

71. These statements were made by Juliana Teixeira Souza about the small traders in imperial Rio de Janeiro; Juliana Teixeira Souza, "Do usos da lei por trabalhadores e pequenos comerciantes na Corte Imperial (1870–1880)", in Azevedo *et al.*, *Trabalhadores na cidade*, p. 218.
72. A number of studies examining the relationship between workers and laws and rights have recently been added to the Brazilian historiography. See, for example, Silvia H. Lara and Joseli Maria Nunes Mendonça (eds), *Direitos e justiças no Brasil: ensaios de História Social* (Campinas, 2006); and Larissa Rosa Corrêa, *A tessitura dos Direitos: patrões e empregados na Justiça do Trabalho* (São Paulo, 2011).

cart drivers, authored by Ana Maria da Silva Moura.[73] In my research, I found that these workers made various submissions to different state institutions about the changes, protested in their places of work, and organized a number of strikes. Of the fifteen stoppages organized by the urban transport workers of Rio de Janeiro over the course of the nineteenth century, nine were linked to questions of remuneration, either to protest for higher wages or to demand the payment of outstanding wages. The main motives for four of the remaining strikes (which this article has analysed) were provided by new laws and police regulations. These were supported by a solid majority of the workers. The strikes organized by the coachmen and cart drivers were able to disrupt an essential service in the urban space and to affect a range of other economic sectors. The strikes also enjoyed popular support and participation, often taking the form of opposition to police repression. These elements help us to understand why transport workers were the sector that experienced the highest number of strikes in Rio de Janeiro in this period.

73. Da Silva Moura, *Cocheiros e carroceiros*.

IRSH 59 (2014), Special Issue, pp. 133–159 doi:10.1017/S0020859014000315
© 2014 Internationaal Instituut voor Sociale Geschiedenis

Rickshaws and Filipinos: Transnational Meanings of Technology and Labor in American-Occupied Manila

MICHAEL D. PANTE

Department of History, Ateneo de Manila University
2F Leong Hall, Katipunan Ave, Loyola Heights, Quezon City,
Philippines

E-mail: mpante@ateneo.edu

ABSTRACT: This article tells the hitherto unknown history of the rickshaw in the Philippines. The Filipinos' encounter with this transport mode was brief and largely revolved around a failed rickshaw business in Manila in 1902. The venture quickly fizzled out, but not without controversy, deeply rooted in the colliding socio-political forces in the city at that time: the reliance on a non-motorized transport system; the consolidation of American colonial rule against the backdrop of an ongoing revolution; the birth of the first Filipino labor federation; and the implementation of a law banning the employment of Chinese workers from unskilled trades. The controversy turned the rickshaw into a disputed symbol. On the one hand, the rickshaw enterprise was criticized by Filipino carriage drivers and nationalist labor leaders, who viewed the vehicle as an essentially foreign apparatus that would enslave Filipinos. On the other hand, the Americans used the Filipinos' opposition to the rickshaw to prove the supposed un-modernity of the lazy native workers, who failed to grasp the idea of the dignity of labor. These disputes were inextricably linked to the clash of discourses between Filipino nationalism and colonial modernity, two competing perspectives both influenced by a comparative transnational frame.

What is presented in this article is the hitherto unknown history of the rickshaw in Manila. A history of the rickshaw still needs to be written for the whole region of Asia,[1] and early twentieth-century Manila might

---

1. Peter Rimmer, "Hackney Carriage Syces and Rikisha Pullers in Singapore: A Colonial Registrar's Perspective on Public Transport, 1892–1923", in *idem* and Lisa M. Allen (eds), *The Underside of Malaysian History: Pullers, Prostitutes, Plantation Workers* (Singapore, 1990), p. 160; David Arnold and Erich DeWald, "Everyday Technology in South and Southeast Asia: An Introduction", *Modern Asian Studies*, 46 (2012), pp. 1–17, 6. A regional history of the rickshaw has been attempted in an as yet unpublished paper by M. William Steele, "Mobility on the Move: The Rickshaw Conquers Asia". I would like to thank him for allowing me to read and cite his manuscript.

just be the appropriate starting point for this huge undertaking. At first glance, selecting Manila as the springboard for a regional history of the rickshaw seems misplaced, if not outright ridiculous, given that there are other cities more deserving of this distinction. A substantial scholarly literature on the history of this vehicle exists, composed of historical accounts set in cities that have had a long relationship with the rickshaw. In contrast, the journey of the rickshaw in Manila was brief and undocumented. Apart from passing mentions in the works of William Henry Scott and Melinda Tria Kerkvliet,[2] there is practically nothing in the academic literature that deals with it. Nonetheless, I argue that, though short, this particular encounter between city and vehicle was significant.

Historical literature on rickshaws has given the vehicle its rightful place in the historiography of colonial cities in Asia. These vehicles did not just form an integral part of the urban fabric of these cities, they also served as a useful analytical tool, as it were, to understand colonial rule. Moreover, a consequence of the increasing prominence of the rickshaw in literature was the centrality conferred upon the workers: the rickshaw-pullers. Once rendered mute in the historical record, pullers and coolies have been given due recognition in James Warren's *Rickshaw Coolie: A People's History of Singapore, 1880–1940*.[3] Warren has shown the value of analyzing the rickshaw in terms of the intersections of modern urbanity and labor relations in the age of Western imperialism in Asia, a mode of analysis that has been demonstrated in subsequent works by other scholars.[4]

This article seeks to contribute to the growing literature on the history of rickshaws by focusing on the transnational understanding of the rickshaw. The transnational character of this vehicle was not just "physical" (manufactured using imported materials and then exported to different cities), but also in terms of the formation of imageries attached to the vehicle as absorbed and deployed by cosmopolitan travelers. The peak of rickshaw use in Asia corresponded to the period of late imperialism, an era characterized by a high degree of physical mobility within the region enjoyed even by certain elite groups among the colonized. The result was the traveling of meanings from one urban center to another. Moreover, the divergence

---

2. William Henry Scott, *The Union Obrera Democratica: First Filipino Labor Union* (Quezon City, 1992), p. 30; Melinda Tria Kerkvliet, *Manila Workers' Unions, 1900–1950* (Quezon City, 1992), p. 10.

3. James Francis Warren, *Rickshaw Coolie: A People's History of Singapore, 1880–1940* (Singapore, 2003).

4. Rimmer, "Hackney Carriage Syces"; Zwia Lipkin, *Useless to the State: "Social Problems" and Social Engineering in Nationalist Nanjing, 1927–1937* (Cambridge, MA [etc.], 2006); Fung Chi Ming, *Reluctant Heroes: Rickshaw Pullers in Hong Kong and Canton, 1874–1954* (Hong Kong, 2005); Michael Tsin, *Nation, Governance, and Modernity in China: Canton, 1900–1927* (Stanford, CA, 2002).

of values attached to the act of rickshaw-pulling was often framed in comparative transnational terms. With the rickshaw seen as an essentially foreign vehicle in Manila, arguing for or against the dignity of labor in pulling a rickshaw necessitated comparisons with non-Philippine urban societies.

As such, I argue here that the brief encounter between Filipinos and rickshaws in the early twentieth century becomes significant only if understood in transnational terms. Contemporary newspaper articles, especially in the *Manila Times*, and travel accounts are the main primary sources due to the absence of archival materials that would have provided more details on this event.[5] Using these sources, limited as they are, I show the convergence of social changes in Manila that intensified an otherwise fleeting encounter between man and machine.[6]

THE RICKSHAW'S JOURNEY INTO THE PHILIPPINES

The pre-World-War-II cities of Asia have a collective urban history with regard to their encounters with the rickshaw. This vehicle has had a long history of traveling from city to city in the region, beginning in the late nineteenth century. Interestingly, the rickshaw is often presented as a traditional vehicle, when to a large extent it is as cosmopolitan as the automobile in terms of both production and consumption.[7] Its position as a ubiquitous vehicle in key Asian port cities during the heyday of Western imperial expansion turned it into a vehicle that gained overlapping meanings, a concept that will be discussed below.

The commonly accepted story regarding the origins of the rickshaw involves an American missionary in Japan who supposedly invented the vehicle in 1869.[8] The vehicle was originally called *jinrikisha*, which literally means "human-powered vehicle", but usually contracted to *rickisha* while Western tourists usually pronounce it as "rickshaw".[9] The rickshaw was an instant success; it was integrated into the transport systems of

5. I have consulted the most relevant administrative sources in this regard: Municipal Board of Manila, *Report of the Municipal Board of the City of Manila for the period from August 7, 1901, to June 30, 1902* (Manila, 1903); Municipal Board of Manila, *Report of the Municipal board of the City of Manila for fiscal year ending June 30, 1903* (Manila, 1904); however, these sources yield nothing about the rickshaw incident. The silence of the Municipal Board in these reports may mean that the authorities regarded the 1902 incident as insignificant or that they wanted to leave no trace of it in the public records.
6. The gender bias toward men in this statement is intentional. Men monopolized the labor force of Manila's urban transport system in the early twentieth century. On this, see Michael D. Pante, "A Collision of Masculinities: Men, Modernity, and Urban Transportation in American-Colonial Manila", *Asian Studies Review*, 38 (2014), pp. 253–273.
7. Steele, "Mobility on the Move".
8. Warren, *Rickshaw Coolie*, p. 14.
9. Mack Cretcher, *A Tenderfoot in the Tropics* (Topeka, KS, 1918), p. 18.

Japan's main cities and it then spread across Asia in the last two decades of
the nineteenth century.[10]
Although rickshaws seem not to have been introduced in Manila in an
enduring way, or in the Philippines for that matter, these vehicles did
arrive in Manila and became a public mode of transportation, albeit for
only a brief period. However, it must be noted that the Filipinos' first
encounter with the rickshaw did not take place in the country; it happened when members of the middle-class intelligentsia, the so-called
ilustrados, began their journeys abroad for further studies. These sojourns
began in the 1880s and continued in the next few decades. Although
Europe was their main destination, almost all *ilustrados* stayed temporarily,
but for a considerable length of time, in Asian cities, such as Hong Kong,
Singapore, and Yokohama.[11] It was in these cities that they first saw and rode
in rickshaws. For example, Jose Rizal, the most well-known *ilustrado* and
Filipino nationalist, mentioned in his letters his experience of seeing and
riding rickshaws in Tokyo.[12]
The actual date of the arrival of the first rickshaw on Philippine shores
cannot be ascertained, but based on the primary sources I have consulted,
the earliest mention of it is in the 1890s. According to *The Straits Times*,
an American company established a rickshaw company in Manila around
August 1899. Based on a report in the Manila newspaper *El Comercio*,
1,000 rickshaw units were imported for this purpose.[13] Interestingly,
the historian Kees van Dijk mentions that in the 1890s an American
businessman tried to introduce rickshaws into the country. Unfortunately,
Van Dijk does not give the sources for this claim, so one cannot verify
whether this is the same incident reported by *The Straits Times*. In any
case, Van Dijk states that the 1890s rickshaw experiment failed, leading
him to conclude that rickshaws "did not become an accepted means of
transportation" in the Philippines.[14] Meanwhile, according to the Briton
John Foreman, who visited the Philippines in 1899, the first person to use
a rickshaw in Manila was a European consul who employed a Chinese
puller.[15] There are also anecdotes about rickshaws pulled by Moros in
Zamboanga City, which is located on the western tip of the southern

10. Warren, *Rickshaw Coolie*, p. 14.
11. Resil B. Mojares, *Brains of the Nation: Pedro Paterno, T.H. Pardo de Tavera, Isabelo de los Reyes and the Production of Modern Knowledge* (Quezon City, 2006). On the well-documented sojourns of *ilustrados*, see *idem, Isabelo's Archive* (Pasig City, 2013), pp. 143–154.
12. Jose Rizal, Letter to Ferdinand Blumentritt, 4 March 1888, in Jose Rizal, *Epistolario Rizalino, Vol. V.1: Cartas de Rizal a Blumentritt en Alemán, 1886–1888* (Manila, 1938), p. 240.
13. "Jinrikishas at Manila", *The Straits Times*, 18 August 1899, p. 2.
14. Kees van Dijk, "Pedal Power in Southeast Asia", in Jan van der Putten and Mary Kilcline Cody (eds), *Lost Times and Untold Tales from the Malay World* (Singapore, 2009), pp. 268–282, 274.
15. John Foreman, *The Philippine Islands* (Manila, 1980), p. 635.

island of Mindanao, in the early decades of the twentieth century.[16] One
observer even stated that Zamboanga was "the only place in the Philippines
where jinrikishas have been introduced".[17]

Despite the existence of personal accounts by American colonial officials
recalling the existence of rickshaws in Manila,[18] what is clear is that these
vehicles never became a popular public transport mode in the country. The
apparent absence of the rickshaw in Manila was a point of contrast when early
twentieth-century Westerners compared the city to its Asian counterparts.
This was not lost on the Americans who began to occupy Manila in mid-1898.
Many of them lamented the lack of a rickshaw system and saw it as an
example of Manila's poor urban transport facilities. There were other transport
modes in Manila at the turn of the nineteenth century, but these were perceived as inadequate by the new colonizers.[19] During this period, the public
urban transport system of the city was dominated by river-based vehicles, such
as *bancas* and *cascos*, which were ridiculed and criticized by Manila Americans
and other Westerners. Even land-based transport, such as the horse-drawn
tranvia and the system of public carriages, did not escape these criticisms.[20]
Public carriages also came under scrutiny because of the Westerners' discomfort
with the *cocheros* (carriage drivers).[21] There were even some Americans who
said that the public transport system was so unreliable that owning a private
carriage became a necessity.[22] The frustration caused by the lack of a rickshaw
system can be felt in Neil Macleod's reply to a question posed by General
Arthur MacArthur regarding the use of rickshaws in the country: "No; they
don't use them [rickshaws]. We are very far behind the times."[23]

16. William Boyce, *The Philippine Islands* (Chicago, IL, 1914), p. 176; Charles Thomson, *Terry: A Tale of the Hill People* (New York, 1921), p. 35.
17. "The Port of Zamboanga", *The Mindanao Herald: Historical and Industrial Number*, 3 February 1909, p. 64.
18. Charles Burke Elliott, *The Philippines to the End of the Commission Government: A Study in Tropical Democracy* (New York, 1968 [1917]), p. 279.
19. Michael D. Pante, "Ang sasakyan at lansangan bilang paaralan: Modernisasyon ng trans-portasyong panlungsod sa lipunan sa Manila, 1900–1941", *Malay: Internasyonal na Journal sa Filipino*, 23 (2011), pp. 111–126, 113; idem, "The *Cocheros* of American-Occupied Manila: Representations and Persistence", *Philippine Studies: Historical and Ethnographic Viewpoints*, 60 (2012), pp. 429–462, 435.
20. US Bureau of Insular Affairs, *Monthly Summary of Commerce of the Philippine Islands, July, 1902* (Washington DC, c.1903), pp. 12–13; Victor Clark, "Labor Conditions in the Philippines", *Bulletin of the Bureau of Labor*, 58 (1905), p. 830; Campbell Dauncey, *An Englishwoman in the Philippines* (London, 1906), pp. 92–93.
21. Pante, "The *Cocheros* of American-Occupied Manila".
22. Arthur Brown, *The New Era in the Philippines* (Nashville, TN, 1904), pp. 93–94; Ronaldo B. Mactal, *Ang pang-araw-araw na buhay sa Maynila sa panahon ng Digmaang Pilipino–Amerikano, 1898–1901* (Manila, 2010), p. 158.
23. US Philippine Commission, *Report of the Philippine Commission to the President, Vol. II: (Testimony and Exhibits)* (Washington DC, 1900), p. 39.

Figure 1. Cover photograph of a travel account written by an American journalist to describe her trip to the Philippines. It shows a rickshaw with a puller and a passenger, although the author did not identify the actual location where this photograph was taken.
From: Margherita Arlina Hamm, Manila and the Philippines: Our Possessions in the East *(London, 1898).*

Such a widespread perception of Manila's urban transport system is a crucial element in understanding American-colonial Manila at the start of the twentieth century. Manila was a highly urbanized and cosmopolitan city, a site for businesses engaged in international trade. The wage-labor system in the city was in the process of replacing old methods of labor mobilization, such as the employment of Chinese coolies (predominant in Manila when the American colonizers first arrived, but already waning by 1902 and about to be rendered illegal by impending legislation, the Chinese Exclusion Act). Commercial activities relied then on Chinese labor gangs, which were secured for businesses by patrons, who handled all payments.[24] While numerous Chinese coolies were still employed in various enterprises in the city, *ilustrados* were organizing the nascent Filipino proletariat into a nationalist working class.[25] This last point was connected to the atmosphere of revolt and frustrated independence cut short by American intervention in the Philippine anti-colonial revolution against Spain. The intersections of these factors and events provide the backdrop for Manila's brief and yet significant encounter with the rickshaw in 1902.

THE 1902 RICKSHAW CONTROVERSY

On 8 January 1902 the Municipal Board of Manila, the capital's American-dominated local government, received from American entrepreneur Carlos S. Rivers an application to import several hundred rickshaws.[26] The application was then referred to a committee of the Municipal Board. In response the Board requested a meeting with Rivers and the Chief of the Metropolitan Police to discuss the matter.

The American community in Manila welcomed the news. An editorial in the *Manila Times*, the so-called voice of the American expatriate community, expressed optimism about the proposal and believed that the plan would be "hailed with rejoicing by the public".[27] The newspaper had long argued in favor of this transport mode, given its editors' frustration with the existing urban transport system. The editors even presented the rickshaw in the same light as the automobile as far as the improvement of passenger mobility was concerned: "With automobiles and rickshas the public should at last be afforded relief from the tyranny of the *cochero* and the general inadequacy of the present system of street conveyances."[28]

24. Greg Bankoff, "Wants, Wages, and Workers: Laboring in the American Philippines, 1899–1908", *The Pacific Historical Review*, 74 (2005), pp. 59–86, 80.
25. Kerkvliet, *Manila Workers' Unions*; Scott, *The Union Obrera Democratica*.
26. "Manila May Have Rickshas", *Manila Times*, 9 January 1902, p. 1; "Mr. Carlos S. Rivers", *El Comercio*, 27 January 1902, p. 5.
27. "Editorial", *Manila Times*, 9 January 1902, p. 4.
28. *Ibid.*

According to the *Manila Times*, Governor-General William Howard Taft himself had advocated the use of rickshaws in Manila even before Rivers's application, but believed that previous conditions in the city would have turned the rickshaw into a controversial issue because "it was then considered by the military authorities [...] that conditions were not sufficiently settled for such an innovation [...]. Now conditions are different, and the only difficulty in the way of the proposition would appear to be in the motive power."[29] Taft's statement was revealing on two counts. First, he resorted to a euphemism (i.e. his use of the term "motive power") to avoid referring to the rickshaw as a transport mode that was propelled by human beings. And secondly, which would also help explain the first point, he supposed a rickshaw system in Manila could have been politically contentious under certain circumstances. His views were not unfounded, as succeeding events would reveal.

By late January the Board had given Rivers the signal to go ahead, but not without some criticism from the American press, which felt that Board President Arsenio Cruz Herrera was too slow in implementing "American urban methods", i.e. approving the rickshaw proposal.[30] The Board issued Rivers's Luzon Jinricksha Company with a permit to import a few hundred rickshaw units and place them in service.[31] The business also obtained financial security when the American Bank agreed to issue shares to potential investors in the company.[32] However, just a few days after these events, rumors spread that certain groups opposed the rickshaw scheme. The *Manila Times* disputed the rumors and reported that, on the contrary, no-one opposed Rivers's plans. The *Manila Times* report, however, was an obvious attempt to protect a business venture that it supported.

On 7 February the *Manila Times* reported Rivers's promise to bring in 1,000 coolies to serve as pullers. The pullers would be divided into two shifts of 500 pullers each (one shift to be dispatched from 6 am to 3 pm, the other from 3 pm to 12 am).[33] A few days after, Rivers petitioned the Municipal Board to allow him to import a further 500 rickshaws – despite the fact that the first consignment had yet to arrive – believing that the business would be a "paying investment".[34] Such a move could be interpreted as unfounded optimism, but if one looks at Rivers's actions in

29. "Manila May Have Rickshas", p. 1.
30. "Pres. Herrera's Stand", *Manila Times*, 23 January 1902, p. 4.
31. "Manila Will Have Rickshas", *Manila Times*, 31 January 1902, p. 1. Rivers's franchise was not exclusive however. Other private entities interested in putting up their own public rickshaw system were allowed to apply for a permit, although primary sources revealed no other individual or company that signified their intention to do so. See "The Ricksha Scheme", *Manila Times*, 7 February 1902, p. 8.
32. "The Luzon Ricksha Company", *Manila Times*, 5 February 1902, p. 1.
33. "The Ricksha Scheme", p. 8.
34. "Wants Five Hundred More Rickshas", *Manila Times*, 12 February 1902, p. 1.

other aspects of his business he was actually preparing for considerable trouble related to issues of labor. Apparently the company already had qualms regarding the feasibility of employing Chinese coolies as pullers, despite their prominence and reputation in Manila at that time as reliable workers. In this regard the company wrote to the Collector of Customs to ask for permission to import Japanese coolies for the said purpose. A glimmer of hope presented itself to Rivers when he was able to have a talk with the Japanese consul in Manila, who was initially reported to have stated that Japanese coolies would be banned from leaving Japan. The consul, however, made it clear to Rivers that Japanese coolies could be obtained for the rickshaw plan. The discussion with the consul was a positive development for Rivers, who had also made arrangements with a company in Yokohama for the importation of coolies. Rivers explained that he preferred Japanese rickshaw-pullers because they were "much more attentive and considerate than the Chinese and not so likely to be insolent".[35]

Meanwhile, Edith Moses, wife of Philippine Commission member Bernard Moses, recognized that the rickshaw plan was facing considerable opposition to the point that the feasibility of importing coolies had been put into question. In her memoirs dated 11 February 1902 she wrote:

> There has been an effort made here lately to start a riksha company, and we thought it would succeed, but the Chinese and Japanese consuls and citizens have protested against "making beasts of human beings", and the company cannot get coolies to pull the rikshas. The rikshas are, I hear, still in the customs house. The English consul uses one, and his coolies seem quite as human as some of the dirty bare-legged drivers who beat broken-down ponies about the streets.[36]

The complexity of the issue of the importation of coolies was initially a legal matter. In a 21 March 1902 in a letter sent by Collector of Customs W. Morgan Shuster in response to a previous letter from the Luzon Jinrikisha Company, which inquired about the legality of importing Japanese coolies, he cited Section 5 of the 1885 US law entitled "An act to prohibit the importation and migration of foreigners and aliens under contract or agreement to perform labor in the United States, its Territories, and the District of Columbia". The restrictions of this law only covered unskilled laborers. He cited this law to conclude that Japanese coolies could not be categorized as skilled workers and that the necessary labor for the rickshaw service could be obtained in the country, given the presence of Chinese coolies.[37] With such legal barriers, the

35. "The Delay in the Rickshas", *Manila Times*, 18 May 1902, pp. 1, 8.
36. Edith Moses, *Unofficial Letters of an Official's Wife* (New York, 1908), p. 213.
37. W. Morgan Shuster, "Importation of Japanese Jinrikisha Coolies Prohibited", in Philippine Customs Service, *Chinese and Immigration Circulars (Annotated): Vol. I, Nos. 1 to 197, December, 1901, to December, 1907: Constructions and Decisions* (Manila, 1908), pp. 35–36.

company lost its case, notwithstanding the fact that it was not the only establishment that wanted to secure Japanese coolie labor.[38]

At this point it was quite apparent that, while the company desperately tried to avoid hiring Chinese coolies, at the same time the idea of employing Filipino laborers was clearly out of the question. But why? The answer lies in the tumultuous and politically charged labor situation in Manila during the early years of the twentieth century. Despite the initial optimism of the Manila American community, opposition to the rickshaw plan intensified in the first half of 1902. And opposition came on two different fronts: Filipino labor groups and Chinese coolies. With Shuster's decision, the rickshaw company was now caught between a rock and a hard place.

Rivers was certainly aware of opposition from Filipino laborers, especially the *cocheros*. On 18 May the *Manila Times* reported that, although the first installment of imported rickshaw units (twelve vehicles) had arrived from Japan on 13 May, the inauguration of the rickshaw business would be delayed due to the "unfortunate jumble in packing pieces in Japan".[39] These units were assembled in Tokyo and were made to "run down on their own running gear", i.e. rolled as complete rickshaws to Yokohama, where they were disassembled again for shipping. However, the most interesting detail in the article was that, when the shipment arrived, Rivers assembled one rickshaw and rode on it "merely as an experiment, to see if any malicious cochero would run him down or if any bellicose hombre would hurl a brick at him".[40] No-one did so; instead, the rickshaw got the attention of Manila City Hall employees. Nonetheless, Rivers's pronouncements revealed his hidden anxiety toward the *cocheros'* possible hostile reception to his business. In another *Manila Times* article, a *cochero* was asked for his opinion about rickshaws. The *cochero* replied that he did not believe rickshaw-pullers could run at the pace Americans wanted.[41]

The *cocheros'* opposition to the rickshaw plan was made more potent by their decision to organize themselves. In 1902 a *cochero* section was established within the Union Obrera Democratica (UOD), the first Philippine labor federation, which was composed mainly of Manila-based unions of lithographers, printers, and bookbinders, and led by well-known nationalists Isabelo de los Reyes and Hermenegildo Cruz.[42] With this development, the anti-rickshaw campaign intensified to the point that it caused the delay of rickshaw operations.[43] On 19 May the UOD

---

38. Edgar G. Bellairs, *As It Is in the Philippines* (New York, 1902), p. 158.
39. "The Delay in the Rickshas", p. 1.
40. *Ibid.*, p. 8.
41. "The Rickshas", *Manila Times*, 22 May 1902, p. 4.
42. Scott, *The Union Obrera Democratica*, pp. 32–33.
43. "Editorial", *Manila Times*, 25 May 1902, p. 4.

released a statement entitled "Los Filipinos no son brutos"[44] [Filipinos are not beasts] as a protest against the planned rickshaw business. The UOD opposed Rivers's plans because they believed that if Filipinos were hired as pullers they would become the slaves of foreigners. Cruz asked his fellow Filipinos not to allow themselves to be employed as pullers, lest they become traitors and submit themselves to this "unholy", "despised and devil-contrived vehicle".[45] He coaxed *cocheros* to launch a *"cochero insurrection"* against the rickshaws, which would have been an alternative transport mode to the carriages the *cocheros* drove. Reacting to the decision of the Municipal Board to grant Rivers a permit, Cruz stated that "God will never forgive him [Herrera] for allowing such satanic monstrosities". Apparently Cruz knew that a number of Filipinos had already committed to serve as pullers, leading him to urge other Filipinos not to use rickshaws if these were pulled by "our brothers". He added that he could not blame Filipino pullers, "whose ignorance and weakness [were] being exploited by certain people".[46]

Rivers's response to Cruz's polemics marked a key point in the debate. Rivers declared that he would not hire Filipinos as pullers because he believed that they were lazy and ineffective workers.[47] Rivers found allies in the editors of the *Manila Times*, who opined in an editorial comment that the "transportation problem" in Manila could not be solved without a rickshaw system, given that *cocheros* were unreliable.[48] Such an inadequacy in labor, from the editors' perspective, was the root of the problem and was even compounded by the recent enactment of the Chinese Exclusion Act.[49] The new law prohibited the employment of Chinese coolies in non-skilled trades. Though Rivers preferred Japanese over Chinese coolies, the legislation was still a big blow to the rickshaw plan and its proponents, for it left them no option but to depend on supposedly unreliable Filipino laborers, who were also being mobilized by Filipino labor organizers to boycott the rickshaw.

Despite the politically charged atmosphere, the Luzon Jinrikisha Company began operations on 24 May at 2 pm. On its first day, out of a total of 300 rickshaw units stored at godowns built inside Puerta Isabel Segundo (located within the walls of Intramuros, the oldest part of the city center of Manila), 20 plied the city streets. In violation of the Chinese Exclusion Act, Rivers decided to employ Chinese coolies as pullers, many

---

44. "Los Filipinos no son brutos", *El Comercio*, 19 May 1902, p. 3.
45. "Appeals to His People", *Manila Times*, 23 May 1902, p. 1.
46. *Ibid.*
47. "Rickshas Are Running", *Manila Times*, 25 May 1902, p. 1.
48. "The Labor Problem", *Manila Times*, 23 May 1902, p. 4.
49. Clark Alejandrino, *A History of the 1902 Chinese Exclusion Act: American Colonial Transmission and Deterioration of Filipino–Chinese Relations* (Manila, 2003).

of them reportedly former stevedores and unemployed coal-handlers,[50] and a few Filipinos, who became "objects of ridicule".[51] The total number of 300 rickshaw units was a drastic decrease from the proposed 500, which would be deployed in 12 stations: Plaza Moraga (100); Pasaje de Perez near Escolta (100); Plaza de Santa Cruz y Goiti (50); Customs House (20); Captain of the Port (20); Plaza de Binondo–Oriente Hotel (40); Malate (20); Ermita (30); Walled City (Intramuros)–Puerta Parian (30); Malacanang Palace (20); City Hall (20); Bridge of Spain, south side (50).[52]

Based on the locations of the rickshaw stations, American customers were clearly the main clientele because the majority of the stations were at centers of government, businesses, and residences of Americans. Their continued strong support for the business was thus not surprising. In its editorial, the *Manila Times* recognized the Filipinos' right to protest against Rivers's venture but qualified it by stating that "they had better not make any demonstration when Americans are riding in the rickshaws or their crusade will be both short-lived and fraught with sorrow".[53] The editorial was harsh and hostile, a reflection of how serious the rickshaw controversy was for the Manila Americans. It also blamed certain Filipinos for scaring off pullers and for the delay in rickshaw operations, and even posited that this issue would set the *Manila Times* against Filipinos. The editors argued that they could not allow Manila's poor public transport system to continue, which was supposedly forcing American women who did not own private rigs, especially those who traveled from home to Escolta and back, to go on foot just to travel within the city.[54]

Notwithstanding the assertive stance of the American press in its support, the rickshaw business found itself already crumbling within the next few days. On its second day, no puller reported for work, and the following day, only one did so. However, this time around, the cause behind the breakdown in operations was opposition not from Filipinos but from the Chinese. The sudden absence of Chinese coolies was supposedly due to pressure from the Manila Chinese community, which felt humiliated by their compatriots who chose to be pullers. Placards were seen posted around the city that served as a "friendly warning" to coolies

50. Edgar Bellairs, Correspondent in Manila from the Associated Press, mentioned that the company began with three Chinese as pullers. Though it was clear that he witnessed the unfolding of the rickshaw controversy in Manila, Bellairs failed to provide a detailed recollection, leading me to put more trust in *Manila Times* articles regarding facts surrounding this event; Bellairs, *As It Is in the Philippines*, p. 159.
51. "Rickshas are Running", p. 1; Scott, *Union Obrera Democratica*, p. 30; Foreman, *The Philippine Islands*, p. 635.
52. "Ricksha Stands", *Manila Times*, 2 February 1902, p. 1.
53. "Editorial", *Manila Times*, 25 May 1902, p. 4.
54. *Ibid.*

VOL. III—NO 63

RICKSHAS ARE RUNNING.

A Score of these Japanese Carts Started Yesterday Afternoon and Fifty Promised Today.

President Rivers of Luzon Jinricksha Company Says Filipinos Are in no Danger of Becoming Coolies, if he Has His Way.

The 'rickshas are out. Twenty of them, drawn by Chinese coolies, made their appearance on the street shortly before 2 o'clock yesterday afternoon. Today it is likely that forty or fifty will be running.

It was announced yesterday noon at the office of the 'ricksha company that the first installment of them would be on the street in the afternoon, Mr. Tuttle, the secretary of the company, went to the Internal Revenue office in the morning and secured licenses for all that they had set up. There was some hitch about the coolies, as some were fearful that they could not make days' wages, while others feared attacks from Filipinos, and still others to be jeered at by their own coun- 'ricksha hung up somewhere. We do not wish to give that kind of service. Sooner than employ Filipinos to draw them, we would lock the 'rickshas up in a godown and keep them there until we could get the kind of help we wanted".

Mr. Rivers first saw Hermenegildo's pronunciamento in El Progreso, and in the same paper he saw a call which that gentleman had issued for a meeting of cocheros to fight against the 'rickshas.

Figure 2. The *Manila Times* headline announcing the start of operations of Carlos Rivers's rickshaw company.
From: "Rickshas are running", Manila Times, 25 May 1902, p. 1. Photograph courtesy of Microform Reading Center, Rizal Library, Ateneo de Manila University.

not to be draught animals for foreigners. Asked to comment, Rivers, who had brought the matter to the police, entertained the idea that Filipino oppositionists put up the placards. The "warnings" also affected the Chinese coolie contractor, who was visited by certain Chinese who

threatened him.[55] Meanwhile, according to Foreman, the Chinese consulate prohibited the employment of Chinese coolies as pullers.[56] Scott
corroborates this point by stating that the Chinese consul himself posted
placards, "in elegant calligraphy hinting that any Chinese who touched
the shafts of a rickshaw would be deported [to Hong Kong] with his
queue cut off".[57] The consulate's actions as narrated by Foreman and
analyzed by Scott seem to contradict the reports of the American press,
which mentioned that the Chinese consul talked to and sympathized with
Rivers expressing disappointment over recent events. According to the
reports, after the two talked Rivers concluded that the placards were the
work of the Chinese and not Filipinos.[58]

Pressure on the rickshaw company mounted in succeeding days. On
May 27 the UOD petitioned for the banning of rickshaws and the strict
implementation of the Chinese Exclusion Act.[59] Although six rickshaws
plied the streets on the day that the UOD released its petition, Rivers now
believed that it was already useless to rely on the Chinese pullers. He
believed that behind all these covert acts to disrupt rickshaw operations
was a "syndicate", which exerted undue influence over Chinese coolies.
He was already desperate at this point, leading him to consider calling
Acting Governor-General Luke E. Wright and asking for action from no
less than the Philippine Commission, especially with regard to his plea to
allow the importation of Japanese coolies.[60]

Reaffirming its support for the rickshaw business, the American press
launched a tirade against the UOD and its supporters. This time the anger
was vented mainly against *cocheros*. The *Manila Times* lambasted the
cocheros for failing to understand the "dignity of labor" that had ultimately kept Manila's urban transport system backward.[61] But just like
Rivers, the *Manila Times* also appeared to have abandoned the idea of
pursuing Chinese coolies. On 28 and 29 May the *Manila Times* released
consecutive editorials that put forward the idea of importing Japanese
coolies to serve as pullers.[62] Knowing that critics would invoke the
Exclusion Law against this proposal, the editors defended their stance by

---

55. "A Ricksha Strike", *Manila Times*, 27 May 1902, pp. 1, 8. One must take note that while the
Manila Times referred to the pullers' actions as a "strike", technically speaking, these acts of
resistance cannot be labelled as such. Perhaps the editors did so in order to cast these pullers in a
negative light.
56. Foreman, *The Philippine Islands*, p. 635.
57. Scott, *Union Obrera Democratica*, p. 30.
58. "A Ricksha Strike", pp. 1, 8.
59. "Wants Higher Wages", *Manila Times*, 28 May 1902, p. 1.
60. *Ibid.*
61. "Filipinos and Rickshas", *Manila Times*, 28 May 1902, p. 4.
62. *Ibid.*; "Ricksha Labor", *Manila Times*, 29 May 1902, p. 4.

stating that rickshaw-pulling should be classified under skilled labor in contrast to the assessment of immigration officials.

On 4 June the Luzon Jinricksha Company held a meeting in its office at Calle San Juan de Letran in Manila.[63] The company sent a petition to the Philippine Commission the following day asking for permission to import Japanese coolies as pullers.[64] However, the reports of the *Manila Times* on the rickshaw business end here. The controversy did not appear in the pages of the newspaper any more in the succeeding months. The silence could only mean one thing: Rivers's plans had fizzled out and died a natural death. In his assessment, Edgar Bellairs, Manila Correspondent of the Associated Press from 1901 to 1902, looked at the issue from the perspective of the Chinese pullers' practical decision-making: "The majority of the Chinese left were making far too much in other directions for them to take to the hard manual labor of rickshaw-pulling. On the other hand, the Filipinos were not only unable, but unwilling." In the end he lamented the demise of a supposed grand plan for Manila's development: "the rickshaws are lying in Manila useless, badly as they are needed in the streets for transportation".[65]

THE DIGNITY OF LABOR

In the aftermath of the controversy it was apparent that the proponents of the rickshaw system had failed in their objective. It is difficult to identify a single factor that led to this failure, but one could assert that the business was not so viable to begin with. First, it was driven by demand from Manila Americans, who comprised a small fraction of the city population. Another factor was its fare rate, which was 10 cents for every 15 minutes. In contrast, *carromatas*, also referred to as the commoners' carriages, charged less than 10 cents for a half-hour ride.[66] Of course, labor politics also worked against Rivers's business, as discussed in the previous section.

Consequently, the vehicles were taken out of the country.[67] By 1904 Arthur Brown had reported that rickshaws were unknown in Manila.[68] In its assessment of the events, the Bureau of Insular Affairs presented its prediction for Manila's transportation system: "[b]ut with the climatic conditions and distances in Manila against it, it is not believed that it will afford any relief to the present congested transportation facilities".[69] Even

63. "Meeting of the Jinricksha Co.", *Manila Times*, 4 June 1902, p. 1.
64. "The Ricksha Coolie Trouble", *Manila Times*, 6 June 1902, p. 1.
65. Bellairs, *As It Is in the Philippines*, p. 159.
66. "Rickshas will Run Today", *Manila Times*, 16 May 1902, p. 8; Pante, "The *Cocheros* of American-Occupied Manila", p. 432.
67. Foreman, *The Philippine Islands*, p. 635.
68. Brown, *The New Era in the Philippines*, p. 94.
69. US Bureau of Insular Affairs, *Monthly Summary of Commerce*, p. 13.

the Singapore press took note of the 1902 rickshaw affair. *The Straits Times*, in an untitled commentary, mentioned that the "strong prejudice against the Chinese there mar[red] the success of the enterprise". It also added: "The Filipinos are too lazy to work at pulling and Filipino drivers molest the pullers. Swell Chinese at Manila fancy that rikisha pulling is degrading to their race."[70] The Englishwoman Campbell Dauncey offered additional insights worth quoting at length:

> One thinks regretfully of the delightful luxury of the rickshaws and chairs of the real Far East, and I was very much surprised to see none of these luxurious comforts when we first arrived in the Philippines. It seems that a company was formed some years ago to introduce them, and got the concession to bring rickshaws and coolies from China, but as soon as these useful institutions appeared in the streets of Manila, the Filipinos stoned them, and at last forced the American authorities to banish the innovation altogether: "For", said the astute and progressive Filipino, "the next thing will be that *we* shall be made to draw these things about, and we will not be treated as animals."
>
> Fancy giving in to them! And fancy thinking of a splendid country and people like Japan, "where the rickshaws come from", and listening to such preposterous nonsense from a Filipino! But these ignorant half-breeds got their way, and the only example they had ever had of energy or of the real dignity of labor was promptly withdrawn to please them.[71]

Clearly, the rickshaw controversy went beyond the issue of physical mobility as hinted in the commentaries of Dauncey and *The Straits Times*. The controversy, albeit brief, turned the rickshaw into a disputed symbol, which saw the overlapping of the issues of race, labor, colonialism, and modernity, a product of layer upon layer of various encounters with the rickshaw experienced by the different actors involved in the controversy. The issue of the dignity of labor was illustrative of the disputed nature of the rickshaw as a symbol because it could be viewed from various competing perspectives, as will be explained in the succeeding paragraphs.

To understand the gravity of the situation from the Americans' perspective, one has to take note of their frustrations with the city, beginning with the then prevailing transport system in Manila. Adding to their disappointment was what they believed was a "backward" system of procuring labor. They were surprised to find out that a free labor market was almost non-existent in the country – even in the capital city of Manila[72] – including the land transportation sector.[73] When it became apparent that most Filipino workers would not agree to be employed as

70. [Untitled], *The Straits Times*, 18 June 1902, p. 4.
71. Dauncey, *An Englishwoman in the Philippines*, p. 93.
72. Bankoff, "Wants, Wages, and Workers", p. 66.
73. Clark, "Labor Conditions in the Philippines", p. 830.

pullers, the American press took this as evidence of their lack of under-standing of the dignity of labor. Taken together with Rivers's depiction of Filipino workers as lazy, the American press chastised the Filipinos for treating pulling as a lowly and degrading occupation.

While Westerners were hesitant to rely on Filipino labor, their demand for Chinese coolie labor was high, especially in Manila.[74] Although a diversity of opinion existed among Western businessmen regarding this matter, their strong opposition to the Chinese Exclusion Act revealed the predominant sentiment.[75] The newspaper articles that reported on the rickshaw controversy of 1902 did not give a detailed profile of the pullers. However, based on the context of early twentieth-century Manila, the pullers employed in Rivers's short-lived business most probably came from the ranks of Chinese coolies who had been employed in elite households since the late nineteenth century and who also made up the labor pool for Singapore's rickshaws.[76] Indeed, the rickshaw controversy demonstrated the prevailing attitude among them. The American press even propounded the idea that rickshaw-pullers were skilled laborers and that, therefore, the Exclusion Law was not applicable in this case. The bias of Western business owners against Filipino workers and their preference for Chinese coolie labor heightened the Americans' frustrations with this new law even more.[77]

In contrast, many Filipinos understood their resistance to the rickshaw business as an assertion of laborers' dignity. A significant point here was that such a stance was articulated mainly by organized labor, namely the UOD, an act that proved critical in the eventual demise of Rivers's business. The significance of the UOD's opposition was its timing: the rickshaw controversy erupted just a few months after the founding of the UOD on 2 February 1902, an event that marked the establishment of the first labor federation in the Philippines.[78] In fact, the controversy happened when the UOD was in the middle of a major labor strike that the federation spearheaded, and in one of the strikers' meetings, orations and speeches that dealt with the ongoing issue were delivered.[79] The rickshaw controversy presented UOD ideologues, particularly de los Reyes and Cruz, with an opportunity to consolidate its ranks and articulate its vision as an organization that fought for Filipino workers.

74. *Ibid.*, p. 861; Julia Martínez and Claire Lowrie, "Transcolonial Influences on Everyday American Imperialism: The Politics of Chinese Domestic Servants in the Philippines", *Pacific Historical Review*, 81 (2012), pp. 511–536.
75. Alejandrino, *A History of the 1902 Chinese Exclusion Act*, pp. 18–20.
76. Edgar Wickberg, *The Chinese in Philippine Life, 1850–1898* (Quezon City, 2000); Martínez and Lowrie, "Transcolonial Influences"; Warren, *Rickshaw Coolie*.
77. Bankoff, "Wants, Wages, and Workers", p. 71.
78. Scott, *The Union Obrera Democratica*, pp. 21, 30.
79. "The Strikers Meet", *Manila Times*, 7 June 1902, p. 1.

Although de los Reyes had already become notorious within the Manila business community because of the workers' strikes he had led at that time,[80] the controversy still served as a litmus test for the nationalist UOD, and even the American press recognized the symbolic value of the issue for Filipino nationalism. A *Manila Times* editorial stated: "The most regrettable feature of the opposition of the Filipinos to the jinricksha movement will be the idea of their own omnipotence which will seize them if they succeed in rendering it a failure."[81] To convince fellow Filipinos of the inhumanity of rickshaw-pulling, Cruz and de los Reyes deployed, borrowing Michael Salman's words, "metaphorics of slavery".[82]

Nevertheless, a number of Americans respected, supported, and praised the Filipinos' resistance to the rickshaw project. W.C. West, in his analysis of the Philippine transportation system, stated that: "Manila and the Philippines certainly have cause to congratulate themselves that every attempt to introduce the jinrikisha or any description of man-propelled vehicle has failed."[83] American surgeon Robert Hart shared West's opinion but with a deeper level of introspection:

> Incidentally, the stranger having previously visited Japan, China, India or the Straits Settlements, will be surprised at not finding the rickshaw in use in the Philippines. They were introduced at one time in Manila but no one, no matter how humble, could be found among the Filipino to draw them, as the native is possessed of a very considerable amount of natural dignity and the substitution of a man for a pony aroused such a storm of indignation that the company who had endeavored to introduce these vehicles were glad to ship them out of the islands.[84]

Hart's views were an articulation of a fairly common tendency among Westerners to perceive the rickshaw as a vehicle that was essentially oppressive to the puller. Also, among Americans in the US and in Manila, there were those who felt that having a rickshaw system was incompatible with the purported modernizing thrust of American colonialism. David Doherty, a doctor from Chicago and an ardent anti-imperialist,[85] who visited the Philippines for several months, went even further by suggesting that the Filipinos were Western in perspective based on their response to the

---

80. Bellairs, *As It Is in the Philippines*, p. 160.
81. "Editorial", *Manila Times*, 30 June 1902, p. 4.
82. Michael Salman, *The Embarrassment of Slavery: Controversies over Bondage and Nationalism in the American Colonial Philippines* (Quezon City, 2001), p. 123.
83. W.C. West, "Highway Transportation in the Philippines", *The Philippine Review*, 1 (November 1918), p. 75.
84. Robert Hart, *The Philippines Today* (New York, 1928), p. 10.
85. Lewis E. Gleeck, Jr, *The American Half-Century (1898–1946)*, rev. edn (Quezon City, 1998), p. 72.

rickshaw system. In his paper presented to the US Senate he concluded, albeit in racist fashion:

> [...] the Filipino, after three centuries of Christian and Spanish influence, and after a considerable race intermixture with Spaniard and Chinese, is no longer a Malay. He really is the outpost of western civilization on the shores of the Orient. His ideals and aspirations are European; his views on the questions of Japanese rickshaws (the attempt to introduce which into Manila was defeated by a storm of popular indignation); of opium toleration (to which he is opposed); of Chinese labor, are certainly western.[86]

Interestingly, Doherty was also vocal in his opposition to the importation of Chinese labor and a believer in the capacity of Filipinos as efficient laborers.[87]

In Manila a number of Americans expressed their concern that the rickshaw system was inconsistent with the supposed values the US was to uphold as a colonizer. The *Manila Times* even had to defend its pro-rickshaw position vis-à-vis Manila Americans who were against it. In a letter to the editors of *Manila Times*, a "constant reader" commented that the *Manila Times* was not being faithful in representing the spirit of the US in the Philippines when it advocated the use of rickshaws. The letter also noted that the *cocheros* could not be blamed, given that demand for transportation in the city exceeded supply. "Constant reader" then shared his/her analysis:

> Let us not retrograde. Of course it is easy to perceive whence the cry for "rickshas" comes. It comes from our British brethren. The "rickshaw" is fast enough for Singapore and Shanghai; but if Manila is to become an American city, the man in the "rickshaw" will be getting there while the man in the "mobile" has gotten there [...]. But let us be modern, let us encourage "mobile" companies, railway companies. Let us move forward, not backward.[88]

Based on this letter to the editor, a certain transnational frame informed the negative view of the rickshaw, a frame shaped by the transnational mobility of Westerners within various Asian cities. This transnational frame provided anti-rickshaw commentators with a comparative vista that lent legitimacy to their remarks, as demonstrated in Hart's identification of a hypothetical (obviously Western) stranger visiting Japan, China, India, and the Straits Settlements. However, the legitimacy of transnational experience also applied to those who advocated the use of rickshaws, as gleaned from a *Manila Times* editorial that criticized the decision of the rickshaw company to import one-seater vehicles, when it could have

---

86. David Doherty, "Conditions in the Philippines", Paper presented to the Committee on the Philippines, US Senate, Fifty-Eighth Congress, Second Session, 27 February 1904, p. 6.
87. Gleeck, *The American Half-Century*, pp. 73–74.
88. "Doesn't Want Rickshas", *Manila Times*, 22 January 1902, p. 4.

imported two-seaters from the Straits Settlements.[89] Interestingly, Foreman shared his observation that there were also other Westerners in Manila who were unfamiliar with the rickshaw, an observation borne out of his expansive knowledge of other urban societies in Asia:

> Other whites, unaccustomed to these vehicles, took to beating the runners – a thing never seen or heard of in Japan or in colonies where they are used in thousands. The natural result was that the 'rikisha man bolted and the 'rikisha tilted backwards, to the discomfort of the fool riding in it.[90]

Nonetheless, many Americans first encountered rickshaws through their experiences in Asian cities, mostly cosmopolitan treaty ports that hosted sizeable Western communities.[91] For example, the members of the Philippine Commission rode rickshaws in Japan while they were on their way to the Philippines in May 1900. In contrast to West and Hart, the commissioners were quite happy with the rickshaws and the Japanese pullers, who were apparently accustomed to tourists. According to Bernard Moses, the Japanese coolies "had their own notion of what [the members of the Taft Commission] should see, derived doubtless from a composite of the demands of by-gone tourists".[92] It is thus not far-fetched to assert that when William Howard Taft stated that he wanted to implement a rickshaw system in Manila, he was basing it on his experience in Japan.[93]

A transnational frame would have allowed tourists to appreciate comparative descriptions such as this one made by a 1930s Manila travel guide: "The carretela and the carromata are to the Philippines, what the ricksha is to Japan and China."[94] But such comparisons meant more than just a juxtaposition of vehicles found in different cities; a transnational frame also provided the space for racialist analyses. As will be elaborated in the succeeding section, the "natural dignity" of the Filipino, displayed in his resistance to rickshaw-pulling, was implicitly compared to the lack thereof among other Asian societies who had adopted rickshaws as a popular transport mode.

OF FOREIGN VEHICLES AND ENSLAVED FILIPINOS

Filipinos, particularly the educated classes, also had their perception of rickshaws shaped by a comparative, transnational frame, given their high

89. "The Rickshas", p. 4.
90. Foreman, *The Philippine Islands*, p. 635.
91. US Bureau of Insular Affairs, *Monthly Summary of Commerce*, p. 13; Cretcher, *A Tenderfoot in the Tropics*, p. 18.
92. Daniel Williams, *The Odyssey of the Philippine Commission* (Chicago, IL, 1913).
93. *Ibid.*, p. 24; Helen Taft, *Recollections of Full Years* (New York, 1914), pp. 57–58.
94. American Express Company, *Manila and the Philippines* (Manila, c.1933), p. 98. The *carretela* is a two-wheeled, animal-drawn freight vehicle.

level of cosmopolitanism. Rizal lamented the fact that in Tokyo humans pulled rickshaws as if they were horses.[95] The *ilustrado* Trinidad Pardo de Tavera was another example, but with a different angle from that of Rizal. In his article published in the *Philippine Review*, he narrated his experiences in early twentieth-century Hong Kong where a Filipino colony had the reputation of being "ungovernable, aggressive, undisciplined, and disorderly",[96] due to their disrespect for the Chinese. So disorderly was their behavior that the police often had to intervene to control them. Pardo de Tavera recounted an incident when, as he passed through a group of Filipino sailors while riding a rickshaw, one of these sailors suddenly jeered at the coolie pulling the *ilustrado's* rickshaw. The sailor called the coolie *caballo* [horse]. Pardo de Tavera requested the puller to stop the vehicle and asked why the sailors were insulting the coolie. One of them replied: "Just because I want to." Pardo de Tavera scolded them and told them to respect the puller since he was "doing work as honorable as yours". According to the account, one of the sailors recognized Pardo de Tavera and told his companions who this person was. Pardo de Tavera said that afterwards, "[t]hey all thanked me for my intervention".

Similar to Pardo de Tavera's account was Ignacio Villamor's report prepared for the Board of Regents of the University of the Philippines in 1916 regarding the state of education in Japan. In that report Villamor expressed his appreciation for the values and industriousness of the Japanese. As an example, he juxtaposed the sense of camaraderie, discipline, and diligence of the Japanese rickshaw-pullers to the recklessness and "impetuousness" of Filipino *cocheros* and chauffeurs, attitudes which, according to Villamor, could not be observed in Japan.[97]

Pardo de Tavera and Villamor deployed the imagery of the rickshaw coolie in terms of hard work, humility, and perseverance vis-à-vis the negative traits of Filipinos. Such a comparison was patently similar to how most Americans viewed the rickshaw controversy. However, from the point of view of those opposed to the rickshaw system, the rickshaw symbolized an entirely different imagery. Still framed in a transnational and comparative manner, anti-rickshaw ideologues saw the rickshaw not only as a metaphor of slavery but also as a symbol of foreignness, and opposition to it stood for independence – freedom from a foreign entity and from enslavement.

Many Filipinos viewed the rickshaw as an entirely foreign vehicle. Indeed, the rickshaw was foreign, in the barest sense of the term. No rickshaws

95. Rizal, Letter to Ferdinand Blumentritt, p. 240.
96. Trinidad Pardo de Tavera, "Recollections of Hongkong, Kowloon, Macao and Canton", *The Philippine Review*, 5 (November 1920), p. 770.
97. Ignacio Villamor, "Japan's Educational Development", in *Fifth Annual Report of the President of the University of the Philippines: Manila, December 15, 1916* (Manila, 1916), pp. 80–81.

were manufactured in the country; all units were imported from Japan. Filipinos probably first heard of the existence of rickshaws from stories about Japan.[98] What is more, at a figurative level, it appeared to many that rickshaws contained a foreign essence, totally alien to Filipinos. In its "Los Filipinos no son Brutos" statement, the UOD claimed that rickshaws should not be used in the Philippines because of the harm they could cause to pullers, given the incompatibility of rickshaw-pulling with the local climate. Comparing the climate of the Philippines with that of Asian countries where rickshaws were common, the statement asserted that in those places the climate was much milder, and yet statistics showed that during the first year of service one-quarter of the pullers died due to sunstroke, fevers, tuberculosis, and other diseases that they contracted due to profuse sweating.[99] Supposedly, the unnaturalness of the rickshaw to the Philippine context could take a much greater toll on the health of potential Filipino pullers. Such an appreciation of the rickshaw as something totally foreign could also be observed in anecdotes even after the 1902 rickshaw controversy.

Though a public system of rickshaws was never attempted again in the wake of the 1902 controversy, on a few occasions rickshaws made their presence felt to Filipinos in different ways, but always understood as completely novel and bordering on the exotic. For example, Filipinos were shocked when on the morning of 28 July 1910 they saw a rickshaw plying the streets of Manila. This event was reported by the *Manila Times* and the tone of the article suggested that Filipinos were amazed by the "strange" vehicle imported from Japan.[100] Stories about Filipinos facing the "alien" rickshaw were not limited to physical encounters.

Published years after 1902, a manual distributed by the Bureau of Education for English teachers in the country contained an interesting sample dialogue presented as an exercise for students. The fictional dialogue featured a Miss Villanueva talking to a Mr Campos, both presumably Filipinos, about her recent trip to Japan. Her story revolved around the experience that she and her mother had with a rickshaw and the accident they met with when the Japanese puller stumbled, fell, and broke his leg as a result. Although she flew into a ditch, Miss Villanueva recounted that she was not hurt. Rather symbolically, "a party of tourists came by in automobiles and took us [the two ladies] back to town". This hypothetical situation curiously juxtaposed the Villanuevas' unfamiliarity with their Japanese pullers – as both mother and daughter could not even "speak a word of Japanese" – and the ladies' "sense of security/comfort"

---

98. James Blount, *The American Occupation of the Philippines, 1898–1912* (New York, 1913), p. 191.
99. "Los Filipinos no son brutos", *El Comercio*, 19 May 1902, p. 3.
100. "Ricksha gives Filipinos Shock", *Manila Times*, 28 July 1910, p. 1.

after automobile-riding foreigners, presumably Westerners, "rescued" them from their predicament in a foreign land.[101]

While educated Filipinos like Pardo de Tavera and Villamor used their transnational mobility as a way of contrasting Filipinos' supposed lack of respect for the dignity of labor to the hardworking attitude of pullers in foreign lands, a number of cosmopolitan Filipinos did the opposite. Enrique Altavas, in narrating his voyage to Japan, related that the rickshaw is one of the first things that attract the attention of the visitor. He also gave his opinion regarding the rickshaw: "La primera vez que ocupé uno de estos rickshaws tuva [*sic*] una impresión desagradable, pues no podía avenirme fácilmente a la idea de 'animalizar', (si cabe la palabra), a un ser humano hecho a imagen y semejanza del Creador."[102] Altavas left his reader with an image of the rickshaw as foreign (Japanese) and inherently degrading.

That a number of educated Filipinos viewed the rickshaw as essentially foreign and enslaving is not a trivial matter. The result of such an over-lapping of meanings is the increased potency of the rickshaw as a symbol of oppression; but oppression not just of a puller-laborer by the rickshaw owner, but also of a colonized nation by a foreign ruler. To see the potency of the rickshaw as a symbol of colonial exploitation one has to go back to events before the 1902 rickshaw controversy. During the early years of American colonialism, an editorial cartoon of a Filipino pulling a carriage, à la rickshaw, with an American passenger circulated among the natives and became popular.[103] At the same time, anecdotal evidence, which Taft himself presented before the US Senate, reported Filipino *cocheros* as expressing their concerns about the new regime in the following way:

> When the American government is established here and the Americanos are in control [...] what kind of cart, wagon, or carromata shall I have to help pull, because I understand the Americans are buying up all the horses in the Philippines with a view to killing them, so that the Filipinos shall be made the beasts of burden.[104]

From educated *ilustrados* to ordinary carriage drivers, it appeared that the subjugation of the Philippines to another colonial power was as

---

101. Mary Helen Fee, *Constructive Lessons in English Designed for Use in Intermediate Grades* (Manila, 1911), p. 70.

102. Enrique Altavas, *Impresiones de viaje* (Manila, 1920), p. 270: "The first time that I rode one of these rickshaws I had an unpleasant impression, as I could not easily reconcile myself with the idea of 'turning into an animal' (if such a phrase fits) a human being made in the image and likeness of the Creator."

103. Blount, *The American Occupation of the Philippines*, p. 191.

104. US Senate, *Affairs in the Philippine Islands: Hearings before the Committee on the Philippines of the United States Senate* (Washington DC, 1902), pp. 269–270. See also Pante, "The *Cocheros* of American-Occupied Manila", p. 455.

degrading as the act of pulling a rickshaw. The intense opposition to Rivers's business was thus not surprising, given these circumstances. One must be reminded that the controversy erupted at a time when the American colonial state had just reached its fourth year and nationalist feeling was still high. Though Manila was quite far away from revolutionary battles and the war against the Americans was already nearing its end, nationalist fervor was still strong among Manila-based oppositionist groups, including the UOD. The wave of militancy that swept Manila during the first months of 1902, articulated by the likes of de los Reyes, was also propagated by anti-US sentiment.[105] From the Filipino perspective, the anti-rickshaw campaign was not just a fight to preserve the Filipino workers' dignity, it also contained remnants of an iconography from very recent anti-colonial resistance.

The persistence of the iconography of the rickshaw from one context to another would be repeated years after the 1902 controversy, this time in an entirely different debate: the debate regarding the independence of the Philippines. In the campaign of Filipino nationalists for political independence, echoes of the controversy could still be heard in rhetoric deployed by Filipino politicians. Though the fight for independence through diplomatic means was something that had been an evident concern from the beginning of the colonial period, it only gained significant momentum with the passage of the 1916 Philippine Act or the Jones Law. In Michael Salman's analysis of the campaign for independence, he noted that Filipino nationalists "wielded definitions of slavery as weapons"[106] to push for their cause. The rickshaw-as-symbol became one such weapon.

In fighting for independence from the US, Filipino politician Isauro Gabaldon stated that a Filipino should be respected for the following reasons:

> I respect the Filipino because he respects himself. There is an innate manliness about him. He has a deep-seated personal pride. No one could ever make a Filipino pull a rickshaw [...]. The present nationalistic movement of this country is an outgrowth of this Filipino trait. Because he respects himself he wishes to govern himself.[107]

Gabaldon's use of the rickshaw as a negative example to illustrate the political maturity of the Filipinos was echoed in the testimony before the US House Committee on Insular Affairs given by James Williams, the editor of various US-based publications who had spent four months in the Philippines. Yet in an ironic twist, Williams's deployment of the metaphorics of slavery was done to praise American colonial rule and

105. Mojares, *Brains of the Nation*, p. 279.

106. Salman, *The Embarrassment of Slavery*, pp. 3–4.

107. Isauro Gabaldon, "Why I Respect the Filipino", in US Senate, Seventy-First Congress, *Independence for the Philippine Islands: Hearings before Committee on Territories and Insular Affairs* (Washington DC, 1930), p. 339.

support its continuation. His testimony was made to convince the US Congress that conditions in the Philippines under Governor-General Leonard Wood were most satisfactory. In his argument, he stated:

> It is a very heartening condition to go through the Orient and finally arrive in Manila and the Philippines and find there that under American sovereignty there are no beggars, and there are no rickshas, in the Philippines. You travel in the Philippines by automobile or by carriage or other vehicle, but a fellow human being does not drag your vehicle through the streets, as he does in some other countries in the Orient.[108]

Apparently, it did not occur to Williams that it was Manila Americans who had pushed for the implementation of a rickshaw system in 1902.

Meanwhile, in an article that extolled the benefits of American colonial rule in the country, Kansas Governor Henry Allen related that when he visited the Philippines in 1927 Filipino leaders preferred the retention of colonial rule over independence that would supposedly leave the country vulnerable to other powers in Asia, including Japan. He then added:

> Even the realization of this danger comes down to the people themselves. I asked the chauffeur who drove me about in Manila what he thought would happen if the United States gave the Philippines their freedom and disavowed further responsibility. He said that he was afraid that in a short time it would mean that he would be "pulling a rickshaw with a Japanese inside, rather than driving an automobile".[109]

Here was an American using the iconography of the rickshaw as both foreign and enslaving in an unprecedented manner: to depict the horrors of possible Japanese colonial rule in the Philippines.

CONCLUSION

In a recent article, David Arnold and Erich DeWald pointed out:

> An argument for the social construction of these technologies in a colonial or semi-colonial context must, therefore, take a different form – in terms of how certain technological goods or practices were locally ignored or rejected, were subjected to significant local emendation and reinvention (like the various forms of the Asian cycle-rickshaw, itself a demonstration of substantial intraregional diversity), were reworked and reappropriated to conform with local cultural norms and social usages.[110]

---

108. US House of Representatives, *Hearing before the Committee on Insular Affairs, House of Representatives, Sixty-Ninth Congress, Second Session on H.R. 16868: A Bill to Clarify and Amend Existing Laws Relating to the Powers and Duties of the Auditor for the Philippine Islands and for Other Purposes, February 3, 4, 5, 7, and 8, 1927* (Washington DC, 1927), p. 110.
109. Henry Allen, "From Jagor to Major General Wood", *The American Chamber of Commerce Journal*, 7 (April 1927), p. 7.
110. Arnold and DeWald, "Everyday Technology in South and Southeast Asia", p. 6.

This article is in part an answer to the call made by Arnold and DeWald. Although the Asian cycle-rickshaw that they mention is totally different from the rickshaws that were introduced in Manila in 1902, their ideas remain significant to this article. Indeed, the evolution of the old rickshaw into the modern Asian cycle-rickshaw show us how transport technology can exist in different reincarnations and reinventions in the polycentric world of Asia from colonial times to the contemporary world, a clear demonstration that innovations are not easily transplanted but are always contested by their recipients.[111] But as the case of Manila demonstrates, even societies that shunned a certain piece of technology can also perform the processes of reworking and reappropriating.

Innovation is not always perceived as positive, for, as shown in the case of rickshaws in Manila, a new form of transportation was rejected. But behind this controversial act of rejection was the creation and deployment of new meanings to otherwise "neutral" objects. As shown in this article, the rickshaw was presented by its opponents as essentially foreign and oppressive, a mechanism to turn pullers into slaves. Significantly, such a depiction of the rickshaw in Manila came decades before the British had foregrounded the same imagery in its campaign to eradicate rickshaws in Singapore in the late 1920s.[112] Manila has illustrated that although the technological diffusion of the rickshaw into the city was very minimal and even rejected outright by key social groups, the meanings ascribed to both the technological artifact and the labor attached to the new technology were highly enriched by transnational movements of people and their ideas.

However, such meanings have been created and deployed mainly by the middle class, such as the articulate leaders of the UOD. One is thus left wondering about the perceptions of both rickshaw-pullers and *cocheros*. How did they view their occupation and the notion of dignity of labor? This question is impossible to answer given that these workers have left us with no letters or memoirs as sources of historical information.[113]

Nonetheless, their actions, as reported by mainstream media and other upper- and middle-class eyewitnesses, allow us to gain more insights about workers, not as individuals, but as active social groups. One such insight is the significance of national ties in securing economic and political interests in a particular locality. While both Chinese coolies and Filipino *cocheros* were subordinate classes whose labor was exploited for the accumulation of wealth, the latter gained a better political position as

---

111. For similar considerations on colonial Africa see Jan-Bart Gewald, André Leliveld, and Iva Peša, "Introduction: Transforming Innovations in Africa: Explorative Studies on Appropriation in African Societies", in *idem* (eds), *Transforming Innovations in Africa: Explorative Studies on Appropriation in African Societies* (Leiden, 2012), pp. 1–15, 7.
112. Warren, *Rickshaw Coolie*, p. 100.
113. Pante, "The *Cocheros* of American-Occupied Manila", p. 456.

they allied themselves with the nationalist labor federation. Unfortunately, the nationalist orientation of the UOD prevented it from establishing ties with the migrant coolies despite apparent class solidarities. And there is an ironic twist: although transnational flows helped shape the UOD's opposition to the rickshaw, it was a strong nationalist agenda that became the primary weapon that led to the demise of the business. As such, while global connectivity transformed Manila by giving it new forms of technology (the rickshaw), labor (Chinese coolies), and capital (American investment), the local context, as defined by a smoldering anti-colonial nationalism, remained crucial in influencing the outcome of historical events.

IRSH 59 (2014), Special Issue, pp. 161–183 doi:10.1017/S0020859014000388
© 2014 Internationaal Instituut voor Sociale Geschiedenis

The First Great Railway Strike: Rereading the Early Labour Movement in São Paulo*

GUILHERME GRANDI

Department of Economics, University of São Paulo
Av. Prof. Luciano Gualberto 908, Cidade Universitária,
05508-010 São Paulo-SP, Brazil

E-mail: ggrandi@usp.br

ABSTRACT: By analysing the first great railway strike in São Paulo (Brazil), this article aims to understand the role of the Companhia Paulista railway workers' movement and its impact on labour relations in the São Paulo state. To that end, I have examined selected newspapers, the minutes of workers' meetings, police investigations into the strike, and the reports of the Companhia Paulista's directors. Differing from the views of other historians who have tended to see the 1906 railway strike as a relatively inconsequential conflict about wages, I interpret it both as rooted in deeper grievances about labour conditions and as a starting point for a period of heightened militancy and changing labour-management relations.

No written social history of the twentieth century is complete without an account of railway strikes. Because it has a strong impact, often long-term, strike activity in general offers a useful observation point for studying changes in labour relations. Although strikes are not the only form of labour conflict (others include sabotage, absenteeism, slowdowns, and boycotts), they remain more visible historically because they are usually better documented than other forms of labour protest. In the United States, for example, many scholars who have examined national strike data have been interested in the long-term relationship between strikes and the development of collective bargaining.[1] According

---

* This article is part of a postdoctoral research project developed at the Centre interuniversitaire de recherche en économie quantitative (CIREQ) at Université de Montréal (Québec, Canada) between September 2012 and December 2013. I want to thank Michael Huberman for his supervision and for his helpful suggestions on earlier versions of this article. I have also benefited from the comments of Jacques Rouillard at the Department of History, Université de Montréal. I owe special thanks to anonymous referees for their comments and suggestions. Responsibility for any error or omission is entirely mine.
1. Shelton Stromquist, *A Generation of Boomers: The Pattern of Railroad Labor Conflict in Nineteenth-Century America* (Urbana, IL, 1987), p. 25.

to Gerald Friedman, strikes are the proving grounds of unions, which survive only when they can significantly increase the bargaining power of workers.[2]

In early twentieth-century São Paulo (Brazil) there was, as in many other places at the time, an inherent association between the militancy of urban workers, the organization of left-wing parties, and the union movement. The strategy of leftist uprisings was accomplished principally by means of strikes organized as mobilizations of workers and through rallies in public spaces. Most such upheavals had the support of the labour organizations that represented the oldest and most numerous types of industrial workers, such as railwaymen. The latter played an especially important role in the trajectory of the labour movement in São Paulo because they constituted one of the first categories to organize themselves against exploitation and to fight for better working conditions. It is for that reason that strike activity has been seen as such a key element in the progress of industrial workers. It is known that the railwaymen were not the only category of rank-and-file workers who went on strike, for at the turn of the century printers, shoe-makers, glassmakers, bricklayers, textile workers, matchmakers, metal-workers, and port workers frequently did the same.

However, it appears that railway strikes were more visible than other labour disputes because they could unify a larger number of employees. Moreover, railway strikes tended to be more disruptive to other economic activities and the repercussions were always greater for society than the effects of strikes in other industries. The interruption of rail traffic and its consequences for the trade and manufacturing sectors made rail strikes particularly serious and commanded extraordinary attention from the state and public, because solutions needed to be found quickly. Railway workers, as well as other kinds of skilled workers, had considerable bargaining power, which enabled them to structure their unions, and they had great influence upon labour movements around the world. All in all, they were one of the few groups who could embody a broadly based labour movement in São Paulo state during the first few decades of the twentieth century.

There is an extensive literature on Brazil's general railway history,[3] but little exists about the formation of the railway working class specifically

---

2. Gerald Friedman, "Strike Success and Union Ideology: The United States and France, 1880–1914", *Journal of Economic History*, 48 (1988), pp. 1–25, 1–3.

3. The most important studies on Brazilian railways are: Julian S. Duncan, *Public and Private Operation of Railways in Brazil* (New York, 1932); Odilon N. de Matos, *Café e ferrovias: a evolução ferroviária de São Paulo e o desenvolvimento da cultura cafeeira* (São Paulo, 1974); Flávio Saes, *As ferrovias de São Paulo 1870–1940: expansão e declínio do transporte ferroviário em São Paulo* (São Paulo, 1981); Liliane Segnini, *Ferrovias e ferroviários: uma contribuição para a análise do poder disciplinar na empresa* (São Paulo, 1982); Colin M. Lewis, *Public Policy and*

and the conflicts involving the railway capital, the early labour movement, and the state's repressive apparatus. The main reason for this lack might be the great difficulty encountered in tracking down the political actions of railway workers in the sources. The railway sector represented an area of early government activity in Brazil, with the financing of construction, promotion of incorporation, and the regulation of operations being only the most prominent aspects of state intervention in the sector from the second half of the nineteenth century onwards. Nonetheless, most of the Brazilian historiography on business enterprises has not focused on the analysis of railway labour–management relations. This article approaches that relationship, which, as a by-product of the state's conflict with labour, eventually brought about a new framework for labour–management cooperation in São Paulo state.

The history of Brazil shows a growing trend towards increased state control over labour relations as working conditions and wage levels were systematically constrained by rules, regulations, and economic policy decisions, all established by a number of government agencies. Furthermore, legislation and the state's repressive power both interfered with and obstructed workers' actions. With the founding of the Brazilian Workers' Confederation (Confederação Operária Brasileira) through the first Brazilian Labour Congress, which took place at Centro Gallego in Rio de Janeiro on 15–20 April 1906, several union representatives tried to organize the labour movement nationally.[4] By organizing meetings and editing newspapers, the partisans of "revolutionary unionism" began to foster people's awareness of the need for better living conditions and basic social entitlements.[5]

Scholars who have studied the history of the Brazilian labour movement have tended to use newspapers as a primary source to investigate the labour movement's path.[6] Dulce Leme's thesis on the first great railway

---

Private Initiative: Railway Building in São Paulo 1860–1889 (London, 1991); William R. Summerhill, *Order against Progress: Government, Foreign Investment, and Railroads in Brazil, 1854–1913* (Stanford, CA, 2003); Maria L. Lamounier, *Ferrovias e mercado de trabalho no Brasil do século XIX* (São Paulo, 2012).

4. The set of resolutions of the First Brazilian Labour Congress are available in Paulo S. Pinheiro and Michael M. Hall (eds), *A Classe Operária no Brasil: documentos (1889 a 1930)*, vol. I, *O Movimento Operário* (São Paulo, 1979), pp. 46–58.

5. A good interpretation of the ideological segmentation and attitudes that characterized early Brazilian unionism can be found in Cláudio Batalha, "Syndicalisme révolutionnaire et syndicalisme réformiste. Les modèles européens dans le mouvement ouvrier brésilien (1906–1920)", in Tanja Régin and Serge Wolikow (eds), *A l'épreuve de l'international* (Paris, 2002), pp. 15–26. On the socialist movement among Italian immigrant workers in São Paulo, see Luigi Biondi, *Classe e nação: trabalhadores e socialistas italianos em São Paulo, 1890–1920* (Campinas, 2011).

6. Sheldon L. Maram, "Labor and the Left in Brazil, 1890–1921: A Movement Aborted", *Hispanic American Historical Review*, 57 (1977), pp. 254–272; *idem, Anarquistas, imigrantes e o*

strike in São Paulo, which was organized by workers at the Companhia Paulista de Estradas de Ferro (CPEF) in 1906, is still a main reference for the study of this conflict.[7] Even though many researchers have commented on this railway strike, most of them offer little more than relatively general observations of it. By analysing the great railway strike of 1906, the objective of this article is to understand the role of the CPEF railway workers' movement during and immediately after the strike. For this purpose, I have examined selected newspapers, the minutes of workers' meetings, police investigations into the causes and consequences of the strike, and the reports of the CPEF's directors. I intend to answer the following questions: how did the first great railway strike begin; what were its causes; what forms of organization and action emerged during the strike; and what were the consequences?

The railway strike of 1906 at the CPEF, the most important privately owned railway company in São Paulo at the beginning of the twentieth century, has previously been interpreted mainly as conflict about wages.[8] As the study by Leme and my own research, however, make clear, it was a personal disagreement between a station chief and one of his subordinates that sparked the walkout. Of course, there were also economic complaints among the workers' demands during the entire duration of the strike, but the kernel of it concerned agitation for the dismissal of certain ruthless managers. The strikers demanded an end to disrespect, threats, humiliation, persecution, and all the arbitrariness that the railway management was practising at that time. If we consider the list of all the grievances expressed by the workers, they were challenging the abuse of the power of patronage, their own harsh working conditions, and oppressive and unfair work rules. In addition, the CPEF's authoritarianism was tempered by a remarkable paternalism as a means of controlling the labour organizations and avoiding the diffusion of militant class-consciousness among workers.

This article is organized as follows: in the first section, I briefly review some of the literature on railway and immigration in São Paulo and discuss the movement that led to the mobilization of labour and, more specifically, of CPEF railway workers. In this initial phase, the labour press and the formation of the first labour organizations had an undeniable importance in

movimento operário brasileiro, 1890–1920 (Rio de Janeiro, 1979); Boris Fausto, *Trabalho urbano e conflito social, 1890–1920* (São Paulo, 1986); Joel Wolfe, "Anarchist Ideology, Worker Practice: The 1917 General Strike and the Formation of São Paulo's Working Class", *Hispanic American Historical Review*, 71 (1991), pp. 809–846.

7. Dulce Leme, "'Hoje há ensaio': A greve dos ferroviários da Cia. Paulista, 1906" (M.A., University of Campinas, 1984).

8. Fausto, *Trabalho urbano e conflito social*; Robert H. Mattoon, "The Companhia Paulista de Estradas de Ferro, 1868–1900: A Local Railway Enterprise in São Paulo, Brazil" (Ph.D., Yale University, 1971).

the process of developing political awareness among railway workers. The second section gives some details of the railway strike of 1906, which resulted from a conflict in the CPEF's labour–management relations. The third section discusses the rise of working-class solidarity in support of the railway strikers and of the outcomes of the strike. The last section summarizes my most significant findings and their implications for the historiographical knowledge about the great railway strike of 1906, in particular, and the labour movement in São Paulo, in general.

RAILWAY EXPANSION, IMMIGRATION, AND THE RISE OF THE LABOUR MOVEMENT

The establishment of railway corporations led to significant changes in labour relations in Brazil. The prohibition on the use of slave labour, the need for a variety of skilled and semiskilled workers, and the presence of a great many immigrants in the service of the railway were all part of the general transition from slave labour to free wage labour. Furthermore, the expansion of the national rail network was related to cycles of growth and downturns in the Brazilian economy and to the seasonal rhythms of a transport system dependent on export-oriented agriculture. José Cechin argues that in Brazil the trains reduced transport costs, expanded markets, and subjected all production units located within their reach to the same inexorable dynamic of competition.[9]

The demand for railway building increased considerably from the 1860s. A huge number of kilometres of new railway were being built and those already in operation required more and more workers for their maintenance and operation. Moreover, due to labour shortages, not only construction gangs but also workers were recruited by subcontractors, and this consequently pushed wages higher. Urban centres, including Rio de Janeiro, the national capital of the time, were not yet the labour reservoirs they would become in the 1890s, and the agriculture sector tended to absorb almost all existing free labour. Finding men in the capital and in São Paulo – the hubs of industry – to wield picks and shovels was not easy, and labour shortages was a difficult and persistent problem in railway building. Therefore, railway contractors received contingents of both slaves and free labourers. The latter was nurtured mainly by internal and external migration.[10]

The foreign-born population made up a large proportion of São Paulo's labour force.[11] In 1893 68 per cent of a total of 54,540 employees in São

9. José Cechin, "A construção e operação das ferrovias no Brasil do século XIX" (M.A., University of Campinas, 1978), pp. 13–14.
10. Mattoon, "The Companhia Paulista".
11. Warren Dean, *The Industrialization of São Paulo, 1880–1940* (Austin, TX, 1969).

Paulo's various industries were foreign. Considering the manufacturing, commerce, and transport sectors, they made up almost 80 per cent of the labour force.[12] Between 1870 and 1920, it is estimated that about 2.5 million immigrants arrived in São Paulo, mostly to work on coffee plantations. Initially, the farmers (or São Paulo's ruling class) had no interest in establishing colonial settlements but only in replacing slave labour with cheap labour.[13] In sum, Brazil was fourth among the New World countries in terms of the number of foreign migrants received from 1870 to 1914.

The expansion of the rail network was essential in contributing to the improvement of the mobility of the incoming workers and to the proliferation of the coffee crop throughout São Paulo state. Indeed, railway building and operations were the principal economic activities listed in the first Brazilian industrial census, and by the 1900s the railway sector's share of the gross value of industrial production in São Paulo was 71 per cent (equivalent to 84,000 contos de réis),[14] and it employed 18,501 people out of an industrial workforce of 25,000. Additionally, railway capital increased from 96,000 contos de réis in 1885 to 360,000 contos de réis in 1910, while investment in the São Paulo textile industry – the second most significant sector – was only 46,650 contos de réis in the same year.[15]

When examining the expansion of the Brazilian rail network as a whole, William Summerhill observed: "The largest percentage increase on an annual basis came in the first decade of operation [...]. In contrast to the large percentage increases in the 1860s, the early twentieth century witnessed the largest absolute increases in track."[16] Table 1 confirms that the first decade of the twentieth century saw the greatest increase in length of railway track, but the most significant increase in São Paulo occurred during the first phase of railway development in the state, during the 1870s. Overall, the national rail network increased 86.3 per cent between 1900 and 1920: from 15,316 kilometres to 28,535 kilometres.

The building of the railways created enormous pressure on a labour supply that was otherwise largely employed in agriculture. At the same time, the demand for "hands for farming" received a great boost with the creation of the Associação Auxiliadora da Colonização e Imigração by the

---

12. Fausto, *Trabalho urbano e conflito social.*
13. Zuleika Alvin, "O Brasil italiano (1880–1920)", in Boris Fausto (ed.), *Fazer a América: a imigração em massa na América Latina* (São Paulo, 2000), pp. 383–418.
14. Until 1942, the baseline Brazilian currency unit was the *mil-réis*. One *mil-réis* was expressed numerically as 1$000 *réis*. A larger unit was the *conto de réis*. One thousand *milréis* was the equivalent of one *conto de réis* and was written as 1:000$000. Thus, 84,000 *contos de réis* would be written as 84:000$000.
15. Wilson Cano, *Raízes da concentração industrial em São Paulo* (São Paulo, 1990), pp. 52–53.
16. Summerhill, *Order against Progress*, p. 55.

Table 1. *Railway track in service in Brazil and São Paulo (kilometres)*

Year	Brazil (1)	Kilometres added in given year	Percentage increase in given year	São Paulo (2)	(2)/(1) (%)
1855	15	0	0	–	–
1860	223	113	51	–	–
1865	498	24	5	–	–
1870	744	7	1	139	19
1875	1,801	517	29	655	36
1880	3,398	457	13	1,212	36
1885	6,930	628	9	1,640	24
1890	9,973	390	4	2,425	24
1895	12,967	707	5	2,962	23
1900	15,316	401	3	3,373	22
1905	16,781	475	3	3,842	23
1910	21,326	2,085	10	5,204	24

Sources and notes: Growth of railway track in Brazil from Summerhill, *Order against Progress*; São Paulo's railway track from Saes, *As ferrovias de São Paulo*. All distances and all percentages rounded to the nearest whole number.

export-oriented bourgeoisie in 1871. Subsequently, in 1886, the settlement programme was further expanded through the establishment of the Sociedade Promotora da Imigração by Martinho Prado, Nicolau de Sousa Queiróz, and Rafael de Barros (three members of the export-oriented bourgeoisie) subsidizing the arrival of foreign workers in São Paulo.

Despite the great encouragement of foreign labour by coffee growers, there were plenty of conflicts involving employers (the export oligarchs and the new industrial bourgeoisie) and employees (foreign and native workers), both on farms and in firms. The first workers in São Paulo and Rio de Janeiro at the beginning of the twentieth century had limited experience of factory life, since a significant portion of the labour force comprised immigrants from the rural areas of southern Europe. Despite their unfamiliarity with industry, however, most of them had some previous experience with political mobilization and many of the workers seemed familiar with the repertoire of labour protests, parties, and unions in Europe.

There is no doubt that European migrants took a prominent place in the early labour movement in São Paulo, when urban workers began to acquire their own working-class consciousness.[17] After Brazil abolished slave labour in 1888 as the last country in the Americas, the protection of

17. It should be mentioned, however, that some historians have challenged the assumption of the essential role of European migrant workers in the rise of organized labour in São Paulo. See, for instance, Michael M. Hall, "Immigration and the Early São Paulo Working Class", *Jahrbuch für Geschichte von Staat, Wirtschaft and Gesellschaft Lateinamerikas*, 12 (1975), pp. 393–407.

industrial workers became a key aim for social activists worldwide.[18] In
São Paulo, the labour press reveals that workers were heavily influenced
by the European revolutionary labour movement, mediated into Brazilian
context especially by Italian immigrants. Also, many railway workers had
originally come from Italy, Portugal, or Spain. Labour conflicts became
more frequent as the labour movement began to take a more definite
shape. Between 1900 and 1903, São Paulo society was shaken by many
disputes, such as the walkouts in the weaving industry (Anhaia e Penteado
factory) and in the glass industry (Santa Maria factory).[19] About the latter,
it is crucial to note that the factory's owner was Antonio Prado, the most
important traditional coffee fortune holder in São Paulo and the chairman
of the CPEF.

During the first decade of the twentieth century, 94.6 per cent of all
newcomers to São Paulo state came from outside the country (dropping
only slightly to 90.6 per cent in the decade 1910–1920), data which give
credence to the view that there was a correlation between the increase in
worker upheavals, which grew from 1901 to 1920, and the high influx of
immigrants.[20] The first attempts of railway workers to organize themselves professionally originated in the late nineteenth and early twentieth
centuries, when worker leagues began to emerge as predecessors of the
modern labour union. Railwaymen, together with printers, shoemakers,
tailors, milliners, and weavers, were the pioneers in founding such leagues,
which organized the first wave of strikes in São Paulo demanding
improved working conditions and some basic level of insurance.

By the turn of the century, labour leaders were meeting under the
auspices of the Brazilian Workers' Confederation, but conflicts between
adherents of anarchist activism and socialist sentiment splintered the
movement, with the result that workers' representatives began to meet
along sector or industrial lines. Although groups were evolving on the

18. Michael Huberman, *Odd Couple: International Trade and Labor Standards in History*
(New Haven, CT, 2012), p. 72. However, the divergence in the labour histories of Old and New
World countries is remarkable and has persisted into the twenty-first century. In Europe,
unions and their representatives succeeded in improving working conditions, embodied in new
labour laws, while in the New World labour and social reformers had less success in pushing
forward the social agenda. According to Huberman, "the asymmetry between Old and New
Worlds' attitudes toward immigration was telling. In the New World, the cry for tighter
immigration controls supplanted appeals for labor regulation and social insurance. In the
relatively open and more inclusive Old World, the call for better labor regulations was louder
than the demand for restrictions on foreign labor. The net result was that population movements within Europe strengthened the continent's attachment to the labor compact, while
elsewhere immigration weakened it"; *ibid.*, pp. 76–77.
19. For more details see Alceste De Ambris, "Il movimento operaio nello Stato di São Paulo",
in Vitaliano Rotellini, *Il Brasile e gli Italiani. Pubblicazione del 'Fanfulla'* (Florence, 1906).
20. Cheywa R. Spindel, *Homens e máquinas na transição de uma economia cafeeira* (Rio de
Janeiro, 1979), p. 129.

same revolutionary political platform, the imagined brotherhood they proposed failed to mask underlying cleavages. According to some historians, one of the causes that limited the development of a broad and effective labour movement was the ideological, social, and gender differences between the leadership and São Paulo's working class. Sheldon Maram, Boris Fausto, and John Dulles all stressed the ambivalent relationship between labour leaders and rank-and-file militancy.[21] Concerning the anarchist-oriented labour activism that was a noticeable mark of the Brazilian Workers' Confederation, Joel Wolfe adds: "Brazil's early anarchist movement owed more to the antistate politics of disaffected Republicans than it did to working-class organizing."[22]

Others have asserted, more strongly, that the "ethnic and national" issue should be considered the "primary cause" of the disorganization and ineffectiveness of São Paulo's labour movement.[23] Throughout the New World, the complaint was that foreign workers diluted labour organization, complicating negotiations of social entitlements, while the high geographical mobility of workers seemed to be another serious challenge to organized labour.[24] The constant lack of stability among foreign workers gave them little opportunity to create ties of solidarity with their fellow workers, and conflicts between immigrant and native groups, as well as between Italian and Portuguese migrants jeopardized the outcomes of collective bargaining.[25] Militant labour's attempts to build links with rural workers and small peasants were equally unsuccessful. The very first labour uprisings were the result of a critical situation that involved a high level of labour exploitation and adverse working conditions. On the more political plane, which developed only subsequently, the labour movement in Brazil, similar to other New World countries, began as a popular struggle for democracy. Battle was joined over the right of every individual to a voice in matters that affected him

---

21. Maram, "Labor and the Left in Brazil"; Fausto, *Trabalho urbano e conflito social*; John Dulles, *Anarchists and Communists in Brazil, 1900–1935* (Austin, TX, 1973).

22. Joel Wolfe, *Working Women, Working Men: São Paulo and the Rise of Brazil's Industrial Working Class, 1900–1955* (Durham, NC, 1993), p. 11.

23. Hall, "Immigration and the Early São Paulo Working Class", p. 398.

24. In a comparison with European countries, Alberto Alesina and Edward Glaeser present familiar arguments to explain why the United States could not have established a US Communist Party: "Successive waves of immigration to the United States of ethnically diverse members of the working class created cleavages across racial and ethnic lines, which 'confused' and diluted the classic class line of Marxism [...]. These immigrants may have had a propensity to find an individual (or individualistic) solution to adversity rather than fomenting a social revolution at home"; Alberto Alesina and Edward L. Glaeser, *Fighting Poverty in the US and Europe: A World of Difference* (Oxford, 2004), p. 9.

25. Kim D. Butler, *Freedoms Given, Freedoms Won: Afro-Brazilian in Post-Abolition São Paulo and Salvador* (New Brunswick, NJ, 1998).

(though seldom her). At the same time, the very ideal of democracy was lost in the separate labour organizations: it was turned into a bargaining chip in the disputes between the workers' leaders and their entrepreneurial opponents gaining material concessions in return for curbing rank-and-file activism.

The labour experience in Brazil had much in common with that in other regions of recent settlement in the Americas. The "soujourner" phenomenon and ethnicity, to take one example, both had a considerable impact on labour organization in the province of Quebec in Canada. Anglo-Celtic, French-Canadian, and Jewish workers predominated in different trade unions, indicating that the ethnic and religious division within the Quebec working class was as commonplace as it was entrenched organizationally. Militancy was further restrained by the inability of workers to put forward a persuasive and unified voice at the political level. As with their counterparts in São Paulo, different political ideologies tended, in a complicated amalgam, to be associated with certain ethnic identities. While French-Canadian workers had a tradition of labourism, i.e. advocating a strict separation of unionism and politics, most socialists were Anglo-Celtic and European migrants.[26] As with the workers in São Paulo, in the dispute between ideals and interests the labourists seem to have had the upper hand, as strongly suggested by the fact that most strikes were conducted by the best-paid workers in order to advance the interests of their own particular craft. The end result was a growing divide between skilled and unskilled workers because the lack of solidarity meant that the bargaining leverage enjoyed by select groups of workers was prevented from being disseminated throughout the whole working class.

The first unions in São Paulo were organized by certain craft workers along narrow lines that excluded ordinary factory workers and rural workers. The unwillingness of entrepreneurs to recognize the autonomy of workers' groups in pursuit of their union organization was one more obstacle faced by the labour leadership – and a daunting one. The new class of industrialists maintained the same approach as the old planters, who had been accustomed to the slave system for so long. That fact, associated with the almost total lack of labour laws, created the conditions for employers to act ruthlessly; and to be sure, during the late nineteenth and early twentieth centuries Brazilian railway management was made up of individuals who saw no benefit in good labour relations. There is

---

26. Geoffrey Ewen, "Quebec: Class and Ethnicity", in Craig Heron (ed.), *The Workers' Revolt in Canada, 1917–1925* (Toronto, 1998), pp. 87–143. Jean Hamelin, Paul Larocque, and Jacques Rouillard have provided a benchmark compilation of Quebec strike data, entitled *Répertoire des grèves dans la province de Québec au XIXe siècle* (Montreal, 1970). Of the total of 227 strikes recorded by various newspapers during the period 1843 to 1900, 30 (13.2 per cent) were related to labour disputes in railway building, maintenance, or operating.

certainly much evidence that labour-related matters were of little concern to employers. Robert Mattoon comments on the case of the CPEF management stating that "the almost total lack of descriptive information about working conditions suggests that the care and well-being of low-ranking employees was less than a constant preoccupation of Company directors".[27]

Faced by growing labour pressures, the CPEF responded in a predictably discreet manner designed to ensure orderly business operations. The company built houses and schools near its workshops in the cities of Jundiai, Campinas, and Rio Claro in order to meet the need to expand its labour force, and with the same purpose it offered training programmes for new employees. The average number of trainees per month grew from thirty-eight to sixty-seven between 1896 and 1901, and, according to the CPEF's chief of workshops, the railway workforce increased by 10 per cent in 1901 due to the successful expansion of the company's training programme.[28] At the same time, it was increasingly difficult for the CPEF to maintain its accustomed paternalistic control, even though it took the initiative in forming a cooperative association of company employees. The Associação Beneficente e Cooperativa dos Empregados da Companhia Paulista (Paulista Benevolent Society) was a typical mutual aid society like others that were emerging in Brazil in those early days of organized labour. Their aims were to provide financial and medical support to the families of workers disabled or killed at work, as well as legal assistance, schools, hospitals, and cooperative stores for working families.[29] In Brazil as a whole, paternalistic control appears to be associated with the rise of early mass-production industries. As with the seniority rules observed in other countries, Brazilian paternalistic management was conducted by foremen as a means of bolstering loyalty while preserving the benefits of a trained workforce.

Initially in São Paulo, the main complaints from railway workers involved the matter of seniority, the laying off of men for belonging to a labour organization, the reinstatement of men following a stoppage, the continuation of wage payments, injuries on the job, and work rules in general. Railway management put a lot of pressure on workers, which sometimes led to the erosion of solidarity and even to divisions between workers. Employees were also highly vulnerable to dismissal for insubordination. Many of them were forced into supporting their foreman's managerial criteria against other workers associated with a radical labour organization. Labour conflicts occurred when some groups

---

27. Mattoon, "The Companhia Paulista", p. 199.
28. Companhia Paulista de Estradas de Ferro, *Relatório da Diretoria da Companhia Paulista de Vias Férreas e Fluviais apresentado à Assembleia Geral dos Acionistas* (São Paulo, 1902), p. 296.
29. Mattoon, "The Companhia Paulista", p. 203.

Figure 1. The CPEF central office: a representation of the power of railway capital. The building, which is one of the first examples of art deco style in Sao Paulo city, completed construction in the 1930s. Today it houses the headquarters of the Secretary of Public Security of Sao Paulo state. *Photograph: Juan Esteves. Used with permission.*

of workers had become sufficiently familiarized with work routines to be able to organize and pursue common goals. In that regard, as mentioned above, the most important step towards the organization of labour on the São Paulo railways was the formation of regional worker leagues, which mobilized the railway working class and encouraged bargaining practices. Despite the high levels of initial investment in the roadbed and capital equipment all railways require, labour was an increasingly important factor in railway output.

The distribution of each grade of CPEF workers is presented in Table 2. Railwaymen were a very diverse occupational group. The variety of skills needed for railway work was remarkable, and no other industry can be found in early twentieth-century Brazil with such diversity of labour tasks. The figures in Table 2 show that while the CPEF white-collar occupations (general officers and office clerks) saw the largest relative increase in their numbers (68 per cent) between 1901 and 1914, the number of jobs related to the actual movement of traffic (including work in and around stations in freight and passengers) provided the largest increase in absolute terms (1,485 new station men and shop men). Furthermore, railwaymen worked under constant disciplinary threat and always faced the risk of being laid off, both by foremen and chief engineers. Despite the potential for occupational advancement, employment conditions may be defined as precarious and unstable, because railway workers had to deal with a working environment where dismissal for technical or disciplinary reasons seemed to be the norm. As a consequence of those hazards, employment insecurity was a constant concern in São Paulo's railway labour market at the turn of the century.

THE OUTBREAK OF THE RAILWAY STRIKE OF 1906

The most probable causes of the first great railway strike in São Paulo were concerns about job security and working conditions, seemingly common in all countries during the early stages of industrialization. Edited for the most part by immigrants, Brazilian workers' newspapers often complained about filthy working environments. Thus, poverty, food shortages, exploitation, low wages, and long hours of work were the main subjects discussed, and, to sum up, the social role of newspaper editing was to raise working-class consciousness and to contribute to the struggle for better working regulations and social entitlements. Labour disputes were not seen as something deserving regulation in terms of effective bargaining mechanisms because they were simply forbidden by the Brazilian state. As a result, the first strikes were illegal and violently repressed by the police.

Dissatisfaction among the CPEF's workers increased considerably from October 1905, when the company forced its staff to take three workdays off per month, citing cost-cutting as the reason. The company's work

Table 2. *CPEF railway workers by grade*

Category	1901 Number	1901 Percentage	1909 Number	1909 Percentage	1911 Number	1911 Percentage	1912 Number	1912 Percentage	1914 Number	1914 Percentage
White-collar	100	2.0	129	2.3	137	3.0	159	3.3	168	3.3
Station men	1,052	20.6	1,214	21.9	1,828	40.8	1,944	40.2	1,947	38.1
Trainmen	284	5.6	342	6.2	–	–	–	–	–	–
Engineers	7	0.1	14	0.3	–	–	–	–	–	–
Conductors	86	1.7	104	1.9	–	–	–	–	–	–
Firemen	90	1.8	103	1.9	–	–	–	–	–	–
Others	101	2.0	121	2.2	–	–	–	–	–	–
Trackmen	839	16.4	1,149	20.7	1,196	26.7	1,229	25.4	1,136	22.2
Shopmen	1,274	24.9	1,188	21.4	1,320	29.5	1,504	31.1	1,864	36.4
Machinists	35	0.7	30	0.5	–	–	–	–	–	–
Carpenters	87	1.7	85	1.5	–	–	–	–	–	–
Others	1,152	22.6	1,073	19.3	–	–	–	–	–	–
Total	5,107	100	5,552	100	4,481	100	4,836	100	5,115	100

Sources and notes: Companhia Paulista de Estradas de Ferro, *Relatório da Diretoria da Companhia Paulista de Vias Férreas e Fluviais apresentado à Assembleia Geral dos Acionistas* (São Paulo, 1902), 30 June 1902, and the corresponding reports for 30 June 1910, 30 June 1912, 30 June 1913 and 30 June 1915. Unfortunately, from the second decade of the twentieth century I could find no further distinction in railway worker categories in the CPEF directors' reports, because the reports began listing only aggregate data on the workforce. Thus, the reports' denomination "Linhas e Edifícios" corresponds to the occupation of trackmen in the table and "Trafego e Telegrapho" is represented by the station men and trainmen grades jointly.

Table 3. *Employees in three railway companies of São Paulo*

Period	Average no. of employees per kilometre of track			Average no. of employees per 1,000,000 tons/km of goods transported		
	Paulista	Mogiana	Sorocabana	Paulista	Mogiana	Sorocabana
1901–1905	4.21	2.81	3.01	38.29	41.57	39.40
1906–1910	3.69	2.83	2.69	22.68	34.90	32.16
1911–1915	4.33	3.18	2.55	18.92	34.41	26.80
1916–1920	4.59	2.69	3.01	16.12	27.84	20.57

Source: Saes, *As ferrovias de São Paulo*, p. 137.

schedule involved a larger number of holidays and shorter workdays – followed by a decrease in wages. At the same time, the railway management began downsizing resulting from the modernization of the company's workshops. Such changes did not affect white-collar and station employees but were concentrated on trainmen, trackmen, and principally on the rail-way shopmen, of whom 159 alone were dismissed between 1905 and 1906.[30]

When comparing different railway companies in São Paulo it is clear that, despite the downsizing of the labour force, the ratio of employees to track length of the CPEF remained higher than that for both the Mogiana and Sorocabana railways. At the same time, its ratio of employees to goods carried was lower, showing that it was the most efficient goods carrier among the railways in São Paulo state.[31] Efficiency, however, translated into high pressure on the work-floor level. A month before the beginning of the strike the workers' press published a series of grievances against the workshop chief, Francisco Paes Leme de Monlevade, who imposed thirteen- to sixteen-hour workdays on the company's staff:

> As if it were not enough working thirteen to sixteen hours a day: every week the workers must work overtime until the end of the working journey, which often finishes at midnight. Sometimes the sentinels become wet and are not allowed to change their clothes. Those who arrive five or more minutes late have a half workday taken off their wages. The employee who is caught talking with either a co-worker or someone else, is seen smoking, or is not at his workplace, even if owing to *force majeure*, will be punished.

> Only one person at a time is allowed to go to the bathroom, and he must ask for permission and explain his reasons. No employee is allowed to take leave for business or illness while another employee is off. The despot who establishes this, and who is very religious, has always done the same wherever he has gone,

---

30. Leme, "'Hoje há ensaio'", pp. 53–54.
31. On the CPEF's efficiency and profitability, see Guilherme Grandi, *Estado e capital ferro-viário em São Paulo: a Companhia Paulista de Estradas de Ferro entre 1930 e 1961* (São Paulo, 2013).

satisfied with his well-being (will it be permanent?) and indifferent to the pain that he causes, with his vexations and his fines.

How can an employee who receives Rs 4$000 per day [...] or who receives Rs 3$000 or 2$600 afford to pay his debts? Is this a wage that a worker can live on, even unpleasantly, without accumulating plenty of debts? This, when food is more and more expensive, when prices are going up while wages are going down![32]

It is evident that among the railway workers' claims the wage question held a prominent place, even though the event that led to the strike was a non-economic matter. The Jundiaí Worker League, which at that time acted like a real railway union, was responsible for recording all worker indictments. This League sent a set of complaints to several newspapers in São Paulo, in which workers accused station and workshop chiefs of disrespect and abuse of authority. Other problems were linked to the downsizing of the workforce, low wages, suspension of promotions, overwork, and the constant threat of dismissal and fines.[33]

Although there was a long list of grievances, the episode that caused the outbreak of the strike was a misunderstanding between the station chief of Jundiaí-Paulista – João Gonçalves Dias – and Thomas Degani, the checker in the same station who had worked at the CPEF for eight years. According to Leme, the checker had twice requested permission from the station chief to visit his family in Itatiba, and only after a third application and following the intervention of the traffic chief and the general inspector of the railway was he granted three days' leave. Nonetheless, when he returned to work he found that he had been posted by Dias to another city, Ribeirão Bonito. Degani was disappointed with so arbitrary a measure because he had begun constructing a house in Jundiaí and his family was completely dependent on him for their livelihood.[34] So began the conflict, and what had originally been an internal corporate disagreement became the largest industrial labour conflict in São Paulo up to that time.

São Paulo's great railway strike of 1906 started on the morning of 15 May when 3,500 CPEF employees stopped work. Services were affected on 1,057 kilometres of track, which carried slightly more than 80 per cent of São Paulo's coffee freight.[35] At the time, the company's rail network connected important coffee districts such as Campinas, Limeira, Araras, Porto Ferreira, Rio Claro, São Carlos, Jaboticabal, and Jaú, to name but a few. The day before the strike, the railway workers had sent a letter to the *Comércio de São Paulo* and *Il Secolo* newspapers explaining the reasons for

32. *A Terra Livre*, 12 April 1906. All translations are mine.
33. *Comércio de São Paulo*, 19 May 1906.
34. Leme, "'Hoje há ensaio'", p. 67.
35. *Gazeta de Piracicaba*, 16 May 1906.

it.[36] Concerning the conflict involving Degani and Dias, the Jundiai Worker League sent two documents to the CPEF's general inspector, the engineer Manuel Pinto de Torres Neves, in which they explained the Degani case and its injustices. In these documents, the League emphasized the checker's personal qualities and demanded his immediate return to Jundiai. Moreover, they denounced the arbitrariness, pressures, and abuses suffered by workers at the hands of Dias and called for his dismissal. Between 24 April, when the first document signed by almost 400 railway workers was issued, and 2 May, when the second was sent to the general inspector, the company had still not acknowledged the workers' complaints. In the second letter, the League board observed that:

> Given the staunch attitude and the general outrage of the employees in the face of the continuous threats and insults uttered by the Jundiai-Paulista station's chief against his underlings, attacking with degrading words a company of which he is unworthy to be part due to his immorality and rudeness, we are forced to ask you to find a solution by Saturday; this worthy corporation of honest workers can no longer be a victim of this ruthless head who does not even deserve to be an employee of an important railway company like Paulista.[37]

In the documents, the railway workers also complained about the fact that work was no longer being done according to the official assignments and, therefore, they had been obliged to assist with or complete jobs unrelated to the activity for which they had been employed. That they were overloaded with tasks was clearly due to the policy of downsizing. They also commented that there was a lowering of wages in relation to the previous period (a period when employment was still guaranteed). Finally, they highlighted the workers' discontent with the traffic chief, Francisco de Monlevade, and the station chief of Jundiai, Henrique Burnier, who were known to be "authoritarian" and "mean".[38] Further, there was another longstanding worker grievance related to the Paulista Benevolent Society, which, according to the workers, hired Monlevade's relatives, who refused the workers their rights of representation and voting in the Society.

After stopping work the strikers' first act was to hand out pamphlets calling on their co-workers to attend a meeting at 8.00 a.m. on 15 May in the São Jose theatre at Jundiai. The gathering was presided over by the League's lawyer, Arthur Guimarães, who addressed a large group of workers, asking them to remain peacefully in their homes and unwavering

---

36. Leme, "'Hoje há ensaio'", pp. 62, 66.
37. Liga Operaria de Jundiahy, *Documento enviado ao inspector geral da Companhia Paulista de Vias Férreas e Fluviais* (Jundiaí, 1906), dated 2 May 1906.
38. *Comércio de São Paulo*, 19 May 1906.

in the face of company pressure to re-establish the railway service. After
that, other members of the League's board gave speeches. For example,
Manuel Pisani detailed the reasons for the strike and mentioned that the
worker leagues of Campinas and Rio Claro, as well as the Worker
Federation of São Paulo (WFSP) had, through its spokesman Edgard
Leuenroth, declared firm support for the strike. He reminded the CPEF
workers that they were not demanding an increase in wages or a reduction
in hours of work. They were simply asking for recognition, respect, and
principled bosses.[39]

The CPEF's president-director (Antonio Prado), who was also the
mayor of São Paulo city at that time, learned about the strike through the
Comércio de São Paulo newspaper. In the early morning of 15 May, Prado
was interviewed by reporters of this newspaper, to whom he said that the
strike was unfair and illegal, since the workers' complaints had never been
brought to his attention. The only claim he acknowledged having heard of
was about the Benevolent Society.[40]

In addition to the other grievances mentioned, the railway workers also
found that their skills and experience, which had been their ticket to
remaining employed, were not honoured as railway companies promoted
their own men from within. While the senior positions and skilled
workers, such as engineers, had opportunities for advancement and
eventually membership of the company's board of directors, the majority
of unskilled workers saw similar advancement as being out of reach.
Indeed, job mobility for unskilled workers was strictly limited, since the
railway managers treated them as subordinates affiliated to a paternalistic
enterprise, as if they were (underage) members of a corporate family. In
that context, the basic wage for linemen rose from 2 to only 3 *milréis* a
day between 1875 and 1910, a period during which the devaluation of the
Brazilian currency and inflation were significant.[41]

WORKING-CLASS SOLIDARITY AND STRIKE OUTCOMES

At 8.30 a.m. the following day, the railway workers held another meeting
in the same theatre, but this time it was chaired by Pisani and was
attended by the Police Lieutenant Augusto Pereira Leite, who had been
invited by the workers. Pisani warned his colleagues of the lies that
some newspapers had been publishing about the strike and took the
opportunity to read telegrams in support of the workers that had been

39. Liga Operaria de Jundiahy, *Acta da assembléa geral extraordinaria realizada no recinto do
Theatro S. José no dia 15 de Maio de 1906* (Jundiaí, 1906), dated 15 May 1906.
40. *Comércio de São Paulo*, 16 May 1906.
41. Robert H. Mattoon, "Railroads, Coffee, and the Growth of Big Business in São Paulo,
Brazil", *Hispanic American Historical Review*, 57 (1977), pp. 273–295, 292.

Table 4. *Strikes in support of CPEF workers (May 1906)*

Enterprise or category	City	Beginning	Ending
Arens Workshops (weaving)	Jundiai	Day 15	–
Globo Shoes Factory	São Paulo	Day 15	–
Campineiro Tannery	Campinas	Day 16	Day 18
Coachmen and wagoners	Jundiai	Day 18	Day 19
Restaurant and hotel employees	Jundiai	Day 18	–
Mac Hardy (machines)	Campinas	Day 19	Day 25
Lidgerwood (machines)	Campinas	Day 19	Day 25
Ramal Férreo Campineiro (railway)	Campinas	Day 19	Day 25
Funilense (railway)	Campinas	Day 19	Day 25
Companhia Mogiana de Estradas de Ferro	Campinas	Day 19	Day 25
Alexandre Sien Mechanical Workshop	Campinas	Day 19	–
Construction workers	Campinas	Day 19	–
Printers' Union	Campinas	Day 19	Day 25
Faber & Irmao	Campinas	Day 19	Day 25
Pedro Anderson	Campinas	Day 19	Day 25
Rio Claro Beer Factory	Rio Claro	Day 19	–
Wagoners	Santos	Day 19	–
Coachmen and tramway conductors (Campineiro Tramway)	Campinas	Day 20	Day 23
[600 workers of different occupation]	Dois Corregos	Day 22	–
Carioca Textile Factory	Rio de Janeiro	Day 24	–
Carioca Tramway	Rio de Janeiro	Day 24	–

Source and notes: Leme, "'Hoje há ensaio'", p. 138. In the case of ten strikes, there are no data available to indicate when they ended.

sent by several labour organizations, including the Workers' Union of Rio de Janeiro. He also said that the milliners and barbers of São Paulo city, as well as the majority of workers and merchants in Jundiai, Campinas, and Rio Claro, had declared their enthusiastic support for the strike. In fact, there were many other categories of worker who went on strike in solidarity with the CPEF's railway workers. Table 4 summarizes these enterprises and occupational categories.

The data from Table 4 illustrate two noticeable features of these strike activities. First, the relatively short duration of the walkouts, approximately five days on average, and second, the peak of the strike movement on 19 May, when the majority of organizations listed on the chart organized their stoppages. Fausto contends that the labour movement achieved its highest level of militancy on 19 May precisely when workers from important companies in Campinas city, such as Mac Hardy, Lidgerwood, and the Companhia Mogiana de Estradas de Ferro joined the strike.[42] Nevertheless,

42. Fausto, *Trabalho urbano e conflito social*.

the strike movement did not reach the São Paulo Railway Company –
another railway company of critical importance as it serviced the link
between port of Santos and the city of São Paulo. Facing the threat that strike
action might extend to port workers, the President of São Paulo state, Jorge
Tibiriça, called for federal intervention. In the meantime, the WFSP supported the worker leagues by sending representatives to the main industrial
cities of the state. Another typical action on the part of the WFSP and the
local worker leagues during the strike was the distribution of pamphlets to
encourage worker solidarity in other trades and industries. Below is an
extract from one such pamphlet, written by the Jundiai Worker League and
published in the *Comércio de São Paulo* newspaper:

WORKER LEAGUE

Comrades! As you know, our friends from the Companhia Paulista are striking
against the despotism and arrogance of the three bosses from that powerful
railway company and the constant persecution and extortion of the workers by
those lords for their own benefit and that of their protégés. [...] So, the
Companhia Paulista's board of directors, which seems to be putting stingy
caprices before the company's interests, and whose management has been
severely damaged, has just declared peremptorily that it will not make any
concession to the strikers. [...] It is necessary that the workers do not lose,
because this would involve an attack on their legitimate rights and therefore the
total discrediting of our honourable class. We invite you, comrades, to strike
tomorrow to increase our moral force. Go ahead, because we hope you will
support our comrades from Paulista until we win. Victory is certain, and if
necessary we will go on a GENERAL STRIKE.[43]

These views clearly suggest that militancy was increasing in São Paulo by 19
May. Not only had the working class demonstrated its support for the railway
workers, in Rio Claro city the businessman Julio Stern distributed several
newsletters in his own beer factory calling for solidarity with CPEF
employees. Leme mentions a large number of organizations that declared their
support for the railway workers.[44] These organizations ranged from worker
leagues to left-wing parties, law students, labour unions, religious groups, and
a few business associations. In general, the level of commitment was significant
if we consider the novelty of this movement at the beginning of the twentieth
century. There were rumours that even the Worker League of Buenos Aires in
Argentina had sent financial aid to the Jundiai Worker League.[45] In São
Carlos, a powerful São Paulo coffee district, there was discontent on the part
of settlers, demonstrating that the movement had reached the agricultural
sector, the heartbeat of the Brazilian economy.

43. *Comércio de São Paulo*, 20 May 1906.
44. Leme, "'Hoje há ensaio'".
45. *Ibid.*, p. 131.

The outcome of the strike might have been better for the strikers if the São Paulo Railway Company workers had supported the CPEF railway strike's cause. If they had endorsed the strike, the whole export–import transport system of São Paulo would have collapsed and the labour conflict within the CPEF would have damaged the heart of the Brazilian economy: the coffee business. The WFSP regretted the behaviour of São Paulo Railway workers, whose collaboration in the transport of troops was seen by the militants as a betrayal of the working class. Some newspapers published the WFSP's bulletin, which urged the railwaymen to join the strike, for that would ensure the victory of the movement in only a few hours. The WFSP mentioned that, four days after the outbreak of the strike, the Mogiana workers, too, marched in solidarity with their CPEF co-workers. The request said: "Let's make the large artery, that gives life to the whole trade of the state, inactive and the victory of workers will be certain and immediate."[46]

According to Maram, the backing by the police reinforced the owners' power, which was key to circumventing the resistance of the workers.[47] In any case all emerging labour movements in Brazil encountered the vociferous bitterness of employers, encouraged by the forces of government. Thus, the CPEF strike movement began to weaken after one week of stoppages, and on 29 May 1906 a tragic episode occurred in Jundiaí city. The meeting, which attracted approximately 100 strikers near the main square of the city (Largo da Matriz), and the purpose of which was to decide what should be done, escalated into violence. As police on horseback approached the group of workers, shots were fired and two strikers, Ernesto Gould and Manoel Dias, were killed, as were a mounted policeman and a soldier named Pedro Evangelista de Araújo.[48] Subsequently, many strikers were imprisoned and the worker mobilization lost the impetus it needed to maintain the already fading railway strike, largely because employees went back to work at the Mogiana railway on 25 May. The efforts of the WFSP to continue to resist failed at the end of May. The strike came to an end as the threats of dismissal became stronger and more frequent. There is no doubt that by the time the strike committee was no longer able to negotiate, the CPEF's board of directors knew that the strike would end in a couple of days. At the end of May, the labour press admitted that: "Anyway, the strike itself does not exist anymore. The backward and unjustified attitude of some workers of our industrial establishments let the number of supporters of a general strike appear too small in the eyes of its proponents."[49]

---

46. *Il Secolo*, 20 May 1906.
47. Maram, "Labor and the Left in Brazil", p. 257.
48. Delegacia de Polícia de Jundiahy, *Inquérito sobre a greve na Companhia Paulista* (Jundiaí, 1906), dated 29 May 1906.
49. *A Platéia*, 29 May 1906.

Even if the consequences of the railway strike were not overly positive at the time due to its relatively short duration and the violent manner in which it was suppressed, I strongly believe that effects, both immediate and long-term, should not be underestimated. For instance, the strike's impact on the trade and economy of São Paulo state as a whole was profound. The roads to Jundiai and the west of the state were over-crowded by the standards of the time. The costs of transport using trol-leys and riders rose substantially. The cost of renting a horse increased to 100 *milréis*.[50] In addition, it is estimated that the CPEF required at least additional 160 workers, principally firemen and conductors, to properly re-establish its railway services, since they were the sectors that remained on strike for the longest time.[51] Much more important, however, were the impulses the strike gave to the further development of the management–labour relations in general and in the railway sector in particular. Even if the railway strike did not settle all of the CPEF workers' claims, it is important to point out that in 1907, the year after the strike, Brazil legally recognized industrial and commercial employee organizations as well as of those of professional people. Furthermore, as had occurred at the Companhia Mogiana, the eight-hour day was established as the pattern of railway work by the CPEF, a clear-cut consequence of the railway strike of 1906.

CONCLUSION

The railway strike of 1906 had significant results – results that have not been fully acknowledged by all previous historiographical assessments. One ensuing development was the regulation of an eight-hour day. Important as this was, it would be too narrow to limit the consequences to this alone and to ignore the further cascade effects that arose from the strike. One of these was a significant upturn for the labour movement in the years to come. Wolfe has thus admitted that the CPEF labour dispute encouraged the organization of other workers and led the labour leader-ship to misjudge the political potential of workers' protests.[52] Further, Maram notes that labour organizations enjoyed rapid growth from 1906 to 1908, and by 1913 the movement had achieved its highest membership – approximately 60,000.[53] It is, in any case, important to stress much more explicitly that this railway strike had a pioneering character in São Paulo's labour history because it was responsible for inaugurating a period of great social unrest involving a large number of urban workers in São Paulo state.

50. Leme, "'Hoje há ensaio'", p. 81.
51. *Ibid.*, p. 150.
52. Wolfe, "Anarchist Ideology, Worker Practice", p. 819, n. 36.
53. Maram, "Labor and the Left in Brazil", pp. 255–256.

As I have sought to show, the railway strike of 1906 implied a growing identity among varying categories of workers and, as a consequence, there was a re-evaluation of the railway companies' labour rules. Stoppages began in the city of Jundiai and spread quickly throughout the CPEF's line and then affected other trades and industries. The strike movement started by company employees mobilized other workers in factories making textiles, matches, cereals, hats, and shoes. Picket lines were set up and there were protests in support of the railway workers. While the organization of the strike was unsophisticated, the strikers' demands were comprehensive: regular hours, better pay, and improved working conditions.[54] In fact, the conflict that gave rise to the strike was related both to maintaining employment and wage levels, and to existing measures that were constraining the autonomy of the railway labour movement.

Apart from the mobilizing effect of the strike among railway workers, it was also shown that many workers from other manufacturing sectors endorsed the CPEF railway strike, which suggests that it played a pivotal role in the process of organizing and raising awareness among São Paulo workers at the beginning of the twentieth century. Also, it was the first time that São Paulo's working class reached a high degree of militancy, demanding fundamental rights and better working conditions. In its context, the railway strike of 1906 undoubtedly provided an effective incentive to the associative spirit among many groups of urban workers. On the whole, the first great railway strike in São Paulo contributed considerably to workers' engagement in their struggles for better working conditions and basic social entitlements. Certainly, it stood as a valuable lesson for the whole of Brazilian industrial relations in the twentieth century.

54. Mattoon, "The Companhia Paulista", p. 204.

IRSH 59 (2014), Special Issue, pp. 185–209 doi:10.1017/S0020859014000339
© 2014 Internationaal Instituut voor Sociale Geschiedenis

Motor Transportation, Trade Unionism, and the Culture of Work in Colonial Ghana

JENNIFER HART

Department of History, Wayne State University
3094 FAB, 656 W. Kirby, Detroit, MI 48202, USA

E-mail: Jennifer.hart4@wayne.edu

ABSTRACT: The emergence of drivers' unions in the 1920s and 1930s highlights the wide range of strategies for social and economic organization available to workers in the Gold Coast. Particularly among workers who operated outside the conventional categories of the colonial economy, unions provided only one of many models for labor organization. This article argues that self-employed drivers appropriated unions and an international discourse of labor organization in the early twentieth century in order to best represent their interests to the colonial government. However, their understanding of the function and organization of unions reflected a much broader repertoire of social and economic organizing practices. Rather than representing any exceptional form of labor organization, drivers highlight the circulation of multiple ideas surrounding labor organization in the early decades of the twentieth century, which informed the ways in which Africans engaged in the wage labor economy and implicitly challenged British colonial assumptions about labor, authority, and control.

In 1935, experienced drivers and local political and religious officials gathered under palm trees along the beach in La, an eastern suburb of Accra, capital of the Gold Coast, to inaugurate a new drivers' union. La was widely recognized by both colonial officials and African workers as the colony's preeminent center for driver training and practice. The new members designated a chief driver and a linguist, who were to facilitate the work of the union, and the new officers swore an oath of office on a steering wheel.[1]

In organizing themselves into a union, La drivers were participating in a broader culture of associational life among entrepreneurial African drivers

---

1. Gene Quarshie (Chairman), P. Ashai Ollennu (Vice-Chairman), and Simon Djetey Abe (Secretary), La Drivers' Union Officers Group, La, Accra, 23 March 2009, interview by the author.

in the 1930s – one that drew both on the international language of trade unionism and indigenous cultures of labor organization. The material and symbolic culture of chieftaincy ("chief driver", "linguist", for example) was the most visible and superficial example of the extent to which local practices of work and authority influenced an emerging union culture among drivers. The organizing strategies and practices of drivers formed the framework of a "mobility system" rooted in cultures of masculinity, respectability, apprenticeship, entrepreneurialism, and state regulation in the region.[2] By adapting these indigenous practices to emerging systems of trade unionism, drivers in La and throughout the colony sought to organize their work to provide better service for passengers and represent their interests to the state.

The culture of drivers' unions and work lives differed substantially from the unionized railway workers, dockworkers, civil service employees, and other waged laborers who followed more conventional models of union organization and who participated in forms of work defined by British colonial capitalism. By transporting goods for trade, drivers were central to systems of exchange and accumulation in the colony, facilitating the expansion of a colonial capitalist economy. While drivers derived socio-economic benefits from this system, which they used to establish lives of masculine respectability and prestige in colonial society, they did so with significantly greater autonomy than other African workers in the colonial economy. Most drivers were self-employed, owning their own vehicles and solely controlling the profits from their business. In transporting both goods and people throughout the colony, drivers, as indigenous entrepreneurs, facilitated the connections and mobility of overlapping entrepreneurial networks. Peasant farmers, market traders, and drivers worked together to reshape the colonial economy and defined a new future for their country, not in political terms, but through the language and practices of economic self-interest. Likewise, drivers, who were largely self-employed, interpreted the function and structure of unions in light of indigenous practices of the organization of labor and the expression and exercise of authority.

The unionization of drivers reflected the culmination of nearly three decades of African attempts to claim control of motor transportation from the colonial authorities and regulate access to it on their own terms. Africans appropriated motor vehicles in large numbers soon after their introduction into the Gold Coast Colony in the first decade of the twentieth century. By the 1930s, motor transportation was well established as an important commercial activity among Africans in the southern Gold Coast, providing economic opportunities for young African men outside colonial pathways of education and respectability and enabling Africans to define their own version of modern mobility. Drivers were entrepreneurs,

2. John Urry, *Mobilities* (Cambridge, 2007), p. 116.

who saved their profits to purchase their own vehicles and attain economic autonomy. By transporting both goods and people and connecting rural villages with urban markets, drivers provided an essential public service, which facilitated the continued growth of the Gold Coast market economy and the prosperity of traders and cocoa farmers throughout the southern half of the colony. At the same time, it challenged colonial attempts to control African mobility and economic activity.

By the 1930s, it became clear to colonial officials that African motor transportation could no longer be ignored. After decades of neglect in road construction and maintenance and limited investment in motor transport regulation and infrastructure, the British colonial state implemented a new and extensive set of motor traffic regulations in 1934, which sought to control motor transportation more directly, defining both driving practice as well as "the type of man who could be a driver". In response, drivers organized themselves into countless local professional associations, such as the Bekwai Transport Union, and national umbrella organizations like the Gold Coast Motor Union. These organizations quickly engaged in strikes, as well as petition-writing campaigns to the colonial Governor, seeking to limit the effects of the shifting parameters of government regulation on drivers' livelihoods.

In forming associations and unions, self-employed drivers appropriated the language and practices of British trade unionism rooted in the experiences of the British working class – waged workers in the employ of industrial capital. Based on such a definition of trade unionism, scholars of African labor unions in the decades immediately following independence criticized these organizing efforts, which in their view, focused too much on either state employees and or the self-employed.[3] The centralized nature of colonial capitalism – in which both labor and resources were concentrated in the extractive structures of the colonial state – limited the growth of African industry and independent waged labor. Thus, unionized Africans directed their activities towards the state, which regulated the conditions of work for both state employees and self-employed groups throughout the colony.

Dockworkers and railway workers, in particular, used their unions to speak out against the abuses of colonial rule and the conditions of life for the African working class in a number of colonies.[4] In part, the success of

3. See, for example, R.B. Davison, "Labor Relations in Ghana", *Annals of the American Academy of Political and Social Science*, 310 (March 1957), pp. 133–141; Jon Kraus, "African Trade Unions: Progress or Poverty?", *African Studies Review*, 19:3 (December 1976), pp. 95–108; Charles A. Orr, "Trade Unionism in Colonial Africa", *The Journal of Modern African Studies*, 4 (1966), pp. 65–81.
4. Frederick Cooper, *Decolonization and African Society: The Labor Question in French and British Africa* (Cambridge, 1996); idem, *On the African Waterfront: Urban Disorder and the*

dockworkers and railway workers' unions lay in their conventionality; these unions mobilized state employees and waged laborers who protested the conditions of their employment and engaged in collective bargaining. However, trade unionism on the continent extended far beyond the limits of the continent's relatively small waged labor force, incorporating entrepreneurs, traders, farmers, and drivers, among others, in a widespread labor movement, which had widely varying political motivations and organizing strategies. The expansiveness and inclusiveness of African trade unionism often drew criticisms from early observers, who argued that the appropriation of the union model by unconventional sectors of the labor force reflected the degree to which Africans failed to understand the meaning and function of unions.[5]

African trade unions were indeed different from their British models. However, trade unionism did not emerge (or arrive) in a vacuum. British trade unionists sent to the Gold Coast met a complex set of societies with their own structures, rules, and logics of labor organization. As scholars like Fred Cooper and Keletso Atkins have demonstrated elsewhere on the continent, African workers often interpreted European conditions and expectations of labor in light of indigenous cultures of work.[6] In taking these indigenous cultures of work seriously, we must also consider "what African workers brought to the workplace".[7] Much like the ways in which Africans appropriated and adapted Western structures to make them locally meaningful in other aspects of colonial society, culture, and economy, unions did not merely appear as an importation but rather emerged from and in collaboration with local cultures and practices of work. Both unions and indigenous forms of labor organization and economic accumulation were transformed in the process.

This article explores the meaning and significance of early union formation among self-employed African drivers in light of these scholarly

Transformation of Work in Colonial Mombasa (New Haven, CT, 1987); Richard Jeffries, *Class, Power and Ideology in Ghana: The Railwaymen of Sekondi* (Cambridge, 2009); Lisa Lindsay, *Working with Gender: Wage Labor and Social Change in Southwestern Nigeria* (Portsmouth, NH, 2003).

5. Roger Scott, "Are Trade Unions Still Necessary in Africa?", *Transition* 33 (October–November 1967), pp. 27–31; Lester N. Trachtman, "The Labor Movement of Ghana: A Study in Political Unionism", *Economic Development and Cultural Change*, 10 (1962), pp. 183–200.
6. Cooper, *On the African Waterfront*; idem, *From Slaves to Squatters: Plantation Labor and Agriculture in Zanzibar and Coastal Kenya, 1890–1925* (New Haven, CT, 1981); Keletso Atkins, *The Moon is Dead! Give Us Our Money! The Cultural Origins of an African Work Ethic, Natal, South Africa, 1843–1900* (Portsmouth, NH, 1993).
7. Ibrahim Abdullah, "Rethinking African Labor and Working-Class History: The Artisan Origins of the Sierra Leonean Working Class", *Social History*, 23 (1998), pp. 80–96, 80; Frederick Cooper, "Work, Class and Empire: An African Historian's Retrospective on E.P. Thompson", *Social History*, 20 (1995), pp. 235–241, 236.

discourses about "indigenous cultures of work" and the emergence of pre-colonial working-class consciousness among artisans and other tradespeople along the West African littoral.[8] In particular, I argue that the emergence of drivers' unions in the 1920s and 1930s, and the structure and function of those unions, highlight the wide range of strategies for social and economic organization available to workers in the Gold Coast. Particularly among workers, such as drivers, who operated outside the conventional categories of the colonial economy (wage laborer, subsistence farmer, slave, for instance), unions provided only one of many models for labor organization. Drivers also strategically drew on indigenous cultures of entrepreneurialism, apprenticeship, and chieftaincy in order to organize their labor and secure respect, authority, and legitimacy, among both African communities and the colonial state. As a result, drivers' unions that formed in the 1930s looked far different from both British models and indigenous practices of labor organization. These new unions facilitated the continued economic autonomy of drivers in the midst of increasing efforts at state regulation.

In order to understand drivers' practices of labor organization, it is necessary to understand the broader culture and economy of which they were a part. This article situates the emergence of drivers' unions within the various coexisting systems of labor organization in the Gold Coast, paying particular attention to the role of entrepreneurialism, apprenticeship, and the state/chieftaincy in local economies of production and trade. Drivers drew on these indigenous cultures and practices of work in order to guarantee their legitimacy and authority among local populations. When the state required union formation and registration in the 1930s as a condition of negotiation, drivers adapted these local practices within a union framework. In the process, they reshaped expectations and understandings of both local economies and union organization.

MULTIPLE LANGUAGES OF LABOR

In the Gold Coast, African engagement with the British colonial cash economy as either waged laborers or entrepreneurs in the nineteenth and twentieth centuries drew on a much longer history of economic activity at local, regional, and trans-continental levels. Similar to the ways in which laborers in southern and eastern Africa brought indigenous understandings of work to the farms, docks, and railways of these British settler colonies, African understandings of labor in the Gold Coast were also rooted in long-standing indigenous cultures of work. In particular, indigenous

---

8. Abdullah, "Rethinking African Labor and Working-Class History"; Peter Gutkind, "The Canoemen of the Gold Coast (Ghana): A Survey and an Exploration in Precolonial African Labour History", *Cahiers d'Etudes Africaines*, 29 (1989), pp. 339–376.

political leaders controlled access to land and resources within local economies that were dominated by entrepreneurs and organized through systems of apprenticeship. Through these systems of labor organization, both leaders and the general population sought to balance the regulation of resources and infrastructure with the values of economic autonomy and entrepreneurialism.

Local labor practices and economic institutions were part of regional and transnational networks of trade and exchange, which connected Africans throughout the western part of the continent and spurred local economic production. Local leaders who sought to profit from these trade networks engaged in often large-scale mobilization and organization of labor for agriculture, trade, mining, and other pursuits.[9] Labor organization for both local production needs and long-distance trade throughout the southern Gold Coast inevitably varied among economic sectors and ethnic groups. Among politically centralized Akan communities in the forests of the interior, agriculture and gold mining tended to be more directly controlled by chiefs, who mobilized the labor of villagers to tend their own farms or work in mines and who controlled access to land and at least a portion of the produce of individual effort in the form of tribute and/or taxes. However, much of the profits from agricultural produce like palm oil and cocoa remained with entrepreneurial cash-crop farmers.

When cocoa production surpassed palm oil as the colony's major export in the nineteenth century, cocoa farmers also had to mobilize and control labor to work their rapidly expanding farms, often accumulating multiple wives and children to provide farm labor and employing local youth and women to tend farms and help with the harvest and transport.[10] While occupations were gendered, the boundaries of that gendered division of labor had shifted by the early twentieth century with the introduction and expansion of cocoa farming. As men left the markets to set up cocoa farms, women took their place, utilizing new technologies of mobility to dominate both local and long-distance trade throughout the region.[11] Young men and women learned trades and skills through formal or informal apprenticeships, assisting (often related) adults in work on farms, at mines, at the market, or in the water. Among less centralized societies

9. As Beverly Grier argues, in pre-colonial societies where land was abundant, but population densities were relatively low, "the struggle to control labor power was at the heart of social and political organization"; Beverly Grier, "Pawns, Porters, and Petty Traders: Women in the Transition to Cash Crop Agriculture in Colonial Ghana", *Signs*, 17 (1992), pp. 304–328, 307.
10. *Ibid.*
11. Gracia Clark, *Onions Are My Husband: Survival and Accumulation by West African Market Women* (Chicago, IL, 1995); Claire Robertson, *Sharing the Same Bowl: A Socioeconomic History of Women and Class in Accra, Ghana* (Bloomington, IN, 1984); Jean Allman and Victoria Tashjian, *I Will Not Eat Stone: A Women's History of Colonial Asante* (Portsmouth, NH, 2000); Stephan Miescher, *Making Men in Ghana* (Bloomington, IN, 2005).

like the Ga, commercial activities such as fishing and the trade in smoked fish were often also organized at the household level, as both men and women collected, processed, and traded the coastal commodity.[12]

Across all of these societies, however, the state played a central role in regulating access to resources and dictating the conditions of possibility for various forms of work. The state often maintained a much tighter control on the activities of traders, who generated significant wealth. In Asante, for example, individuals had to obtain the permission of the Asantehene (King of the Asante) in order to travel for the purposes of trade. Although Asante traders were, to a large extent, entrepreneurs, they represented the Asante state in their trading activities.[13] Other groups of "artisans", including weavers, blacksmiths, goldsmiths, and musicians, were often employed directly by the royal court, which protected access to privileged royal symbols and technical skills passed down through formal apprenticeships.[14]

Despite the importance of the state in regulating economic conditions and possibilities, however, Kwame Arhin argues that even in politically centralized states like the Asante, "[t]here were [...] no landlords and tenants, owners of capital and labourers. There were husbands and wives as owners of farms, master craftsmen, and long-distance traders, and their *nnipa* (sing. *onipa*), lit. 'human beings', but in this context dependants, who did not belong to socially or politically opposed groups."[15] For some members of Asante communities, these small-scale economic activities enabled them to take their places within a relatively hierarchical Asante state and society. However, for others, the relative autonomy of the Asante economy made it possible to establish themselves as "indigenous entrepreneurs".[16]

These "indigenous entrepreneurs" played a significant role in shaping the social, political, and economic possibilities of Asante society – a significance acknowledged by their distinguished status as *obirempon* (Asante Twi: "big men"). As Dumett explains through his analysis of African merchants, the category of "entrepreneur" should not be casually applied to every small-scale economic agent. However, "[a]n entrepreneur certainly does not have to be an industrialist; he can be a trader, farmer, or

12. Robertson, *Sharing the Same Bowl*.
13. There are, of course, exceptions to this general statement, as illustrated by Kwame Arhin, "Trade, Accumulation and the State in Asante in the Nineteenth Century", *Africa*, 60 (1990), pp. 524–537.
14. J.H. Kwabena Nketia, *Drumming in Akan Communities of Ghana* (London, 1963).
15. Kwame Arhin, "Rank and Class among the Asante and Fante in the Nineteenth Century", *Africa*, 53 (1983), p. 5.
16. Raymond Dumett, "Tropical Forests and West African Enterprise: The Early History of the Ghana Timber Trade", *African Economic History*, 29 (2001), pp. 79–116, 92.

skilled craftsman." Entrepreneurs are "change agents" who organize production and distribution in novel ways.[17] Entrepreneurialism does not,
however, negate the importance of the state in organizing and regulating
economic activity and access to capital and resources. Even in "port cities"[18]
at the edge of the Sahara and on the coast, where a professional class of
traders operated for personal profit rather than as direct agents of the state,
local leaders, colonial officials and European merchant houses often heavily
mediated access to both goods and transport.[19]

While indigenous understandings of work and economy profoundly
shaped early interactions with Europeans, the increase in European trade
and the introduction of the cash economy beginning in the fifteenth
century also introduced new forms and understandings of work and
economic accumulation. Early coastal trading interactions spawned a
number of new occupational categories or expanded existing occupations,
including but not limited to traders, canoe men, and carriers. Africans
who engaged in the earliest forms of casual waged labor at the coast
organized for the purposes of bargaining for better pay and working
conditions. Their importance as a labor force was crucial to the functioning of the colonial economy, adding extra weight to their demands
in interactions with early European traders and colonial officials in
the eighteenth and early nineteenth centuries. Canoe men, for example,
who, in large part due to their autonomy as casual workers, could
withdraw their labor in protest over conditions and pay, regularly
halted economic activity at the coast to the detriment of European
commercial interests.[20] However, these casual workers also largely
followed indigenous patterns of labor organization, rooted in the efforts
of individual entrepreneurs and their apprentices, operating within
limitations imposed by the colonial state and the demands of merchants
operating at coastal ports.

CULTURES OF WORK AND THE MOBILITY OF MOTOR TRANSPORTATION

Early economic interactions between Europeans and Africans laid the
foundation for a colonial economy in the nineteenth and twentieth centuries
that was heavily dependent on the economic contributions of African
entrepreneurs in agriculture, mining, trade, and transportation. While some

17. *Idem*, "African Merchants of the Gold Coast, 1860–1905: Dynamics of Indigenous
Entrepreneurship", *Comparative Studies in Society and History*, 25 (1983), pp. 661–693,
662–664.
18. Ghislaine Lydon, *On Trans-Saharan Trails: Islamic Law, Trade Networks, and Cross-
Cultural Exchange in Nineteenth Century Western Africa* (Cambridge, 2012).
19. Dumett, "African Merchants of the Gold Coast".
20. Gutkind, "Canoemen of the Gold Coast".

of these sectors experienced significant transformation in response to new technologies and resources, both colonial officials' and African workers' expectations of the colony's economic future were rooted in indigenous economic practices and networks. African men took up work as motor transport drivers in this context of broader economic activity in the Gold Coast. In particular, the expansion of motor transportation and driving as an occupational category grew directly out of the activities of cocoa farmers, who viewed motor vehicles as a wise investment in the 1920s and 1930s.[21]

By the cocoa boom of the 1920s, farmers, traders, and a new category of African transport owners and drivers began to construct their own networks and means of transportation, often outside colonial government control and contrary to government interests. Motor transportation not only provided a new form of entrepreneurship that was accessible to Africans in the Gold Coast, it also allowed farmers and traders to assert greater control over the production and trade in primary commodities such as cocoa.[22] Parallel to this increasing demand for vehicles, after World War I the Gold Coast was also home to a much larger population of drivers. While deployed in East Africa during World War I, half of the Mechanical Transport Unit of the Gold Coast Regiment received training as drivers. Many of those who returned found work as drivers in the booming cocoa industry of the 1920s. Soon drivers began establishing independent services, purchasing vehicles and hiring out their services to traders, farmers, and other travellers. By 1930, 4,987 vehicles were licensed in the Gold Coast Colony.[23]

Emerging systems of training for drivers also reflected both the continuities and broader transformations in the colonial economy. Much like the apprenticeship systems that had traditionally served to train young men and women in adult occupations, drivers developed systems of

---

21. As Polly Hill argues, lorry ownership and operation were some of the only "common forms of economic enterprise which sprang directly from cocoa farming". By the beginning of what Hill characterizes as the "lorry age" in 1918, "it became the fashion, for those who could afford it, to travel by lorry for most of the way" during their migrations as cocoa farmers; Polly Hill, *The Migrant Cocoa-Farmers of Southern Ghana: A Study in Rural Capitalism* (London, 1998), pp. 190, 234.

22. The lorry is so important to the rise of cocoa that Polly Hill uses the advent of the lorry to establish periodization in her study of migrant Akwapim cocoa farmers. She argues that 1918 marked the end of the pre-lorry age, which corresponds with evidence of an increase in the number of drivers post-World-War-I as well as the increased investment in road building as a result of Guggisberg's Ten Year Development Plan. See Hill, *The Migrant Cocoa Farmers of Southern Ghana*, p. 6.

23. Public Records and Archives Administration Department, National Archives of Ghana, Accra, Ghana [hereafter, PRAAD-NAG], Colonial Secretary's Office [hereafter, CSO] 14/2/329 Road Transportation Board – Formation of.

Figure 1. "Mammy Trucks", 18 July 1968. A driver's mate stands beside a mammy truck loaded with passengers in Accra. While the photograph dates from the 1960s, this type of vehicle had been in use since the 1930s, with the structure of the vehicle generally unchanged from the earliest forms of mass-produced vehicles. Both drivers and passengers referred to these vehicles as "Bedfords", after the British truck manufacturer, which dominated early imports. "Bedford" came to represent a category of vehicle, consisting of an imported metal chassis and a locally constructed wooden body. Drivers and mates could easily change vehicles from passenger to goods transport depending on the nature of their trips.
Photograph: George A. Alhassan. Copyright: Ministry of Information (Ghana), Information Services Photographic Archive, ref no. R/R/9175/13. Used with permission.

training through which apprentices would learn the craft and skill of driving work. These apprentice drivers, or mates, entered into relationships that were similar in many ways to indigenous apprenticeships among skilled artisans. Families often presented masters with drinks (beer, gin, and/or *akpeteshie*),[24] cigarettes, and cash in payment for their services, which then indentured the young man to the master as his "mate".

---

24. *Akpeteshie* is a type of local gin distilled from palm wine. For more information on the history of *akpeteshie*, see Emmanuel Akyeampong, "What's in a Drink? Class Struggle, Popular Culture and the Politics of *Akpeteshie* (Local Gin) in Ghana 1930–67", *Journal of African History*, 37 (1996), pp. 215–236.

Being a mate entailed a number of responsibilities, including the basic maintenance and cleanliness of the vehicle (washing the vehicle, checking vehicle fluid levels, for instance), loading and unloading goods, obtaining passengers (i.e. fighting for passengers) in lorry parks, aiding the master in repairing the vehicle, and other domestic responsibilities in the master's household, including ironing, pounding *fufu*,[25] sweeping, and cleaning. In exchange, mates were often given lodging and food, as well as driver training. Driving apprenticeships were also highly gendered, and driving was considered inherently masculine work that required both physical and mental strength to survive the difficulties and dangers of the road.

For those who grew up in communities like La (a suburb east of Accra), which was closely associated with driving in the first decades of the twentieth century and where driving had been established as a dominant occupation since at least the 1910s, young men saw driving as a desirable and respected family tradition. As a result, entering into an apprenticeship as a driver's mate seemed like a natural extension of local economies and cultures of work. For drivers like J.F. Ocantey, growing up in a household and community of drivers exposed him to the profession and its skills early and the sons of drivers often followed their fathers, uncles, or elder brothers into the profession. Driving, for Ocantey, was a "hobby" from an early age, and early exposure gained through helping relatives inculcated a passion for driving work and provided him with early training.[26]

When Ocantey later entered into an apprenticeship under master driver N.V. Labadi he fully understood the profession in both its technical and social dimensions, and he benefited from the support and encouragement of family members. As Ocantey describes, for those who grew up in La, driving was "in their blood":

> For the driving, they born us in the driving work because where we were born from, driving is the work that most of the people have been doing. That is the reason why – our area here in La, we like driving. You should understand that La people are the people who brought driving into the system because the first driver in Ghana here, he come from La. Before it spread around the whole of Ghana – it's La it started from. The thing is, this man sitting here – his father is a driver, so he was born in the driving work because his father is driving, and I myself too, my senior brother was a driver so any time he always bring cars to the house so even if he's not there and I enter the car, once you spark the car and you accelerate it, the car will move. So that is what we've been doing – once our fathers or brothers brought the cars to the house for us to wash, we would be

25. *Fufu* is a local food staple, most commonly made by pounding cassava and plantain (though also sometimes with yam). *Fufu* is pounded with a large mortar and pestle and often requires two people – one to pound and one to turn the product.
26. Ibrahim Ato, Anum Sowah, Yii O. Yem, J.F. Ocantey, La Drivers' Union Group Interview, Accra, 26 March 2009, interview by the author.

sparking the cars and that brought our interest, so that make us to have the interest of the driving work.[27]

For those young men without any family connections to the driving profession or who did not come from a community of drivers, driving work was appealing precisely because of its novelty. Young boys like Coblah Nimo who lived in farming and fishing communities often stopped work to watch as "mammy" trucks and other motor vehicles passed. Mammy trucks, which were named for their most frequent passengers (market women, aka "mammies"), were hybrid vehicles, consisting of an imported metal engine and chassis and a locally constructed and painted wooden body. In the first half of the twentieth century, mammy trucks dominated Gold Coast roads, as drivers carried market women into the interior to purchase produce from farms and regional markets or to transport the produce of wealthy cocoa farmers to coastal ports. Traveling past villages and farms, these vehicles captured the attention of many young boys who were working or playing along the roadside. The fascination with cars extended into play, as boys pretended to be drivers, improvising imagined vehicles and "blowing" horns (*porpor*) as they traveled back and forth to collect water.[28] When motor vehicles arrived in their villages, children swarmed around them, looking at themselves in the reflection of the metallic chassis and sitting behind the steering wheels pretending to drive.[29] Many of those who ultimately became drivers described themselves as completely occupied – if not spellbound – by the vehicle and its driver, and saw driving as a calling or vocation that was "in their heart".

However, for boys in rural areas outside driving communities, the pursuit of driving and the experience of apprenticeship as mates marked a distinctly different occupational path from that of their families.[30] While many parents ultimately sought out connections through extended family to secure apprenticeships for their sons with respected masters, such training often implied relocation – as mates looked for masters in major cities like Accra, where most drivers were based. For these young men and their families, embracing motor transportation as an occupation and engaging in the apprenticeship system marked a significant diversion from local economies and communities, even as their mobility connected these communities to larger markets and systems of economic exchange. Regardless of their background, however, most young mates received the same training in the technical and social skills of driving work. Saving

27. *Ibid.*
28. *Ibid.*
29. Anonymous Circle Odawna Driver, Accra, 27 August 2009, interview by the author.
30. Ibrahim Ato, Anum Sowah, Yii O. Yem, J.F. Ocantey, La Drivers' Union Group Interview, Accra, 26 March 2009, interview by the author; Abraham Tagoe, Teshie Linguist, Accra, 5 August 2009, interview by the author.

money through their work as mates and apprentices, young drivers sought to purchase their own vehicles. Validated by both their masters and the licensing test of the colonial state, young drivers entered the professional world of commercial motor transportation as professional, skilled workers and self-employed entrepreneurs, ready to take advantage of the possibilities for accumulation and respectability that driving promised.

By the 1930s, these drivers had established themselves as an important commercial industry, undermining the profits of the state-owned railways and dominating the colony's transport industry. Their popularity reflected the degree to which drivers successfully used the emerging technology of the motor vehicle to provide essential services for African economic agents. Unlike railways, which represented British understanding of mobility and economic productivity, motor transportation corresponded more directly with the needs and values of African entrepreneurs, who sought to minimize cost and maximize profit for their produce or trade goods. Drivers connected rural African farmers with urban coastal markets and provided a crucial link that transcended the divides between rural and urban life, which characterized the infrastructure, bureaucracy, and economy of indirect rule. In providing a new way for Africans to express the needs and desires of mobility and profitability, drivers acted as the "change agents", altering the economic and social landscape for both Africans and Europeans in the Gold Coast at the same time as they drew on indigenous cultures of occupational training and commerce.

REGULATING AND ORGANIZING DRIVERS IN THE BRITISH GOLD COAST

The consolidation of motor transport as a legitimate commercial activity in the Gold Coast was paralleled by a professionalization of driving and drivers as both government officials and drivers themselves created rules and codes of conduct that regulated the industry and its participants. Drivers and government officials embraced the apprenticeship system as an important means by which young men became professionalized as drivers. Viewed through the lens of indirect rule, state appropriation of the indigenous apprenticeship system facilitated a more effective means of vocational training than colonial schools or vocational institutions in a wide range of occupations without additional state investment in educational infrastructure or occupational training.[31] However, government disengagement with driver training was also part of a larger dismissal of the emerging motor transport industry throughout the first decades of the twentieth century.

31. PRAAD-NAG (Accra) RG 3/5/1134 "The Gold Coast Apprenticeship System", Annual Report of the Department of Labour, 1938–1939, Commissioner of Labour to the Colonial Governor.

Having invested heavily in the railways as the colony's new means of evacuating the produce of farms in the interior for export at coastal ports in the late nineteenth and early twentieth centuries, colonial officials at this time sought to discourage the growth of motor transportation, refusing to build roads or maintain infrastructure, as part of an attempt to address the empire-wide problem that Colonial Secretary Lord Passfield termed "road vs. rail competition".[32] When these initial efforts failed to deter African drivers and passengers, colonial officials instituted a system of road breaks and passes that would limit African access to roads and undermine the profitability and ease of motor transportation.[33]

Government lack of interest in encouraging the growth of motor transportation and their attempts to protect their investment in the railway as the colony's primary form of transportation created opportunities for investment and entrepreneurialism for Africans who appropriated new technologies to meet the needs of an increasingly mobile African public with disposable income. If vehicles numbered only 16 in 1908, by 1932 there were 4,141 commercial motor vehicles and 1,618 private cars and taxis registered on the Gold Coast. By the end of the 1930s, there were over 5,501 commercial vehicles and 2,076 private cars and taxis.[34]

The growth in car ownership and commercial motor transport practice in spite of government attempts to suppress it meant that, instead of shaping the industry through regulation from the beginning, colonial officials had to impose regulations on an industry that was already well-established in its own system of occupational practice. In implementing these regulations, colonial officials were motivated by a complex set of goals that reflected the often contradictory ideals of the colonial project. On the one hand, transportation was central to the profitability of the colonial economy, which colonial officials sought to control through the railways. The growth of motor transportation undermined government control over the movement of people and goods in the colony and threatened state profits from the railways, even as it facilitated trade. On the other hand, the popularity and affordability of motor vehicles brought increasing numbers of vehicles to Gold Coast roads, and advances in technology enabled drivers to carry heavier loads at higher speeds than ever before.

32. The National Archives (United Kingdom) [hereafter, TNA]: PRO CO 323/1339/8 Transport – Road and Rail Competition, 1935; PRAAD-NAG (Accra) CSO 14/2/23 1930–1931 Road and Rail Competition; TNA: PRO CO 937/49/4 1947 Transport – Road and Rail Competition; TNA: PRO CO 323/1393/3 1936 Transport – Road and Rail Competition; TNA: PRO CO 262/652 Sierra Leone Railway-road competition, Gold Coast Model 1936.
33. PRAAD-NAG (Accra) CSO 14/2/150 1929–1947 Road Policy.
34. PRAAD-NAG (Accra) CSO 15/1/65 1932–1940 Registration Statistics of Motor Vehicles Abroad – Forms for.

Figure 2. "The driver, Murphy, waits patiently for his turn while his mate cleans the bonnet". There was no date attached to this photograph recorded in the archival record. Apprenticeship systems trained prospective young drivers or "mates", pairing them with master drivers. Mates performed basic maintenance on the vehicles, and often also performed chores for their masters. By observing the work of their masters, mates gradually gained the knowledge and skills required for driving work. As this image and its caption also highlight, drivers' work was just as often defined by immobility and waiting for passengers.
From A Day in the Life of a Tro-tro Driver. *Photograph: Ben Kwakye. Copyright Ministry of Information (Ghana), Information Services Photographic Archive, ref. no. PS/1877/6. Used with permission.*

These changes undoubtedly presented an existential danger of accidents for passengers and pedestrians on and alongside the colony's poorly maintained roads in rural and urban areas. Both African leaders and colonial officials sought to mitigate these dangers in the name of public safety and "public interest", implementing new restrictions on the speed and roadworthiness of vehicles and investing in road construction and improvements. Drivers, however, argued that these new regulations placed an unfair burden on drivers, who sought to mitigate the risk posed by poorly constructed and maintained roads while also maximizing profits. Colonial interest in regulating drivers in the 1930s also appeared hypocritical in light of several decades of government disengagement and economic sabotage.

Government attempts to regulate motor transportation culminated in the 1934 Motor Traffic Ordinance. Government regulations had long mandated the size, weight, and speed of vehicles. However, by requiring drivers to be literate (i.e. be able to read and understand the Motor Traffic Ordinance and to read road signs), undergo physical examinations, and submit certificates of competency, the colonial state increasingly attempted to dictate who could and who could not be a driver. By asserting control over the access to and use of their vehicles and by defining the qualifications necessary to be a driver, the colonial state and its representatives also asserted control over the possibility and prosperity of drivers' work. The colonial government subsidized the price of petrol, as well as essential imported goods like tires and spare parts. Thus, even if drivers owned their own vehicles, the ability to run those vehicles commercially and profitably was highly dependent on the actions of government – both through its institutions (Legislative Assembly, Ministry of Transportation, Ministry of Trade, etc.) and through individual representatives (licensing officers, police officers, etc.).

Increasing state efforts to control drivers and define the conditions of their training, qualifications, and work coincided with the growing professionalization of drivers, who had begun to view themselves as a powerful social and economic force by the 1930s. The professionalization of driving as an occupation and socio-economic category was manifested most clearly in the emergence of unions. While drivers' associations had undoubtedly existed prior to 1930, the formation of the Gold Coast Motor Union, the Ashanti Motor Transport Union, the La Drivers' Union, and others in the 1930s marked the first large-scale attempts at organizing the multitude of individual (African) owner-operators who comprised the largest proportion of the motor transport industry in the Gold Coast. Dominated by ex-servicemen who had been trained to drive while serving in the Gold Coast Regiment in the 1920s, these new unions established rules of personal behavior (how to drive, how to conduct yourself with passengers, how to dress, how to maintain your vehicle, etc.) as well as rules of procedure (training drivers, resolving disputes, punishing bad behavior, organizing in the lorry park, setting fares, interacting with the police, petitioning the government, etc.).[35]

Driver appropriation of the language and structures of unions reflected both the influence of African radical politics and the importance of British trade unionism in interwar colonial governance. Throughout the 1930s, radical African political activists like Bankole Awooner-Renner and Isaac Theophilus Akunna (I.T.A.) Wallace-Johnson sought to organize workers

---

35. PRAAD-NAG (Accra) CSO 17/1/24 1935–1937 Motor Traffic Ordinance and Regulations 1934 – Petitions against.

into unions as part of a broader political project of anti-colonial resistance.[36] As the historian Denzer notes, "For a radical journalist and trade unionist, Accra in the 1930s was perhaps the most dynamic place in West Africa for political debate."[37] Wallace-Johnson joined other activists including J.B. Danquah and Nnamdi Azikiwe in the Gold Coast to form the West African Youth League (WAYL) in 1935. Both within and outside the confines of the WAYL, Wallace-Johnson and others worked to organize African workers from a number of different sectors (including drivers) into unions, which he believed would mobilize Africans against colonial rule and raise awareness about social, political, and economic rights among the African public.[38]

Awooner-Renner and Wallace-Johnson drew on Marxist and Leninist ideas from the Soviet Union and European labor movements, as well as earlier labor movements within the continent itself. In the Gold Coast, the first miners' strike occurred in 1919, and a number of labor unions – the Gold and Silver Smiths' Association, the Gold Coast and Ashanti Motor Union, and the Carpenters' and Masons' Union – all formed in the 1920s. The La Drivers' Union itself emerged in 1935 in response to these efforts at labor organization, drawing together drivers in the heart of the motor transport industry. However, the La Drivers' Union and other motor unions, like many other early labor organizations that formed in the first decades of the twentieth century, did not fit comfortably within conventional definitions of labor unions promoted by British trade unionists working within the colonial government.

Concerned about the strikes by railway workers and other types of labor unrest across the continent in the 1930s and pressured by a metropolitan Labour Party government, British colonial officials in the Gold Coast and elsewhere brought in trade unionists to train workers in union organization.[39] Government officials in Britain and the Gold Coast argued that the labor unrest was the result of lack of organization and training among early unions in the art of collective bargaining, which lay at the foundation of British trade unionism.[40] Eager to curb strikes that were crippling the colonial economy, trade unionists arranged "education" sessions for African union officials and sponsored representatives of the largest unions to travel to Britain for more advanced training.[41]

---

36. LaRay Denzer, "Wallace-Johnson and the Sierra Leone Labor Crisis of 1939", *African Studies Review*, 25:2/3 (1982), pp. 159–183, 162.
37. *Ibid.*, p. 165.
38. Leo Spitzer and LaRay Denzer, "I.T.A. Wallace-Johnson and the West African Youth League", *International Journal of African Historical Studies*, 6 (1973), pp. 413–452.
39. R.B. Davison, "Labor Relations in Ghana", p. 135.
40. *Ibid.*
41. *Ibid.*; PRAAD-NAG (Accra) CSO 14/1/711 1940–1946 Courses of Instruction in Labour Problems.

In order to facilitate collective bargaining and to maintain some control over emerging workers' organizations, colonial officials encouraged the centralization of smaller unions into larger umbrella structures, which were then registered with the government beginning in the early 1940s. Such efforts were geared toward limiting the influence of the radical politics of people like Awooner-Renner and Wallace-Johnson. The formal recognition and registration of trade unions also enabled colonial officials better to control and influence the politics of labor organization in the colony. Colonial officials would negotiate only with those unions officially registered with the government, making it difficult for new unions to influence negotiations and enabling the colonial state to marginalize more radical unions in the bargaining process.[42] Entrepreneurial drivers, who directly experienced the consequences of government reforms and regulations, constituted two of the first four unions to register with the government.[43]

Much of the collective bargaining and union organizing of workers in the colonial economy involved the state directly. Colonial capitalism, which centralized economic authority and wealth, privileged the state as the primary source of both jobs and capital.[44] For state employees, like railway workers, collective bargaining over wages, benefits, and working conditions required negotiations with colonial officials. Drivers, by contrast, represented a very different kind of worker in the colonial capitalist economy. As self-employed entrepreneurs, drivers were not "employees" and received neither wages nor benefits directly from the colonial state. However, state actions often produced dramatic changes in the working conditions and profit margins of drivers. As the first real attempt to regulate driver practice, the 1934 Motor Traffic Ordinance marked one of the earliest examples of this relationship, mobilizing drivers across the country to protest government regulations that would redefine "the type of man who could be a driver".[45]

UNIONS AT WORK

In organizing themselves against the state, drivers drew on indigenous understandings of economic regulation and labor organization. As entrepreneurs, drivers operated on a basic assumption that the authorities should provide the appropriate conditions under which their businesses might grow and thrive – an assumption rooted in pre-colonial systems of

42. PRAAD-NAG (Accra) CSO 14/1/789 1943 The Bekwai Motor Transport Union.
43. PRAAD-NAG (Accra) CSO 25/3/132 1942–1946 Trade Unions – Registration of.
44. Davison, "Labor Relations in Ghana", p. 133.
45. PRAAD-NAG (Accra) CSO 15/7/13 1939 Moses Acquaye – Motor driver request for restoration of his driving licence.

political and social organization. For motor transportation, such conditions most obviously included roads – the construction and maintenance of which were necessary in order to reach customers in rural farming communities and markets. Good quality roads also minimized wear on vehicles, necessitating fewer repairs, and allowing a driver to use a vehicle for a longer period of time. The necessary conditions for their work also included inputs like petrol, tires, and spare parts. Drivers relied on subsidized costs for such inputs in order to keep fares low and compete in the transport market. In this sense, the rationale of the drivers was similar to that of other indigenous entrepreneurs: Drivers anticipated that the colonial government would guarantee the basic infrastructure of their work and enable them to secure preferential access to basic resources in the larger service of the public as well as of their own profit. Also, much like other indigenous entrepreneurs, drivers expected significant autonomy on the road itself, regulating their own training and practices to maximize profits and services.

For drivers, unions provided an opportunity not to engage in collective bargaining with the state but rather to pressure the state to limit the regulation of drivers and maintain their focus on what drivers considered a right to basic infrastructure and resources. Particularly in the aftermath of the 1934 Motor Traffic Ordinance, drivers' unions became mouthpieces for complaints about the new regulations and their impact on driver autonomy. Having been officially recognized by the state, many of these unions had the ear of colonial officials, who were obligated to consider and respond to union concerns. Both registered and unregistered motor transport unions engaged in petition-writing campaigns to the colonial Governor, Arnold Hodson. Drivers' protests focused primarily on new literacy requirements that were central to the new physical, social, and intellectual characteristics of "competency" introduced by the 1934 Motor Traffic Ordinance.

According to Chief Transport Officer Cruickshank, the examinations by which applications for Certificates of Competency were evaluated were "held with a view to make sure that the applicants are familiar with the control of a Motor Vehicle and also that they know the Road Signs. This will eventually reduce the number of serious accidents on the roads where many passengers are injured."[46] In practice, however, the new literacy requirements significantly redefined the accessibility of driving as a profession. Before 1934, the skills of drivers were defined by their ability to handle a vehicle.[47] This new literacy requirement – and the

46. PRAAD-NAG (Accra) CSO 15/7/18 1934 Adjei Badoo, Motor driver – Complaint against ETO Mr (Cruickshank).
47. PRAAD-NAG (Accra) CSO 15/7/7 1930 Tetteh Amartey, Motor driver – Complaint against confiscation of his driving licence and 10s fee paid to licensing officer.

broader conversations about competency of which they were a part – reflected an expansion in the understanding of what it meant to be a driver, as well as the state's attempts to control driver practice.

The experiences of drivers themselves directly challenged the clarity and appropriateness of the new requirements. While drivers had long been required to have knowledge of road signs, many of those licensed before 1934 were classified as "illiterate". The new ordinance stipulated that any driver who had obtained his license before the 1934 Ordinance was enacted was exempt from the literacy requirement. The continuing operation of old, illiterate drivers alongside the more recently licensed literate drivers provided a direct challenge to colonial justifications of the literacy requirement. As the Ashanti Motor Union argued, "many of our best drivers are illiterate".[48] In petitioning Governor Hodson, drivers protested what they viewed as a government that was overstepping its rights to regulate driver practice and implementing laws that did not reflect the interests of either drivers or passengers. However, drivers' petitions did not result in any fundamental changes to colonial regulation. Rather, the 1934 Motor Traffic Ordinance was only the first of a series of government efforts to regulate, rationalize, and restrict drivers' practices in an attempt to define African spatial realities and mobility both within and outside the colony's major cities.

Out of frustration, drivers in Accra finally went on strike in 1938. Chief among their complaints was the inadequate provision of lorry parks, which reflected neither the extent of the driver population in the city nor the ways in which people in Accra used lorries.[49] The mobility made possible by motor transportation resulted in increasing numbers of traders bringing goods to sell in the large markets of major urban centers such as Accra.[50] These traders and the mammy trucks/wagons that bore them overwhelmed existing lorry parks, forcing drivers to park illegally in the streets surrounding the city's major market.[51] Furthermore, alternative

48. PRAAD-NAG (Accra) CSO 17/1/39 1935–1938 Ashanti Motor Transport Union, "Petition from Motor Transport Union Ashanti (W.W. Taylor, Secretary) to the Chief Commissioner of Ashanti, November 29th, 1937". See also PRAAD-NAG (Accra) CSO 15/7/81 1939 Mr Kofi Baah – Petition praying for grant of Gold Coast driving license: "I have seen on many occasions that there are some lorry drivers who does not know how to read and write but are Drivers." For other petitions from unions concerning the 1934 Motor Traffic Ordinance and its subsequent amendments, see CSO 15/7/99 1938 Motor Traffic Regulations – Amendments to; CSO 17/1/13 1934 Regulations under the Motor Traffic Ordinance; CSO 17/1/24 1935–1937 Motor Traffic Ordinance and Regulations1934 – Petitions against.
49. PRAAD-NAG (Accra) CSO 14/1/270 1938–1939 Lorry parks, Accra.
50. This period also resulted in a noted shift in the gendered distribution of trading – from men to women, as men increasingly pursued wage labor work and cash-crop farming that had increased throughout the 1910s and 1920s.
51. PRAAD-NAG (Accra) CSO 14/1/270 1938–1939 Lorry parks, Accra; PRAAD-NAG (Accra) CSO 17/4/6 1940–1941 Native Administration – Lorry parks.

markets such as London Market and Salaga Meat Market developed in various parts of the expanding city, and traders in these new markets demanded motor transport to carry their goods.[52] The colonial government quickly responded to the striking motor drivers' demands – seeking out land for new lorry parks and expanding existing lorry parks.

Early strikes were considered troublesome because of their economic impact – a clear indicator of the degree to which the colony had become reliant on motor transportation to facilitate movement both between and within rural and urban areas. The success of the strikes required a strong network of social support from passengers and the broader community. Social sanction of driver protests was rooted in their identification as representatives of working-class African communities as well as the role that motor transportation played in facilitating the growth and prosperity of local economies in both rural and urban areas. In large part, the identification of drivers with the broad base of working-class Africans and indigenous entrepreneurs in the Gold Coast reflected the degree to which unionized drivers also continued to participate in indigenous cultures of work.

However, some unions appealed more directly to local understandings of labor organization and authority. Unions in La and Teshie appropriated the symbols of chieftaincy, and the social and political legitimacy that such symbols implied, to highlight the public responsibilities of drivers and the importance of their role in local communities. The head of the union was known as the "Chief Driver". Chief Drivers were confirmed in their office through a public ceremony, in which the La Manche (chief) (and sometimes even also the Ga Manche or Ga paramount chief), colonial government officials (such as the District Commissioner of Accra), and the larger La community gathered at union offices to witness the new Chief Driver swearing an oath on a steering wheel.[53] This very public investiture emphasized the responsibility that drivers – and in particular the Chief Driver – had in protecting and ensuring the safety and interests of the larger community.[54] Chief Drivers also appropriated the material culture of chieftaincy, appearing in photos wearing leopard-print hats, carrying fly whisks, and speaking through a "linguist", who represented

52. PRAAD-NAG (Accra) CSO 14/1/270 1938–1939 Lorry parks, Accra; PRAAD-NAG (Accra) CSO 14/1/271 1938–1939 Land at Salaga Market Required for a Lorry Park – Ownership of.
53. For more information about Ga governance structures and traditional offices, see John Parker, *Making the Town: Ga State and Society in Early Colonial Accra* (Portsmouth, NH, 2000).
54. Gene Quarshie (Chairman), P. Ashai Ollennu (Vice-Chairman), and Simon Djetey Abe (Secretary), La Drivers' Union Officers Group, La, Accra, 23 March 2009, interview by the author.

Figure 3. Here the first Chief Driver of Teshie was photographed in the mid-1930s wearing kente cloth and a leopard-print hat, both symbols of chieftaincy widely recognized throughout the Gold Coast. Although the Teshie union has since been absorbed into the national Ghana Private Road Transport Union, the photograph is prominently displayed in the Teshie branch office, Accra, Ghana.

Photographed by the author, 2009. Original photograph, property of the Teshie Branch of the Ghana Private Road Transport Union (GPRTU).

the Chief Driver in public appearances and carried his own linguist's staff at public ceremonies, topped with a wooden image of a mammy truck to represent the "clan" of the drivers.[55]

The structure of the La Drivers' Union drew directly from the structure of chieftaincy, which, as a British-invented tradition among Ga communities, had characterized political organization in La and greater Accra since at least the mid-nineteenth century.[56] By appropriating and mobilizing the language and symbols of chieftaincy, motor transport unions in La and Teshie explicitly allied themselves with the people – establishing themselves as the guardians and protectors of the community and their interests. Colonial state regulations of motor transportation that were enacted in what colonial officials understood as the "public interest" failed to grasp not only how drivers were trained and ran their businesses but also what kind of services the public valued. However, the appropriation of the material and symbolic culture of chieftaincy was only the most superficial and visible example of a much broader connection between drivers and local economic and cultural practice. As is clear in the 1938 strike, in organizing themselves into unions and protesting these state regulations, motor transport drivers acted to protect not only their interests but also, perhaps more indirectly, the economic interests and values of their passengers and the broader "culture of work" of which they were a part.

CONCLUSION

In appropriating and adapting trade union structures and practices to reflect indigenous cultures of work, drivers participated in a widespread phenomenon of African trade unionism, which simultaneously bound workers to the state while providing opportunities and foundations for worker resistance to state control. African workers adopted trade-union models in an attempt to counterbalance the power of a centralizing, extractive colonial state that sat at the core of the colonial economy. The characteristics of this colonial economy – the extractive and centralizing nature of colonial capitalism – from the start distinguished Africans' experiences from their trade-union colleagues in Britain. In encouraging the growth of unions, British colonial officials sought "to create, if not people, then societies in their own image"; however, they failed to

---

55. *Ibid.*; Abraham Tagoe, Teshie Linguist, Accra, 5 August 2009, interview by the author.
56. For further information about chieftaincy and the *okyeame*, see Kwesi Yankah, *Speaking for the Chief: Okyeame and the Politics of Akan Royal Oratory* (Bloomington, IN, 1995); Steven J. Salm and Toyin Falola, *Culture and Customs of Ghana* (Westport, CT, 2002); Irene K. Odotei and Albert K. Awedoba (eds), *Chieftaincy in Ghana: Culture, Governance and Development* (Accra, 2006). For discussions of chieftaincy outside Akan communities, see Paul Stacey, *Traditional Uncertainty; Chieftaincy in Northern Ghana: Land Control and Ethnic Conflicts, 1901–1996* (Saarbrücken, 2009); Parker, *Making the Town*.

recognize the extent to which both the foundations of colonial capitalism and the values and practices of indigenous economies differed from metropolitan models.[57] Rather, colonial officials introduced unions in the hope that they would limit strikes and bring workers under the control of the state, by encouraging collective bargaining. In practice, however, the unionization of African workers from various sectors legitimated worker protest and forced the state to reckon with the realities of life for African workers or face resistance.

At the same time, drivers are distinguished from the unionized African workers that have most commonly captured the attention of Africanist scholars. Unlike railway workers and dockworkers, who were often in the direct employ of the colonial state, drivers were self-employed entrepreneurs. Autonomy and entrepreneurialism enabled drivers to craft a culture and practice of unionism and work distinct from British colonial expectations and models. In fact, their work, which made possible new forms of mobility and economic prosperity among Ghanaians in both rural and urban areas, undermined the very assumptions about African inferiority and the necessity of European assistance on which British colonial rule in the Gold Coast was founded and reasserted African control over economic activities.

While it is tempting to see drivers' unions as proto-nationalist organizations, drivers and union leaders did not see their actions as explicitly political, and they did not participate in the nationalist mobilizations of railway workers' unions, for example, in the decades leading up to independence. Individual drivers, of course, could participate in politics, and many did. But drivers' unions were not structures of political mobilization in the early nationalist movement. These choices by union leaders to remain "above the fray" likely reflected the degree to which they believed that, as entrepreneurs who required preferential access to resources in order to remain profitable, their relationship with the state must be productive. This implies some sort of co-optation of union leaders into the structures of state governance. However, their unwillingness to engage in political resistance and nationalist organizing should not detract from the very real implications of their actions for the logics and practices of colonial governance. The entrepreneurialism and autonomy of drivers, their importance to the colonial economy, and the social sanction of their actions provided a powerful check on the colonial state's efforts to remake African economies in the Gold Coast and ignore indigenous economic priorities and practices.[58]

---

57. Davison, "Labor Relations in Ghana", p. 135.

58. I argue elsewhere that these actions represent citizenship claims in the context of colonial rule, rather than resistance – demands for belonging and protection rather than calls to revolution. See Jennifer Hart, "Suffer to Gain: Citizenship, Accumulation, and Motor Transportation in Late-Colonial and Postcolonial Ghana" (Ph.D., Indiana University, 2011).

The unionization of drivers, and the particular union cultures that derived from their organization and registration with the state, highlighted the degree to which drivers very much saw themselves as entrepreneurs defined by their autonomy and control over systems of training and regulation. While they operated within a broad framework of state infrastructure and expected access to subsidized resources, drivers used formally recognized unions to protect their autonomy and economic prosperity in the face of efforts at state regulation and control. The logics and motivations of driver action and the relative success of their petitions and protests were profoundly shaped by indigenous economic values and practices of apprenticeship, entrepreneurialism, and the state/chieftaincy. Much like the union model, drivers also adapted these forms of indigenous economy to better fit the realities of the emerging mobility system of motor transportation. As a result, perhaps even more than their peers in other waged labor occupations, the experiences of drivers suggest that the development and success of trade unions in the Gold Coast reflected not merely an adaptation of an imported metropolitan model, but rather the negotiation of diverse forms of African labor organization.

IRSH 59 (2014), Special Issue, pp. 211–235 doi:10.1017/S0020859014000340
© 2014 Internationaal Instituut voor Sociale Geschiedenis

"Human Telephone Lines": Flag Post Mail Relay Runners in British Southern Cameroon (1916–1955) and the Establishment of a Modern Communications Network

WALTER GAM NKWI

Department of History, University of Buea
PO Box 63, Buea, Republic of Cameroon

E-mail: nkwiwally@yahoo.com

MIRJAM DE BRUIJN

African Studies Centre, Institute for History, Leiden University
PO Box 9500, 2300 RA Leiden, The Netherlands

E-mail: m.e.de.bruijn@hum.leidenuniv.nl

ABSTRACT: The flag post mail relay runners, a communications system established in Cameroon during British colonial rule, laid the foundations for the communications structure of this colonial state. They were a remnant of a pre-colonial communications system and, with the advancement of "modern" communications structures such as roads, telephone lines, and post houses, the flag post runner gradually disappeared. This article explores the role of the runners for the colonial administration in Cameroon and is based mostly on archival research. It describes the runners' system and how it influenced the colonial communications landscape. In addition, the questions of how these runners were involved in the colonial state and what forms of resistance emerged among runners are analysed. Finally, the article discusses the degree to which the subsequent construction of roads, telegraphic communications, and postal networks reflected the role played by mail runners in the British colonial period up to the 1950s.

INTRODUCTION

Communication is one of the backbones of governance and power relations,[1] and therefore understanding communications systems and changes

---

1. Manuel Castells, *Communication Power* (Oxford, 2009); James Gleick, *The Information: A History, a Theory, a Flood* (London, 2011); Mirjam de Bruijn and Rijk van Dijk (eds), *The Social Life of Connectivity in Africa* (New York, 2011).

therein will reveal insights into expected and unexpected power relations and the "making" of power in colonial history. In this article, communications systems comprise all the various ways of organizing communication through the exchange of mail and information with the aid of communications technologies. Important issues include the question of who defines and organizes communications systems and their access rules. What is the history of the communications technologies, and on which and whose ideology are they based? Whose needs are served through this system? The introduction of colonial communications technologies was part of the "modernization" project, of which colonial policies were also part, opening up the hinterland and organizing a "modern" state, a new form of governance. This was not without its problems, including the need to overcome the obstacles of inaccessible roads, long distances, and underpopulation in the larger part of the territory in order to get information and mail moving, and also new forms of resistance.

For British colonial Cameroon, transport and mobility have been little studied. Walter Gam Nkwi's study is an exception, and forms a starting point for the present article.[2] Based on archival research conducted in the Buea National Archives in Cameroon, the Mission 21 Archives in Basel (Switzerland), and the Mill Hill Archives in Oosterbeek (The Netherlands), this article describes the communications systems in Cameroon during the British colonial period from 1916 until the 1950s, focusing on the flag post mail runners. These constituted a kind of "human telephone line". Grasping the reality of this "human telephone line", both in its role as a communications operation and as a lived reality for the runners themselves, is the main aim of this article.

The central question is how this communications system – based on human labour rather than technical devices – formed the basis of later communications technologies, such as the telegraph, road networks, and the telephone. How did the organization of these "human telephone lines" represent flows of information? Probably most importantly for our enquiries here: who were the runners, and how was their labour organized? And how did this organization lay the foundation for a future communications network? One of the ideas underlying this article is that previous systems of communication influence subsequent ones.[3] How did the network of runners and their organization lay the foundations for the communications system, therefore contributing to the foundation of power relations in the late colonial and postcolonial Cameroonian economy and society?

2. See Walter Gam Nkwi, *Kfaang and its Technologies: Towards a Social History of Mobility in Kom, Cameroon, 1928–1998* (Leiden, 2011).
3. Aad Blok, "Introduction", *International Review of Social History*, 48 (2003), Supplement 11, "Uncovering Labour in Information Revolutions, 1750–2000", pp. 1–11.

This article aims to contribute to the knowledge of communication and labour in the social history of Africa, specifically in Cameroon, and seeks to understand power relations between the colonial administration and the mail runners, for whom working for the colonial administration was a way to accumulate wealth and thus enhance their position and power. The world of the mail runner has, at the same time, to be understood as part of a global labour force, which emerged in this period in the context of the colonial system of domination, strongly characterized by exploitation and various forms of forced recruitment, and by systematic attempts by the colonial powers to regulate and control labour relations, which is a characteristic, of course, of every labour regime.[4]

Literature on the topic, especially in relation to labour, is scant. Allied to our topic are the scarce publications on roads and transport. For instance, Stephen Rockel was one of the first researchers to write on transport and transport routes in east and central Africa.[5] The flag post mail runners in Cameroon were not a unique phenomenon; various kinds of runners, messengers, and other communications workers have also existed in other regions of the British Empire, notably in India, and have attracted some attention from historians. Chitra Joshi, for instance, has shown how a similar system of runners played a role in reordering communications networks during the British colonial administration in India. Others have studied the role of the runners, messenger boys, and other workers, and their forms of resistance.[6] These studies have been very useful in helping us to understand the communications systems among human runners in British Cameroon in the early twentieth century.

This article draws on both official and non-official sources.[7] It will first trace the beginnings of the flag post mail runner system and how it drew

---

4. Jan Lucassen (ed.), *Global Labour History: A State of the Art* (Bern, 2006); Marcel van der Linden, "Labour History: The Old, The New and the Global", *African Studies*, 66 (2006), pp. 169–180.

5. See Stephen Rockel, *Carriers of Culture: Labor on the Road in Nineteenth-Century East Africa* (Portsmouth, NH, 2006).

6. Chitra Joshi, "Dak Roads, Dak Runners, and the Reordering of Communication Networks", *International Review of Social History*, 57 (2012), pp. 169–189; Deep Kanta Lahiri Choudhury, "India's First Virtual Community and the Telegraph General Strike of 1908", *International Review of Social History*, 48 (2003), Supplement 11, "Uncovering Labour in Information Revolutions, 1750–2000", pp. 45–71; Gregory J. Downey, *Telegraph Messengers Boys: Labor, Technology and Geography, 1850–1950* (New York, 2002).

7. The bulk of the material collected for this article was gathered from the Buea National Archives and the Provincial Archives of Bamenda, Cameroon. We examined files on flag post relay runners that had not so far been consulted. As is the case with many archives in Africa that had been set up by colonial administrations, the documents are now in poor condition as storage systems are inadequate, and many files have been destroyed by vermin. However, archival information alone cannot recount the whole story, and information provided by people willing to share with us their memories of the runners system was invaluable. The combination

on traditional forms of communication to become an established and vital organization in the colonial administration. The second section moves on to the position of the runners themselves and considers who they were, their labour conditions, and how they and their position were perceived by the administrators and their co-subjects in the colonial society of the day. The third part examines the relationship between the runner system and the administration: its evolution, its moments of conflict, and its eventual disappearance.

THE ORGANIZATION OF BRITISH COLONIAL CAMEROON AND THE FLAG POST MAIL RUNNER SYSTEM

Before delving into the details of the mail runner system, an introduction to the organization and administration of this part of Cameroon in the early twentieth century is needed. After the end of World War I, the former German colony of Cameroon was divided into two parts. The western part, comprising about 15 per cent of the whole territory, came under British rule and the rest was mandated to the French. The British section was administered as an appendage to the British colony of Nigeria. British Southern Cameroon, which is the focus of this article, was made up of the divisions of Bamenda, Kumba, Victoria, Ossidinge (later Mamfe and Tinto), Nkambe, and Dschang.[8] Kumba, Ossidinge, and Victoria were in the forest region of Southern Cameroon, while Bamenda and Dschang were in the grasslands region (see Figure 1).

The divisions were split into subdivisions administered by Assistant Divisional Officers (ADO), who reported to the Divisional Officers (DO), who were responsible for the divisions. The DO answered to the Resident, who, in turn, reported to the Lieutenant Governor General in Enugu, Nigeria. He answered to the Governor General in Lagos and the Governor General reported to the Secretary of State for the Colonies

of these different sources helped to counterbalance the dominant voices of the colonial authorities found in the colonial archives. The photographs from the Mission 21 Archives in Basel and the Mill Hill Archives in Oosterbeek reproduced in this article do not show people running with mail, but rather runners carrying the heavier parcels of the colonial administrators to the hinterland. Walter Nkwi and Mirjam de Bruijn have worked together in Cameroon on the history of communications technologies and on recent developments surrounding the introduction of mobile telephony. For details of Walter Nkwi's Ph.D. research, which was funded by NWO–WOTRO (Project no. W 01.67.2007.014) and supervised by Mirjam de Bruijn, see http://mobileafricarevisited.wordpress.com/.

8. Dschang did not remain in British Southern Cameroon and was transferred to French Cameroon during the 1922 boundary changes agreed between France and Great Britain. See Neville Rubin, *Cameroun: An African Federation* (London, 1971).

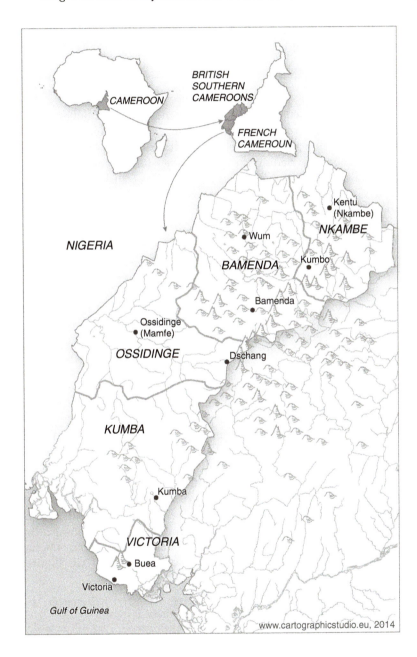

Figure 1. Overview of British colonial Cameroon.

in London.[9] The flag post mail runner system developed within this administrative hierarchy.

The importance of mail

The objects transported comprised mail, as messages, and bulkier parcels/ goods. Mail as referred to in this article could therefore entail both messages in envelopes, and parcels and other smaller goods to be transported – the latter carried on the head of the runner. It could include the goods of colonial residents/missionaries going on transfer, or just arriving in the territory by sea to continue onwards into the hinterland. In both situations, mail runners were used to transport the goods.

The flag post mail runners were employed in the service of the British colonial administration to handle the movement of mail by running with it from one place to the next using a relay system. Each flag post was provided with a flag for the hut, hence the "flag post" in the system's name.[10] Each district had different coloured flags, and the relevant colour was put on the envelope, waybill, or parcel bag. For instance, Bamenda division used red; white was for Dschang; Ossidinge was blue; blue and white were Kumba; and Buea was red and white. This meant that all mail addressed to Bamenda was labelled red and that Bamenda, in turn, would use the colours of the stations to which the mail was addressed.[11] The colours were intended to avoid confusion when people who were unable either to read or write dispatched mail to the different districts. Introducing colours was one way in which the colonial system managed its subjects. It preferred to put colours on mailbags instead of teaching the "human telephone lines" to read and write in the colonial language. The few who were taught to read and write were intended to fill the posts of clerk, teacher, or bookkeeper that were essential to the colonial administration.

The flag posts were divided into two regions. The southern system included Buea–Rio, Buea–Tiko, and Victoria–Tiko and covered 195 miles. The northern sector covered Buea–Kumba–Tinto–Ossidinge–Ikom, Buea–Kumba–Tinto–Bamenda–Kentu, Buea–Kumba–Tinto–Dschang– Mbo, and Dschang–Bamenda, a distance of 570 miles[12] (see Figure 2).

9. National Archives Buea [hereafter, NAB], File no. Cb (1917) 7, Report no. 3–1917 Cameroon Province Annual Report for Year ended December 1917.

10. In this article, "runners" and "carriers" are used synonymously. They will be used interchangeably since their job descriptions were identical.

11. NAB, File no. Ag/1 Memorandum no. 901/10 from Resident's Office Buea, 23 December 1916, Kumba–Victoria–Ossidinge–Chang–Bamenda.

12. NAB, Memorandum no. 354/1916 from the Resident's Office, E.C. Duff, Resident, Cameroon Province, Buea, 5 December 1916, to Post Master General, Lagos. The information on the number of total miles covered is taken from the original source. The method used to calculate the figures is not made explicit there.

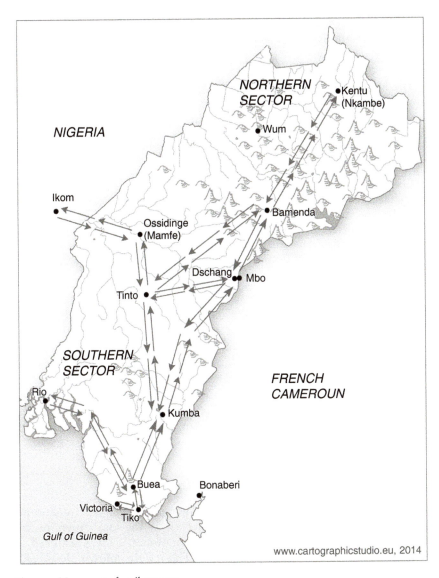

Figure 2. Movement of mail runners.

Each post had a hut that was staffed by three "boys", who worked in the hut for a month before being replaced.[13] Displaying the flags, houses or huts became "intimidating structures" that constantly reminded the

---

13. NAB, File no. Ad/6, Memorandum no. 339/15/17 from Assistant District Officer's Office, Kumba on Tour at Buea, 28 June 1917, to the Resident, Buea, titled "Flag Posts".

population and the mail runners of the presence and importance of the colonial administration. It was not the hut itself that was intimidating, though. Rather it was what the population saw in the presence of the hut, namely colonialism.

The importance of mail and the role of the mail runners were captured in a memo from the Resident of the British Cameroon, E.C. Duff, to the Governor General, Lagos, on 5 December 1916. He wrote as follows:

> I have the honour to confirm my telegram No. 934 of 3 December 1916, which stated that there was four hundred pounds worth for carriage of inland mails. As you are aware, the distances in this Province are very great indeed, and communications so bad at present that the administration is greatly hampered by the delay in forwarding mail. The flag post mail runner system is infinitely quicker and the only way for the administration to solve the problem of mail. A day's run by mail runners can rarely be over 25 miles owing to the hills, rivers and forests but they must still cover 60 miles which is a great distance owing to the urgency of the mail difficulties and challenges notwithstanding [...].[14]

Colonial officers, including the DO, ADO, and the Resident, were given instructions from their superiors and needed to know whether their annual revenues had been received by the Colonial Office in London. Also, all the other actors of colonial domination – businesses, missionaries, the police, travellers, doctors, and engineers – communicated by mail. The mail runners became the "lines" by which the colonial administration and European residents could ensure effective communication. In 1916 the total value of mail for the Bamenda division was estimated at £2,400, which amounted to 23 per cent of the total budget of £10,280 and shows why the colonial administration attached so much importance to the system.[15] Bamenda division was the largest region, and heavily populated.

The origins of the flag posts

The colonial mail runners were based on the well-established pre-colonial communications system that had been set up by the local rulers in this part of Cameroon, where inter-chiefdom communication was achieved, in effect, using runners bearing messages. They were known as *chindas* or *chisendos* in the Grassfields region and carried royal messages and goods in relay to the next traditional polity. With the greater distances in the forest regions, the *ngumbas* (as the runners were called there)

14. NAB, File no. 23/Ag Memorandum no. 354/1916 from Resident's Office, E.C. Duff, Resident, Cameroon Province, Buea, 5 December 1916, to Post Master General, Lagos. In most of the original sources found in the archives in Cameroon, first names were abbreviated. Most of the names in the present article, including E.C. Duff, are written thus.
15. *Ibid.* For the budget figures see NAB, Cb 1918/2, Bamenda Province Annual Report for 1916–17 by L.S. Ward, ADO, and Major H.E.H. Crawford, DO.

were charged with messages alone and never carried heavy loads for long distances.[16]

Another much older but related method of communication used in the territory were the talking drums, large, all-wood instruments made from a single log featuring hollow chambers and long narrow openings.[17] Resonant tones are produced when they are struck with wooden sticks, and there are often small stands under each end of the drum to keep it off of the ground and to allow it to vibrate more freely. The bigger the log from which the drum is made, the louder the sound produced and thus the farther away it can be heard. A talking drum can be tuned to produce a lower or higher note. The drum's edges are hit with sticks as the drummers beat out rhythms of high and low notes. In the past, messages produced by a talking drum could reach the whole of a region. Messages were sent further on by those who were the last to receive them, and they would relay them to those still further afield. Within a short time, a message could be disseminated across a large region.

Both the older system of the pre-colonial messenger and the talking drum were based on covering huge distances in a short time: one through the carrying of sound, and the other through the human runner. The colonial administration was able to construct its own communications system on the basis of these earlier methods.

The operation of the flag post mail runner system

The operation of the mail runner system was detailed in a letter written by the Resident of the Cameroon Province, P.V. Young, to the Secretary-General, Southern Provinces, Lagos, Nigeria. He wrote as follows:

> The system at present working in theory is that the Transport Officer at Calabar wires to the District Officer, Ossidinge, and the details of loads for each Station. On receipt of this telegram by the District Officer, he wires details of the loads to the District Officers at Bamenda and Dschang who send off flag post mail carriers from their respective stations to Ossidinge. They are then sent down by the District Officer Ossidinge (75 miles) to meet the launch at Ikom and bring up the packages; but what in reality happens is that the telegraph is so uncertain that it very often takes days before a wire sent from Calabar reaches Ossidinge. The result of this is that days of delay arise before these boys are got off. The distances approximately are Ikom to Ossidinge 75 miles; Ossidinge to Bamenda 90 miles; Ossidinge to Dschang 85 miles; these mail runners so to say therefore travel from Ossidinge to Ikom and back 150 miles; Bamenda to Ossidinge and

16. Bamenda Provincial Archives, Bamenda, File no. Ad (1948)/22 Dr Phyllis Kaberry, Lady Anthropologist. Intelligence Report on Wum and Nsaw, 1948 (NAB); Ba 1927/1 Cameroon Province League of Nations Annual Report for 1927.

17. Shirley Deane, *Talking Drums: From a Village in Cameroon* (London, 1985).

Table 1. *Partial timetable showing mail departures and arrivals, and approximate distance and time taken.*

Departure	Day	Arrival	Day	Total no. of Days/Miles
Kumba	Wednesday	Tinto	Monday	6 days/100 miles
Tinto	Tuesday	Kumba	Sunday	6 days/100 miles
Tinto	Tuesday	Dschang	Thursday	3 days/46 miles
Dschang	Saturday	Tinto	Monday	3 days/46 miles
Tinto	Tuesday	Bamenda	Sunday	6 days/100 miles
Bamenda	Wednesday	Tinto	Monday	6 days/100 miles

Source: NAB, File Rg (1917) 2 Flag Post System, with approximate distance and time taken.

> back 180 miles; Dschang to Ossidinge and back 170 miles. As regards this system, I would ask that the Transport Officer at Calabar be asked to promptly notify the District Officer, Ossidinge, of the number of packages and their destinations, care being taken by him to give the exact number of loads of each station and the number of boys needed. Thus it could be twenty loads for Bamenda and ten loads for Dschang.[18]

This excerpt emphasizes, first, the degree to which riverboat transportation and the mail runner system were interlocked (see Figure 4); second, it shows how difficult the mail runner system was in practice. It evidently operated within the limitations posed by the boats that brought in the mail and other goods from the metropolis. It also had to compensate for the deficiencies in telegraph lines in the territory. At places where the steamers or boats terminated, the flag post mail runner became vital to the colonial administrators. He was condemned to clear the thick bush before passing with his load or smaller parcels.

However, before examining the connections between water and mail runners, it is helpful to understand the rough timetable to which the mail runner was tied (see Table 1 above).

River transport was crucial to the effective operation of the system. All inland mail and other goods came by boat and were then transported further on to the various stations. The main stations for this boat transport were Tiko, Victoria, Ikom, and Bonaberi. Water tides determined when the launches anchored and set sail, and therefore influenced the times when the mail runners were able actually to take on the mail. The role water transport played, and its limitations, and the role of inter-imperial, British–French cooperation in transport are echoed by the Resident in the following:

> An alternative which I might suggest, and which might take some reconsideration is that all transport shall be done via Victoria, Tiko and then to Bonaberi, thence

18. NAB, File no. 17/1917; Rg (1917) 2 Flag Post System, Letter no. 318/377/1917.

Figure 3. Carriers on trek in the Grassfields.
Mill Hill Archives, Oosterbeek (The Netherlands). Used with permission.

by the French Railway to Nkongsamba, by this route an enormous saving of
carrier transport is affected. The distance from Nkongsamba to Dschang is about
52 miles and from Dschang to Bamenda 53 miles. The connections would be as
follows: from Calabar there is a monthly boat running to Victoria and very often

Figure 4. Transport water–rail–road.

Tiko, there is the ordinary Mail Steamer Service to Victoria about once in five weeks, from Tiko to Bonaberi there is the French weekly service between Bonaberi and Tiko which leaves every Wednesday, the train service to Nkong-samba leaves Bonaberi every Monday and Thursday. In my opinion this is the one and only satisfactory way for mail and packages to be dispatched.[19]

19. NAB, File no. 11/1917; Bb (1917) 3 Flag Post System.

Figure 5. Mail runners bearing inland mail crossing a flooded river, 1953.
Mission 21 Archives Basel (Switzerland). Used with permission.

A mail relay runner arrived in Dschang from Nkongsamba every Saturday with mail for Dschang and Bamenda. In the initial stages there was no flag post between Bamenda and Dschang and so the mail had to be sent via Tinto. The port of Douala (located opposite Bonaberi, on the other side of the Wouri river) and the Nkongsamba railway terminus were vital links for mail destined for Dschang and Bamenda (see Figure 4).

THE FLAG POST RUNNER

As can be seen in Governor General Duff's memorandum quoted above, the task of the mail runner was difficult. Distances and loads were excessive: twenty-five to sixty miles on foot on a regular basis is challenging, even without having to carry a load, and the terrain was not easy to "run" due to the preponderance of rivers, hills, and forests. Southern Cameroon is mountainous, with peaks ranging from 3,000 to 4,500 metres above sea level. Regardless of whether the terrain covered forests, fast-flowing streams, and high peaks, the colonial administrator expected the mail to be forwarded without delay. The Resident in Bamenda, G.S. Podevin, aptly captured it thus: "At whatever hour of the day or night a letter or message or parcel is received, it is the duty of that post mail runner to forward it onto the next without any delay whatsoever."[20] The British colonial administration depended on the mail runners, and the runners had to follow the instructions of the colonial administration regardless of the weather, or the time of day.

The physical condition of the mail runner was important. As a result, doctors were employed by the colonial service to certify that mail runners were fit enough to carry out their duties. As far as the physical nature of the mail runner was concerned, Captain L.W.G. Malcolm, writing in 1917, said: "In physical appearance, the men are well built and in many cases are of excellent physique. It is an extraordinary thing that whenever men have been recruited [...] they always turn out to be first-class shots. This has been remarked over and over."[21] Such an encomium appeared to be something of an embellishment. This admiration for the physique of the runner co-existed uneasily, as we will see below, with equally regular complaints about his sluggishness.

Recruitment and speed

The mail runners were recruited by the chiefs, who were the representatives of the indigenous administration and mediators between the colonial administration and the indigenous population. Colonial statistical sources show that in 1917 Bamenda division alone employed a total of 135 "boys" at 45 flag posts.[22] The high numbers in the Bamenda division might be explained by the fact that it was the largest of all the divisions and had a tradition of strong centralized kingdoms. The mail runners supplied by the chiefs were mostly the sons of palace guards and came from influential families in their chiefdoms.[23] The chiefs signed the contracts on behalf of the mail runners.

Once recruited, the "first commandment" given to the mail runner was speed. Speed was essential because mail was a central form of communication for the colonial administration. In addition, this administrative mail – colonial reports, League of Nations and United Nations Trusteeship reports,[24] and other types of dispatch – needed to be transported onwards by ship; ships or

---

20. NAB, Confidential Report, no. 1/1916, Bamenda, 28 February 1916, Flag Post by G.S. Podevin.

21. Captain L.W.G. Malcolm, "Notes on the Cameroon Province (with Special Reference to the Bamenda Division", *The Scottish Geographical Magazine*, 36 (1920), pp. 145–153.

22. NAB, File no. 60/16 Cb 1916, 9 Bamenda District: Administration 1916–1917.

23. NAB, File no. Ag/235, Flag Post System in British Administration: A Commentary.

24. The League of Nations (1919–1939)/United Nations (1945–) Trusteeship reports merit some attention here. In 1919, the year in which the League of Nations was created, Cameroon became a Mandate "B" territory. The League of Nations was charged with overseeing the political, social, and economic development of the territory. In 1945, the League of Nations ceased to exist and was replaced by the United Nations. Like the League of Nations it oversaw the economic, social, and political development of the territory. But it differed from the League of Nations in that it was to prepare the territory for self-government and independence. The League of Nations sent its reports to its headquarters in Geneva, while United Nations reports were sent to its headquarters in New York.

Figure 6. Mail carriers carrying loads for European administrators, and sometimes even carrying Europeans themselves, 1945.
Mission 21 Archives, Basel (Switzerland). Used with permission.

steamers could not wait once the tides were right, and any mail had to arrive on time. There were two main ports in British Southern Cameroon: Tiko and Victoria. Elders & Fyffes ships left Tiko once a month carrying mail, first-class passengers, and bananas from the plantations. Elder Dempsters, in turn, maintained a monthly service between Victoria and various Nigerian ports and their ships. Together with those of other well-known West African Lines such as Palm Line and Guinea Gulf Line, these provided a regular inter-continental service between Victoria and Great Britain and Europe.[25] It was because of these ships' schedules that speed was central to the transportation of mail within the territory. At the same time, when compared to other parts of the empire, like India,[26] the notion of "speed" in British Cameroon was not properly defined or standardized and was thus difficult to calculate.

Any mail runner carrying mail was, as his title suggests, supposed to move at speed, and there was to be no break or conversation with anybody along the way. The colonial administration sanctioned any mail runner who was caught in conversation while transmitting the royal mail. Colonial laws

25. NAB, File no. Ba (1921) 4, British Mandate for the British Cameroon.
26. See Joshi, "Dak Roads, Dak Runners", p. 175.

were severe when it came to punishing defaulters who delayed the mail, be it either through conversation with others or through rests. For instance, a mail runner was sentenced to five years' imprisonment and a fine of £10 in Bamenda division in 1931 because he was caught conversing, instead of running with the mail. Another was sentenced to ten years in prison in 1941 because he was caught resting under a tree in Kumba division. Such cases of imprisonment became rampant. People who saw mail runners conversing or resting were encouraged to report them immediately to the nearest administrative station and were subsequently rewarded for their reporting of cases with a few shillings.[27]

There were also exceptions to the rule. Some mail runners had to alternate their duties by carrying the luggage of European administrators who had just arrived in the territory by ship and were going to work in the hinterland. In such situations, they were required to rest with their European superior, who was not used to travelling long distances on foot. Even those officials who were transferred within the colony needed mail carriers to help them transport their belongings and their children.[28]

Wages and image of the mail runners

Wages varied from division to division. Between 1916 and 1922, in Kumba division, the three flag post "boys" received £2 each[29] for covering the distance of the three flag posts. In Dschang division it was £1 for three posts; in Ossidinge division they received £10 a month for twenty-one posts. Bamenda division, covering the largest area and having the highest population density, had the largest number of flag posts and also employed the highest number of runners, who received £15 per month.[30]

It is clear that in the early years (1916–1922), the wages of the mail runners were not standardized, and each government official proposed an amount that he was willing to offer. But in later years, for example in 1937, the Resident for Cameroon Province, G.H. Findlay, suggested a rate of £15 per month, though he was ready to pay up to £17 6 s a month,[31] on condition that better and stronger men were made available to the service.

27. Interview with Benedicta Young Mukalla, Bamenda, 23 October 2010.
28. Mission 21 Archives, Basel, File no. BMCA–E–30.87.056, Transportation of Missionary goods, child in his baby cot to the hinterland station.
29. NAB, File no. Ba (1921) 4, British Mandate for the British Cameroon.
30. See NAB, Memo no. 88/2/18 from Divisional Office, Ossidinge, to the Resident, Buea, 20 March 1918; File no. 14/37/1918 from the DO Dschang Cameroon Province to the Resident Buea, 16 February 1918; File no. 339/15/17 from District Officer's Office Kumba on Tour at Buea, 28 June 1917, to the Resident, Buea titled "Flag Posts".
31. The abbreviations used are: £ = pound, s = shillings, and d = pence; £1 = 20 shillings, and 1 shilling = 12 pence.

Figure 7. Resting with the mail and parcels destined for the hinterland, 1946.
Mill Hill Archives, Oosterbeek (The Netherlands). Used with permission.

One wonders why he opted to pay more, but one might speculate that mail runners were in short supply because of a corresponding increase in the demand for labour on the coastal plantations, with promises of a secure wage and less risk. For instance, labour statistics for the plantations suggest that between 1937 and 1938 the number of workers of British Cameroon origin rose from 13,924 to 17,799, a significant increase of 3,875.[32] In some cases, as in Bamenda division in 1918, the Resident, G.S. Podevin, was already giving an advance of 2 marks to ten men who were recruited and another eight were advanced 3 marks.[33] He also proposed that recruited mail runners be paid £17 6s in English currency or the equivalent in marks. In 1918, the Resident offered 7d or 8d a day for mail runners.[34]

32. Simon Joseph Epale, *Plantations and Development in Western Cameroon, 1885–1975: A Study in Agrarian Capitalism* (New York, 1985), p. 113.
33. NAB, File no. 416/17, Qe (1917) 4, Mail runners Permanent. Although this was a period of British control of the territory, the German mark (and not sterling) was used as a medium of exchange.
34. NAB, File Rc 1956/2 Cameroon Road Programme Policy. See also The National Archives, Kew, London [hereafter, TNA], PRO CO 583/248/11 Cameroon Report on Road Communication; NAB, File no. Qc (1960), Kenneth E. Berill to J.O. Fields, The Economy of the Southern Cameroon: A Report Submitted to J.O. Fields, Commissioner of Southern Cameroon, 25 August 1960.

Table 2. *Official one-way journey rates for the runner, 1920.*

Division	Shillings	Pence
Bamenda to Dschang	1	9
Bamenda to Tinto	2	11
Bamenda to Nkongsamba	4	8
Bamenda to Ossidinge (Mamfe)	4	8
Bamenda to Bagam	1/2	5
Bamenda to Ikom	8	2
Ossidinge to Dschang	4	6
Ossidinge to Bamenda	5	0
Ossidinge to Buea	7	6
Ossidinge to Ikom	3	0
Victoria to Kumba	8	0

Source: NAB, File no. Qe (1920) 2, Approved Rates of Mail Runners Southern Provinces – Current from 1st January 1920. General Orders – XVIII – Paragraphs 34, 1920.

It is interesting to note that both pounds and marks were used at the same time during the early years of British colonial administration, but as the British established their authority over the territory the pound completely replaced the mark. Cameroon's first colonial administrator was German, and after World War I the territory was partitioned between France and Britain. Bamenda fell under British control, and during the nascent years of its administration both currencies were in circulation. The increase in pay, whether in pounds or marks, was meant to lure runners and discourage them from going down to the plantations. This seems to have met with very little success.

Wages were ultimately standardized. For instance, approved rates of payment for mail runners were established in 1920 for Cameroon Province (see Table 2 above, for one-way transport). Day rates were also established. For instance the daily rate for the Victoria division was 8d when the runner was carrying a load and 4d when he was not carrying a load. Elsewhere in the province, the daily rate for mail runners was 6d and 3d respectively.[35] A "retention" rate – a rate paid when runners had to wait before continuing with the transportation of goods – of 3d a day was paid in Victoria division and of 2d elsewhere in the province. This rate was payable in lieu of a daily rate for days of employment when no running was involved or when there were compulsory halts on special journeys. Officers could engage mail runners at a lower rate than the ones above, depending on such aspects as the type of terrain and the type of

35. NAB, File no. Qe (1920) 2, Approved Rates of Mail Runners Southern Provinces – Current from 1st January 1920. General Orders – XVIII – Paragraphs 34, 1920.

load to be carried. The rate paid depended, above all, on the budget at the disposal of the colonial officer. This depended on the Native Authorities, which were the basic units of the British administrative system and used partly in generating revenue.[36]

Table 2 provides data on special journey rates for the one-way transportation of loads. In this case, the carrier had to make the arrangements required for any return journey on his own. These rates were calculated according to the distance covered by the runners. The lowest was from Bamenda to Bagam, a territory that was transferred from British to French Cameroon in the 1920s. There were three possible reasons why the runners to Bagam received the lowest rates. In the first place, the distance to Bagam was 22.2 km, while the distance to Dschang was 37 km. Second, the terrain from Bamenda to Bagam was low lying, grassy, and void of any big rivers. Another reason could just have been the whims and caprices of the colonial administrator. Later, in 1947, the Secretary of the Eastern Provinces of Nigeria and the Cameroon laid down approved rates for the payment of mail runners. From then on, mail runners received 9d a day when they were loaded, 4d a day when they were not, and 2d a day retention rate. The Bamenda DO at that time had proposed payment of 1 s per day for loaded mail runners, 6d per day for unloaded mail runners, and 4d a day as retention pay.[37]

There were serious implications for social change as a result of paying wages to mail runners. With wages came new forms of life in the economy. Having money meant that the mail runners could pay the colonial taxes that were used to grease the colonial machinery. They could also afford better medical treatment for their families, and, above all, pay school fees for their children. Acquiring new clothes, building new types of houses, and buying bicycles and gramophones, the mail runners adopted a lifestyle that gave them a new position in their society. The introduction of wages, and the possibility of acquiring "modern goods" led to a change in power relations and social hierarchies and gave way to the emergence of a new social group, a middling class considered advanced in comparison with other "traditional" social categories.[38]

The mail runner's job brought him close to the colonial administration, which, in the eyes of onlookers, translated into prestige. The mail runners were thus variously known in indigenous parlance as *gheliikfaang, mikallade, wulbara,* or *wulmukalla,* all meaning "modern people". The notions contained in these expressions – *kfaang, mukalla,* and *mikallade* – all denote newness, innovation, or novelty in thinking and action, as well as the material indicators and relationships that result from it.[39]

36. *Ibid.*
37. NAB, File no. C. 174/74, Qe (1947) 1, Mail Runners Rates of Pay.
38. John Iliffe, *The Emergence of African Capitalism* (London, 1995).
39. Nkwi, *Kfaang and its Technologies,* p. 1.

Secondly, the challenges of the job and the robust constitution of the
mail runners brought them respect among their kin. One of our interview
respondents suggested that they were proud people.[40] They felt socially
superior because they carried the royal mail and also because they were
among the first people to wear western clothes.

MAIL RUNNERS AND THE COLONIAL
ADMINISTRATION: RUPTURES AND CONTINUITIES

Mail runners' acts of resistance

Given the challenges faced by the mail runners, one would expect some
resistance to have emerged in response to these conditions and, more specifically, to European administrators. Mail runners were exposed to all types
of danger: rugged terrain, high peaks, flooded rivers, thick forests, while
running without rest in all weather at all times of day and night. These and
various other individual and collective grievances did, in fact, lead to
resistance to the colonial administration. Compared with other places and
more advanced technologies, for instance in India where "class solidarities in
the telegraph strike were formed directly through the communication system",[41] the heterogeneity and relative isolation of the mail runners in
Cameroon tended to induce more individual forms of resistance. This could
vary from sluggishness at work to abandoning mail and even stealing from
the mailbags they were carrying. The contention was thus subtle in nature
and belonged more to the sphere of "everyday forms of resistance".[42]

The Resident's in-tray was full of memoranda from the DO complaining about the activities of mail runners. A few cases might serve to
illustrate the point. The DO of Victoria wrote to the Resident in Buea on
23 November 1921 as follows:

Dear Sir,
Several complaints regarding the mail runners' service between Buea and
Victoria have been made and I have actually seen three mails and five parcels
that have been lying at the flag post hut for ten days now [...]. This delay is
excessive on the part of the mail runners and the necessary action needs to be
taken to remedy the situation.[43]

---

40. Ngongtum Janarius, Interviewed by Walter Nkwi, Kom, Bamenda, 20 August 2009.
41. Choudhury, "India's First Virtual Community and the Telegraph General Strike of 1908",
p. 47.
42. James C. Scott, *Weapons of the Weak: Everyday Forms of Peasant Resistance* (New Haven,
CT, 1985). For observations about resistance forms among another group of communications
workers, telephone operators, in colonial British Cameroon in that period, see Walter Gam
Nkwi, "Telephone Operators' Resistance to British Colonial Administration in the Cameroons
Province, 1917–1931", *Lagos Historical Review*, 10 (2010), pp. 50–67.
43. NAB, Rg (1919) 6 Letter from DO Victoria to the Resident Buea, 23 November 1921.

To have abandoned mail was unforgivable in the eyes of the colonial administrator. This was contrary to one of the most important maxims of the system, which stated that at "whatever hour of the day or night a letter or message or parcel is received, it is the duty of that post mail runner to forward it onto the next without any delay whatever".[44] Although many factors outside the influence of the runners might have delayed mail, longer delays, such as the one insinuated here by the DO, make it plausible to interpret them as mail runners actually contesting their working conditions.

The theft of a mailbag appeared to be one of the most serious forms of resistance among mail runners. Destroying the royal seal or making a hole in a royal mailbag upset the colonial administration, which responded accordingly. On 5 July 1930, the Acting Divisional Officer of Bamenda, L.L. Cantle, reported a case of mailbag robbery. While writing to the Health Officer, Banso, he wrote: "On your mail box being opened today and the cash inside checked it was found that the bag contained £2:14 only and not £7:14 as stated in your cover letter." This led to an inquiry into the mail runner who had transported the mailbag and what happened while the mailbag was being transported. On 10 July 1930, the medical officer wrote back to the DO: "I have made extensive enquiries and there is no doubt whatever that the amount £7:14 was placed into the bag [...]. Taking all the evidence, I consider either Ngo is the thief or he is in collusion with the thief. I have thus locked up his quarters and am confining him in the barracks."[45]

The colonial administrators interpreted these incidents less as acts of resistance than as reflecting a lack of energy and responsibility on the side of the mail runners, as we can read in this extract from a letter from the DO of Bamenda, W.E. Hunt, to the Resident:

> I admit that the mail service is very slow due to the sluggishness of the mail runners [...]. I am very strongly opposed to the present corps of mail runners who have proved themselves very unreliable and have also become insubordinate. Sooner or later again a theft will take place and/or a mail bag abandoned and it is practically impossible to fix responsibility when the mail bag passes through a score of different hands.[46]

Nevertheless, the colonial administration also reacted to these practices of mail runners in a way that indirectly reveals that they, in fact, read them

---

44. NAB, Confidential Report, no. 1/1916, Bamenda, 28 February 1916, Flag Post by G.S. Podevin.
45. NAB, File Rg (1930) 2, Letter from Assistant Divisional Officer, L.L. Cantle, to Medical Officer, Banso.
46. NAB, File Rg (1931) Letter from DO of Bamenda, W.E. Hunt, to Resident, 30 December 1930.

as expressions of grievances, if not outright resistance. Thus, in a meeting
of colonial administrators, six points were advanced by the DO to remedy
the situation:

> 1) That there should be uniformed mail runners at villages about 12 miles distant
> from each other and paid 10/- a month. 2) They would have nothing to do but
> to pass the mail bags as received to the next post and return. 3) The mail runners
> would have to go day and night. 4) The mail runners will also be natives of the
> towns to which they are posted. 5) These new mail runners will have nothing to
> do but a weekly journeying or two to the next post. 6) The dismissal of all the
> present mail runners and the appointment of others who are obedient to the law
> and who will be bound by signed contracts signed by the mail runners them-
> selves and not chiefs.[47]

The sewing of uniforms, the harmonization of wages, and the signing
of contracts by mail runners themselves and no longer the chiefs were
definitely improvements. They showed that subtle resistance on the part
of the runners could yield dividends.

Continuation of the mail runner system in "modern" communication

Mail runners followed particular paths and tracks. Through constant
use, these tracks became worn pathways along which roads would later
be constructed. And some of those places in which flag post huts
were originally located became prominent post houses in postcolonial
Cameroon. Anecdotal archival evidence mentions the survey for the road
network linking Victoria, Kumba, Mamfe, and Bamenda, with the
Resident writing as follows: "The most important line of communication
in the territory is the trunk road linking the port of Victoria in the South
with Kumba–Tinto–Ossindige–Mamfe–Bamenda in the North. Rather
than looking for new passages, I suggest we follow the mail runners'
roads."[48] The Resident's words were taken seriously and the road
network was constructed along the route of the bridle paths used earlier
by the mail runners. The telegraph construction across the territory
relied heavily on the paths used by the mail runners, albeit with some
deviations. The engineer in charge of surveying and wiring the territory,
Lawson, sent a telegram to the foreman, W.W. Breaden, indirectly suggesting that there were going to be deviations from the original paths
used by the mail runners. "Expect reach Ossidinge tomorrow. Stop. Road

---

47. NAB, Report by Her Majesty's Government in the United Kingdom of Great Britain and
Northern Ireland in the General Assembly of the United Nations on the Administration of
Cameroon Under United Kingdom Trusteeship for the year 1946.
48. NAB, File no. Rc 1956/2 Cameroon Road Programme Policy (NAB). See also TNA, PRO
CO 583/248/11 Cameroon Report on Road Communication; NAB, File Qc (1960) Kenneth E.
Berill to J.O. Fields, The Economy of the Southern Cameroon: A Report Submitted to J.O.
Fields, Commissioner of Southern Cameroon, 25 August 1960.

from Nguti to Aschum is very difficult hilly country. Shall probably have to erect telegraph line along Nguti–Tinto–Ossidinge road but will advise you later. Stop."[49]

Although not very explicit about the deviation, the telegram indicates that the telegraph wires would not follow the exact routes used by the mail runners but that the mail runners' paths would serve only to indicate an initial direction. The wiring of the territory received additional attention in the mid-1930s, a period that can be seen as the heyday of colonial rule. The construction of such telegraph lines also called for labour. Writing to the DO of Dschang apparently asking for labour, the telegraph engineer, G.B. Hebden, said: "Instructions from His Excellency the Governor General are that the telegraph line between Buea-Kumba and Ossidinge is to be rushed with the greatest speed and I am in need of more labour. Can you send to me 1000 carriers?"[50] The request seems to have had the desired effect as the DO for Dschang sent 1,020 carriers in response to help move telegraph poles, wires, and water. "I am sending this morning 1020 carriers, the extra 20 to allow for any leakage."[51] The telegraph lines were to be constructed from Kumba along the same paths used by the mail runners. However, "beyond Mabanda, the track passes through a very hilly country and [is] impracticable for the telegraph, thus there will be a slight deviation".[52] It can thus be ascertained that the telegraph lines across the territory largely followed the old tracks created by the mail runners. Further, post offices sprouted up where the flag post huts had been. The post offices found today in Tiko, Victoria, Buea, Kumba, Ossidinge, Mamfe, and Bamenda are at the spots where flag post houses were initially situated. The mail runner system was thus the precursor of the modern communications system in British Southern Cameroon.

The twilight of the mail runners

With improvements in the territory's communications network, the system of mail relay runners gradually became redundant. With the initiatives in mind that had led to the birth of the mail runner system in the first place, it is clear that its success was due to the inadequate road and telegraph system in British Southern Cameroon. By 1955 the situation had drastically improved. A large part of British Southern Cameroon

49. NAB, File no. Rg (1933) 1, Surveying of Telegraph Construction Communication in the British Occupied Territory of Southern Cameroon.
50. NAB, File no. Rg (1935) 3, Telegraph Construction, British Occupied Territory Cont'd.
51. *Ibid.*
52. *Ibid.*

was linked by a motorable road network.[53] In addition, Austen lorries were already making their presence felt in the territory.[54] This meant that the loads carried by the mail runners on their heads and backs could now be transported by motorized vehicles. British colonial administrators justified the construction of new and wider roads on the grounds that mail runners were generally more expensive than the motorcar. Frederick Lugard, 1st Baron Lugard, often known as the father of indirect rule and who had worked in India, Uganda, and Nigeria as the British Governor, had stated as early as 1926 that human beings carried less, ate too much, and were liable to sickness and tiredness much more than had been expected.[55] By 1955, the mail runner was extinct, having been replaced by roads and modern post offices.[56]

CONCLUSION

For the colonial administration, the British-initiated mail runner system was vital in the transportation of mail by means of a relay system across the colony, and the flag posts became signposts on which today's modern road communications systems were constructed. They were the embodiment of the modern colonial state and the precursors of the contours of the modern present-day administration, as they underpinned the territorial communication that was one of the essential building blocks in the making of the state.

This article has demonstrated how, both as a communications technology and as a labour force, the runners were an indispensable part of the colonial administration. Although some resistance and/or insubordination to the system can be found, this was never organized beyond the level of individual resistance. Improvements in working conditions were made to maintain the system. Although the runners acquired a special social status in

53. See NAB, Report by Her Majesty's Government in the United Kingdom of Great Britain and Northern Ireland in the General Assembly of the United Nations on the Administration of Cameroon Under United Kingdom Trusteeship for the Year 1951.
54. The history of the motor car in Sub-Saharan Africa has been studied for a long time. By 1940, French West Africa had about 10,000 vehicles. The expansion of the motor car in British West Africa was even more rapid. The number of vehicles imported into the Gold Coast and Nigeria in the 1920s more than doubled and was twice the number arriving in the French colonies. See Anthony G. Hopkins, *An Economic History of West Africa* (London, 1973).
55. See Frederick D. Lugard, *The Dual Mandate in British Tropical Africa* (Abingdon, 1926), pp. 472–473.
56. NAB, Files Ab 79, Report by His Majesty's Government in the United Kingdom of Great Britain and Northern Ireland to the Trusteeship Council of the United Nations on the Administration of Cameroon under United Kingdom Trusteeship for the Year 1949; Ab 81, Report by His Majesty's Government in the United Kingdom of Great Britain and Northern Ireland to the Trusteeship Council of the United Nations on the Administration of Cameroon under United Kingdom Trusteeship for the Year 1950.

the colonial state, they never developed to become a more coherent social group capable of collective action, as appears to have happened elsewhere in British colonial territories, as research from India shows.

An interesting conclusion can be drawn from Castells's notion in *Communication Power* of communication as the backbone of power relations of the modern state.[57] The flag posts that were defined and situated by the British colonial administrators have always determined the communications system of anglophone Cameroon. Communication lines link geographical spots that have become hotspots and political/urban crossing points in the modern state. It is interesting to realize that these are based on power relations that date from colonial times and that today's road networks and other communications networks are linked to colonial governability.

57. Castells, *Communication Power*.

For EU product safety concerns, contact us at Calle de José Abascal, 56–1°, 28003 Madrid, Spain or eugpsr@cambridge.org.

www.ingramcontent.com/pod-product-compliance
Ingram Content Group UK Ltd.
Pitfield, Milton Keynes, MK11 3LW, UK
UKHW020329140625
459647UK00018B/2080